Alina Nychyk

Ukraine Vis-à-Vis Russia and the EU
Misperceptions of Foreign Challenges in Times of War, 2014–2015

With a foreword by Paul D'Anieri

UKRAINIAN VOICES

Collected by Andreas Umland

34 Vira Ageyeva
    Behind the Scenes of the Empire
    Essays on Cultural Relationships between Ukraine and Russia
    With a foreword by Oksana Zabuzhko
    ISBN 978-3-8382-1748-2

35 Marieluise Beck (ed.)
    Understanding Ukraine
    Tracing the Roots of Terror and Violence
    With a foreword by Dmytro Kuleba
    ISBN 978-3-8382-1773-4

36 Olesya Khromeychuk
    A Loss
    The Story of a Dead Soldier Told by His Sister, 2nd edn.
    With a foreword by Philippe Sands
    With a preface by Andrii Kurkov
    ISBN 978-3-8382-1870-0

37 Taras Kuzio, Stefan Jajecznyk-Kelman
    Fascism and Genocide
    Russia's War Against Ukrainians
    ISBN 978-3-8382-1791-8

The book series "Ukrainian Voices" publishes English- and German-language monographs, edited volumes, document collections, and anthologies of articles authored and composed by Ukrainian politicians, intellectuals, activists, officials, researchers, and diplomats. The series' aim is to introduce Western and other audiences to Ukrainian explorations, deliberations and interpretations of historic and current, domestic, and international affairs. The purpose of these books is to make non-Ukrainian readers familiar with how some prominent Ukrainians approach, view and assess their country's development and position in the world. The series was founded, and the volumes are collected by Andreas Umland, Dr. phil. (FU Berlin), Ph. D. (Cambridge), Associate Professor of Politics at the Kyiv-Mohyla Academy and an Analyst in the Stockholm Centre for Eastern European Studies at the Swedish Institute of International Affairs.

Alina Nychyk

UKRAINE VIS-À-VIS RUSSIA AND THE EU

Misperceptions of Foreign Challenges in Times of War, 2014–2015

With a foreword by Paul D'Anieri

Bibliografische Information der Deutschen Nationalbibliothek
Die Deutsche Nationalbibliothek verzeichnet diese Publikation in der Deutschen Nationalbibliografie; detaillierte bibliografische Daten sind im Internet über http://dnb.d-nb.de abrufbar.

Bibliographic information published by the Deutsche Nationalbibliothek
Die Deutsche Nationalbibliothek lists this publication in the Deutsche Nationalbibliografie; detailed bibliographic data are available in the Internet at http://dnb.d-nb.de.

Cover image: © copyright 2023 by Kostiantyn Shyptia

ISBN-13: 978-3-8382-1767-3
© *ibidem*-Verlag, Stuttgart 2023
Alle Rechte vorbehalten

Das Werk einschließlich aller seiner Teile ist urheberrechtlich geschützt. Jede Verwertung außerhalb der engen Grenzen des Urheberrechtsgesetzes ist ohne Zustimmung des Verlages unzulässig und strafbar. Dies gilt insbesondere für Vervielfältigungen, Übersetzungen, Mikroverfilmungen und elektronische Speicherformen sowie die Einspeicherung und Verarbeitung in elektronischen Systemen.

All rights reserved. No part of this publication may be reproduced, stored in or introduced into a retrieval system, or transmitted, in any form, or by any means (electronical, mechanical, photocopying, recording or otherwise) without the prior written permission of the publisher. Any person who does any unauthorized act in relation to this publication may be liable to criminal prosecution and civil claims for damages.

Printed in the EU

Foreword by *Paul D'Anieri*

When analysts discuss the events following the Russian assault on Ukraine in 2022, the careful ones often refer to "Russia's full-scale invasion," recognizing that Russia had first invaded Ukraine in 2014, and that war had not ceased since then, though it was much less intense between 2015 and 2022. This chronology creates puzzles for those who study the war and would seek to explain it. If the massive escalation that took place in 2022 was an extension of the war that began in 2014, what is the relationship between the events? Do they constitute a single war, two distinct wars, or something in between? What is the relationship between explaining what happened in 2014 and explaining what happened in 2022? Complicating matters further is the fact that in 2014, Russia effectively made two distinct decisions to invade Ukraine, first using special forces to seize Crimea, then fomenting rebellion in Donbas before invading with regular army forces when its proxies were on the verge of defeat.

While the scale, brutality and global implications of the 2022 escalation have naturally drawn sustained attention from media around the world and from scholars who previously paid very little attention to Ukraine, the 2014 invasions faded from front pages relatively quickly. However, understanding why Russia invaded in 2014, and invaded not only Crimea but also Donbas (and tried to set conditions for seizing a much larger swath of eastern and southern Ukraine) is essential if we want to understand why Russia saw the need to escalate in 2022. Similarly, the extent of Russian aggression in 2022 offers evidence relevant to claims about Russia's goals and motives in 2014.

While much focus is on Russia's decisions, it is equally important to understand how Ukraine responded to Russia's invasions. One of the major victories of Russian propaganda, avidly abetted by many western scholars and commentators, is the prevailing discussion of the war as essentially between Russia and the West (or particularly the United States). While western support has been crucial in helping Ukraine resist Russia, the notion of Ukraine as a western proxy effectively deprives Ukraine of its agency and distorts the historical record. In 2014 Ukraine's resistance was initially weak enough to allow Russia to seize Crimea and to capture important swaths of Donbas, but then recovered to force a major adjustment of Russia's aspirations and tactics. In 2022, when the US was urging President Zelenskyy to flee, the Ukrainian government's decision to remain and fight, and the tenacity with which Ukraine's army and society resisted, again completely changed the nature of the conflict. Treating the war as one between Russia and the West is not, of course an analytically neutral move. In addition to being a distortion of what happened it feeds the belief that Ukraine is merely an object of others' actions, rather than a subject in its own right. This is exactly what the Russian government (and some in the West) have long contended.

Alina Nychyk's book goes a long way to correcting that misimpression in the case of the crucial months in 2014 following the culmination of the "Revolution of Dignity in Kyiv." As Viktor Yanukovych fled Kyiv, Russian special forces began the takeover of Crimea. The exact timing of the decisions by Yanukovych to flee Ukraine and by Putin to seize Crimea remains opaque. The assumption is that the first caused the second, and Nychyk's chronology fits with this view, but we still do not know exactly when Putin ordered the seizure of Crimea.

Nychyk addresses the equally important question of how and why the new Ukrainian government responded, first to the invasion in Crimea, and then to the nascent rebellions across eastern and southern Ukraine. This analysis rightly puts Ukraine at the center of the picture, for while Russia obviously took the initiative in starting the war, Ukraine had a range of options in responding. The choices it made help explain why the two sides arrived at the Minsk protocol in September 2014 and at the revision of that agreement, "Minsk 2," in February 2015.

Ukraine's response to the invasions of Crimea and Donbas represents two contradictory phenomena—the near collapse of the Ukrainian state versus the ability of the state and society to quickly reconstitute a fighting force that thwarted Russia's ambitions both in Donbas and across "Novorossiya." While the Ukrainian parliament quickly replaced the departed Viktor Yanukovych with Oleksandr Turchynov, much of the top level of the government fled. Many others in key positions, especially in Crimea, joined Russia. After Turchynov appointed Denis Berezovsky the new head of the Black Sea Fleet on March 1, Berezovsky defected the next day, and a few weeks later was named deputy commander of the Russian Black Sea Fleet.

As a result, the levers which Ukrainian leaders could pull in these crucial first days were limited. The new Ukrainian leaders faced the immense power of the Russian military just as their own military command and state apparatus had crumbled. This appears to have deterred Ukraine from challenging militarily the annexation of Crimea. Not only did Ukraine appear militarily incapable of retaking Crimea, but there was fear that if Ukraine tried to do so, Russia would respond by invading eastern Ukraine. The memory of Russia's invasion of Georgia in 2008, in which Georgia's response to provocations by Russian proxies was used to justify a large-scale Russian invasion and occupation, deterred Ukraine from challenging the annexation of Crimea. Western governments urged Ukrainian leaders not to "overreact". The fact that responding to an invasion was seen as justifying further invasion demonstrates the extent to which Russia had won the information war before the actual war even began. As it turned out, of course, Russia invaded eastern Ukraine anyhow.

Despite these early problems, Ukraine rallied and checked Russian moves in eastern and southern Ukraine. Government forces were deployed to Donetsk and Luhansk to challenge the building occupations and secessionist movements. Equally important, non-governmental actors filled gaps created by state weakness, deploying paramilitaries to help combat separatism. The far-right political orientations of some of these "volunteer battalions" fed Russian propaganda about Ukrainian fascism, and these groups were gradually integrated into the Ukrainian armed forces. Moreover, government and business elites in several cities, including Mariupol and Kharkiv, worked to foil efforts by pro-Russian forces to take over those cities. In Odesa, pro-Russian forces were also defeated by local Ukrainians, but dozens of people, mostly pro-Russian activists, died in the conflict.

Thus, while Russia took the initiative in driving conflict in Ukraine in 2014 and again in 2022, and while the West's policies created both opportunities and costs for Ukraine, the Ukrainians themselves played a crucial and neglected role in the story. Literature in international conflict reminds us that war begins and continues only if two sides are willing to fight. Ukraine steadfastly resisted Russian entreaties after 1991, whether those entreaties were backed by positive inducements or by threats. In 2014, Ukraine decided not to fight for Crimea, but to fight for Donbas. While much research has focused on explaining Russian choices, not enough has focused on exploring how Ukrainians saw the problems, how they evaluated and debated the possible responses, and how successfully they executed their decisions. This book provides much-needed analysis of these questions.

Prof. Paul D'Anieri
University of California, Riverside

Contents

Foreword by *Paul D'Anieri* 5
Acknowledgements 13
Introduction 15

1   Framing the analysis: A review of key scholarship and a proposal for a game theory-based framework 25
    Introduction 25
    1.1. The conflict in Ukraine within a broader theoretical perspective 27
        1.1.1. The EU-Ukraine-Russia relations 27
        1.1.2. The armed conflict in Ukraine 31
    1.2. Foreign policy decision-making through a game theoretical toolkit: Information, trust, payoffs, and resources 36
        1.2.1. The role of information in foreign policy decision-making 38
        1.2.2. Trust in interstate relations 43
        1.2.3. Analysis of payoffs in international interactions 48
        1.2.4. The importance of resources in international relations 52
    Conclusion 56

2   A backward look: Ukraine's relations with the European Union and Russia in 1991-2014 61
    Introduction 61
    2.1. Ukraine's independence and its foreign policy in 1991-2004 63
        2.1.1. International recognition and territorial disputes with Russia 63
        2.1.2. Integration options for Ukraine 69
        2.1.3. The impact of Ukraine's domestic situation on its foreign policy 74

	2.2. The EU-Ukraine-Russia relations after the Orange Revolution 77
	2.2.1. Post-revolution expectations and challenges 77
	2.2.2. The failures of the Yushchenko presidency 82
	2.3. The Yanukovych regime and its fall (2010-2014) 85
	2.3.1. The bargaining between East and West 85
	2.3.2. Euromaidan 91
	Conclusion 94
3	Crimean *Blitzkrieg* (21st February – 26th March 2014) 101
	Introduction 101
	3.1. Information: The problem of a knowledge vacuum 103
	3.2. Trust in international law 108
	3.3. Miscalculation of payoffs 113
	3.4. Low awareness of resources 120
	Conclusion 127
4	Donbas on fire: Improvement of Ukraine's crisis management (April – August 2014) 133
	Introduction 133
	4.1. Information: Partial mprovement 136
	4.2. Trust: Gradual decrease 145
	4.3. Payoffs: Limited awareness 151
	4.4. Resources: Development of Ukraine's resources and learning about those of others 158
	Conclusion 168
5	Efforts in reaching peace: The post-Minsk crystallised image (5th September 2014 – 12th February 2015) 175
	Introduction 175
	5.1. Information: Good awareness 177
	5.2. Erosion of trust 183
	5.3. Payoffs: 'Eyes wide open' 188
	5.4. Resources: Good awareness 194

- Conclusion 200
- Conclusions 205
  - Introduction 205
  - Theoretical and methodological contribution 207
    - Theoretical contribution 207
    - Methodological contribution 215
  - Empirical findings 216
    - Information about interlocutors' preferences 218
    - Trust in interlocutors' signals 223
    - The payoff structure 227
    - Resources 231
  - Broader implications 235
    - The role of the US in the armed conflict 236
    - The EU as a foreign policy actor 237
    - The role of Russia in Europe 238
    - Lessons for Ukraine's foreign policy 239
- Epilogue: Russia's full-scale invasion in 2022 243
  - Information: The same underestimation of Russia's commitment to fight 247
  - Trust: Disbelief of Russia's brutality 249
  - Payoffs: Destroyed *status quo* 251
  - Resources: International anti-Russian coalition 252
- Annex 1. Interview guide 257
- Annex 2. Changes in Ukrainian leaders' decision-making in relations with Russia and the EU in February 2014 - February 2015 263
- List of interviews 267
- Bibliography 271

Acknowledgements

This book is proof that dreams come true if one fights hard for them. This doctoral research could be done only after years of struggle to find a funded doctoral position for someone with Ukrainian citizenship. It was a struggle against the world, in which passports matter more than one's education, abilities and motivation, and the only advice women get to solve this is to find a husband with the 'right' citizenship. It was a long road to be accepted by the world without the need to adapt to discriminatory regulations. I wish that one day everyone on this planet will have a chance to realise her/his potential with fewer obstacles.

I am happy that my persistence allowed me to achieve my goal and that you have a chance to read the results of my research. I am thankful to my family, that pushed me to overcome my limits. I am thankful to my great supervisors, Prof Dimitris Papadimitriou and Dr Olga Onuch, who showed their faith to me from the beginning of my PhD path, supported me until I received my doctoral title and beyond. I am grateful to the University of Manchester, that provided me with a full scholarship and supported my research in all possible ways during these four years. I also appreciate the help of my amazing examiners, Dr Paul Tobin and Dr Anna-Sophie Maass, who suggested adding the last valuable bits into my PhD dissertation, which made it a better academic work. The quality of my expression in English was improved due to the valuable help of Dr Lynne Attwood, who proofread my whole dissertation, and Dr Precious N Chatterje-Doody, who proofread my acknowledgements and epilogue. The wonderful cover of my book was painted by a talented Ukrainian painter from my hometown, Sumy—Kostiantyn Shyptia (https://shyptia.sumy.ua/). I would also like to express great thanks to Prof Paul D'Anieri, who kindly agreed to read my full manuscript and gave me many valuable comments and suggestions on how to better turn my dissertation into a book. Addressing these comments improved the manuscript and made it more accessible for readers. Lastly, I would like to thank Ibidem

Press and Dr Andreas Umland for support in publishing this work.

I hope this book will inspire others to fight for any life path they wish to have. I hope the book will provide the readers with new facts and novel analysis of the Russian-Ukrainian war, EU-Ukraine-Russia relations and Ukraine's foreign policy. I hope my scholarly findings will push other academics and students to ask more questions and to search for new solutions. I hope the knowledge and thinking the readers will get, will inspire them to build a better world for all of us.

Introduction

Armed conflicts around the globe challenge humankind. Why a solution could not be reached before a truly dangerous situation was triggered is a puzzle to both scholars and policy-makers. The core role in the development of conflicts is played by individual decision-makers, whose perceptions of the environment and of the actions of their foreign counterparts, and consequent foreign policy decisions, result in the escalation/de-escalation of tensions and violence. The war in Ukraine, which began in the spring of 2014, has caused a massive upheaval in European politics and a substantial deterioration in security on the entire continent. Though Russian unprovoked full-scale invasion of Ukraine on 24th February 2022 shook the world. International law was brutally broken and hopes for stability and peace in post-Cold War Europe were destroyed. Yet Ukraine's brave fight against this aggression in 2022 impressed the world and was somehow different to the slow response to the annexation of Crimea and the war in Donbas in 2014. Thus, to understand the seemingly irrational Russia's decision to invade the neighbouring country, Ukraine's defensive strategy and the world's reaction, it would be helpful to investigate the history, in particular the beginning of the war in 2014. I offer this trip into the recent past—the analysis of EU-Ukraine-Russia interactions during the annexation of Crimea, the first months of the war in Donbas, Minks I and II Peace Agreements.

Whilst the war in Ukraine has attracted much attention even before 2022 full-scale invasion (R. Allison 2014; Averre and Wolczuk 2016; Dragneva-Lewers and Wolczuk 2015; Haukkala 2015, 2016; Mearsheimer 2014; Sakwa 2015a; Samokhvalov 2015), no research has focused on the perceptions and actions of individual policy-makers and their roles in the escalation or de-escalation of events in the first year of the war. Scholars also have not investigated the specifics of Ukraine's foreign policy, its improvement over time and its permanent issues. To fill this gap, I explore decision-makers' (and specifically key Ukrainian policy-makers') perceptions of other actors, namely Russia and the EU, with my focus placed on actors from Europe, and how this led to changes in their decisions, actions, and interactions with their counterparts at different points in time throughout the first year of the armed conflict.

My analysis and argument build on, and fill in the gaps of, what is already an extensive literature on the unfolding of the conflict that resulted in the annexation of Crimea in March 2014 and on the ongoing war in Donbas. Part of the literature looked at normative issues, such as legality and fairness. The annexation of Crimea by Russia was seen by some as a threat to European security (Gehring, Urbanski, and Oberthür 2017; Haukkala 2016). Others analysed the way in which Russia interpreted its own actions in Ukraine in terms of international law (R. Allison 2014; Dubinsky and Rutland 2019). Another approach was to examine the EU's foreign policy in relation to Ukraine. Some scholars pointed to issues such as internal divisions, the lack of a strategic view and the limited application of hard mechanisms in the EU's foreign policy (Averre 2016; Haukkala 2016, 2018; Sobczyk 2015). Others argued, however, that the EU's incursion into Russia's 'sphere of influence' left Russia with no choice but to attack Ukraine (Charap and Colton 2017; Kissinger 2014; Lukyanov 2016; Mearsheimer 2014; Sakwa 2015b). This explanation highlights the view that Russia perceived itself as a protector of its sphere of influence, and that its actions could be observed through this prism (Åtland 2016; Flores, Alejandro, and Campoamor 2016; Haukkala 2015; Tsygankov 2015). In this light, it has also been understood that the EU's policy of normative hegemony over Russia might have created hostility in Russia (Gretskiy, Treshchenkov, and Golubev 2014; Haukkala 2015, 2016; Lukyanov 2016; Wiegand and Schulz 2015). There have been limited attempts to apply game theory in order to explain these actions and interactions between the West and Russia during the war in Donbas (Ericson and Zeager 2015; Veebel and Markus 2016). This book offers a focus on actors' perceptions and how they spark different calculi (e.g., whether to invade to protect a sphere of influence or not), which, in turn, were heating and cooling the conflict during different moments in time. This could help to avoid attributing blame to either side, and to promote a more nuanced understanding of the armed conflict of 2014-2015[1].

It is worth noting that the majority of the scholars I have mentioned above examined relations between the EU and Russia regarding Ukraine and paid less attention to Ukraine's own actions, sometimes even providing Ukraine with no agency. Most focused on either the West or the EU's relations with Russia regarding Ukraine (Alcaro 2015; Birchfield and Young 2018; Charap and Colton 2017; Ericson and Zeager 2015; Haukkala 2015, 2016; Kudelia 2019; Sakwa 2015a), with only a few exploring Ukraine's relations with both sides (Averre and Wolczuk 2016; Dragneva-Lewers and Wolczuk 2015; Samokhvalov 2015), or Ukraine's internal drivers of the war (Katchanovski 2017; Kudelia 2014, 2016; Wilson 2016). This leaves Ukraine's foreign policy during the war relatively understudied and it would be worthwhile to cast a scholarly eye on how Ukrainian politicians were steering the country's relations with its crucial neighbours during these stormy times. Whilst an analysis of the first year of this armed conflict might also include a study of the US, Canada (the West) and other global actors such as China, in this book I focus solely on the actors who were most central in the events that unfolded in 2014: the EU, Ukraine, and Russia. This is the first major conflict in Europe since the immediate post-communist period in the 1990s and thus a focus on the European actors' involvement and understanding of the events as they unfolded is optimal, as it is these actors who were and are most directly affected by the conflict.

This book predominantly contributes to research on foreign policy analysis and specially to literature, which focuses on foreign actors' perceptions and interactions during times of conflict, −something that has not been examined in the case of the armed Russian-Ukrainian conflict. While I look at relations between EU-

---

1 The book focuses on events of 2014-2015 (with several links to 2022), other scholars' views on those events and my original research. Due to the changed context of 2022 Russian invasion of Ukraine, some statements, concepts, and arguments may sound inappropriate. I ask my readers to keep in mind that we are looking into the history and this history will help us to make sense of the situation in 2022.

Ukraine-Russia during the first year of the war in Ukraine (2014-2015), I also enrich scholarship on Area Studies and its sections — European and Ukrainian Studies. In addition, my employment of a game theory-inspired analytical framework to Ukraine's decision-making offers an alternative usage of game theory (beyond formal modelling) in foreign policy analysis. Previously, game theory has not been consistently applied in this way in this geographical region and in particular in analysis of Ukrainian leaders' foreign policy steps in their relations with the EU and Russia during this war.

Even though the above-mentioned sections of the literature point to very important aspects of this armed conflict, we still lack a systematic and theoretically informed understanding of what key actors did during the conflict, and in particular, a systematic analysis of Ukraine's foreign policy steps. Whilst scholars analysed Russia's geostrategic goals, the failures of the EU's foreign policy and the illegality of Russia's actions in Ukraine, less attention was directed to internal crisis management. The decision-making process of the politicians who determined their countries' foreign actions based on their personal analysis and perceptions of the situation has been particularly under-studied. Most notably, we know little about Ukrainian policy-makers' thinking and their decisions about interactions with the EU and Russia in the course of the escalations and de-escalations of the first year of the conflict, from the annexation of Crimea up until the Minsk II Agreement.

Looking at the decision-making process of Ukrainian policy-makers will allow us not only to better understand how Ukrainian leaders were making their decisions in times of crisis, and how these decisions influenced the direction of this armed conflict but could also help with the analysis of other international conflicts. This focus on individual policy-makers' perceptions, decisions and interactions with their foreign counterparts reveals how countries' foreign policy decisions are dependent on individuals and their subjective assessments of the situation. Thus, this book will seek to answer the following research question: *Which factors shaped the response of Ukrainian policy-makers in their relations with the EU and Russia during the first year of the conflict in Ukraine (February 2014 – February 2015)?*

In order to answer my research question, I take elements central in game theory and apply them to the development of a novel framework for the analysis of foreign policy decision-making. I do not use game theory in a formal manner here, so you will not see any formal models. What I do in this focused application of the theory is identify four themes—information, trust, payoffs, and resources—which guide and structure my analysis. Firstly, scholars argue that there is a need for policy-makers to have information on other countries' preferences, while flawed perceptions about them may lead to conflict (Bennett 1995; Fearon 1995; Putnam 1988). Secondly, the role of trust in inter-state relations is underlined (Booth and Wheeler 2008; Fearon 1995b; Kydd 2000; L. Thompson 1995). Thirdly, there is analysis of how actors should analyse the payoffs of the other participants before making their decisions (Axelrod 1985; Bennett 1995; G. H. Snyder 1971; Tsebelis 1990). Fourthly, I consider how resources and the willingness to use them also has an influence on international relations (IR) (Clausewitz, Howard, and Paret 1976; Moravcsik 2010; G. H. Snyder 1971). Based on these four themes, I build a framework to explain the decision-making process of Ukrainian policy-makers in their relations with Russian and EU interlocutors in February 2014 – February 2015. In doing so, I switch from a focus on countries as IR actors (which is what the majority of scholars offer) to an exploration of how foreign relations are built by individual policy-makers' understandings, perceptions and interactions with their foreign interlocutors and how these processes influence the unfolding of wars.

My novel approach uses elements of game theory to construct an analytical framework that allows me not only to focus on key actors but also key factors (trust, information, resources, payoffs) to provide a more nuanced understanding of actors' perceptions, decisions, actions, and interactions. The book will explore the following sub-questions:

1. *What was the type and quality of information available to Ukrainian policy-makers regarding the preferences of the EU and Russia during different points of escalation/de-escalation in the first year of the conflict?*
2. *To what extent was trust towards their interlocutors in Russia and the EU important in determining the strategy of Ukrainian policy-makers during different moments of the escalation/de-escalation of the conflict?*
3. *How did Ukrainian policy-makers perceive Ukraine's, Russia's, and the EU's payoffs in different periods during the first year of the conflict in Ukraine?*
4. *How aware were Ukrainian leaders of Ukraine's (and others') resources and readiness to use them at different points of escalation/de-escalation of the conflict?*

These questions will allow me to employ a game theory framework more effectively, will guide my analysis and enable me to answer my overarching research question.

In terms of its research design, this study involves a single-case design, in which the case under study is *the first year of the Russian-Ukrainian conflict*, with its points of escalation and de-escalation. The study's subject is Ukrainian policy-makers who were involved in decisions on the country's foreign relations, and its object is their perceptions, analysis of the situation and interactions with foreign interlocutors at different points of escalation/de-escalation. The benefit of this design is that it allows me to look in more detail at how Ukrainian foreign policy developed, but at the same time it enables me to introduce some comparative elements, when I discuss policy-makers in the EU and Russia, their perceptions, and decisions. Broadly speaking, then, this is a study of foreign policy decision-making during crisis times. I look at the first (most turbulent until 2022) year of the armed conflict – 21st February 2014 to 12th February 2015, I identify the peaks of escalation/de-escalation throughout the period, and I focus my analysis on actors' perceptions and foreign interactions in those key moments. In Ukraine's foreign policy responses, I include negotiations with the EU and Russia regarding the conflict (e.g., peace negotiations, asking for the EU's support); Ukrainian leaders' inaction (e.g., during the events in Crimea and in the beginning of spring 2014 in Donbas) and their actions in relation to Russian-supported insurgencies in Ukraine, such as the introduction of the Anti-Terrorist Operation in April, the counteroffensive in June 2014.

As noted above, the book does not engage with all foreign actors involved in this conflict but focuses on Ukraine's relations with the European Union and Russia. One reason for this is that the conflict situation between the EU, Ukraine, and Russia regarding the prospective EU-Ukraine Association Agreement (AA) had been developing for years. This makes these three actors and their interactions crucial for the origins of this war. The second justification is that due to Ukraine's desire to integrate with the EU, many of Ukrainian policy-makers considered that the EU (but not the US) had an 'obligation' to support Ukraine in the face of Russian aggression. Thirdly, these three actors are directly involved in the conflict. The war is on Ukraine's territory; Russia annexed Crimea, supports the insurgents in Donbas, and was present during all the peace negotiations; the EU was directly influenced by the conflict since it borders Ukraine, has been involved financially in support of Ukraine, and has been involved politically by introducing sanctions against Russia and having a partial presence during peace negotiations. Although one may argue for the inclusion of the US in this study—and some of my respondents viewed the US as an important decision-maker in this armed conflict (e.g., due to Russia's perception that Ukraine and the EU were dependent on the US)—in this research I focus on core European actors (in 2022 the role of the US was far larger) and analyse Ukrainian policy-makers' relations with their interlocutors in the EU and Russia.

My contribution to scholarship consists of offering a nuanced discussion of individual policy-makers' understanding of their foreign interlocutors' preferences, resources, and other elements during the decision-making process. Inclusion of more actors would have complicated the analysis and reduced its depth. Another essential issue is my definition of the EU in this book. The EU as an actor and in particular its foreign actorness is a complicated topic that is discussed and debated in the literature

(Bretherton and Vogler 2005). In my research, I take a very holistic approach by looking at everything that the EU institutions and member-states did in Ukraine and how they were specifically perceived by Ukrainians to be 'the EU'. As will become clear in the analysis that follows, Ukrainians did not always distinguish between different types of EU actors and member-states in a way that might be expected in the literature, but rather referred to Polish politicians as the EU, the Council as the EU, or the ambassadors of EU member-states in Kyiv as the EU (Int-1 2020; Int-5 2020; Int-22 2020; Int-27 2020). Since these Ukrainian perceptions are core to my approach, I considered the actions of both the EU institutions and member-states, focussing slightly more on the former.

My application of a game theory-inspired analytical framework to the Ukrainian case is then explored empirically and tested by means of in-depth elite interviews designed not only to capture these elements of game theory, but also to allow the tracing of key decisions and actions and to understand how they were the product of major misunderstandings and misperceptions on the part of Ukrainian policy-makers of other actors' strategies. I will begin by analysing primary material consisting of in-depth elite semi-structured interviews, which I conducted in Kyiv, Brussels and via Zoom between February 2020 and May 2021. Altogether, I conducted 38 interviews with EU, Ukrainian and Russian policy-makers (13 Ukrainian, 16 EU, eight Russians, and one American), who were officials, politicians, journalists, diplomats, analysts, and social activists. I have reached people who were either involved in EU/Ukraine/Russia decision-making, or directly witnessed the events I am studying. Respondents were chosen from different backgrounds and across the political spectrum so as to incorporate diverse opinions. I contacted people directly, via gate keepers or by use of snowball sampling. Interview questions were designed in accordance with my game theory analytical framework: information, trust, payoffs, and resources. The questions can be found in the appendix. Respondents were asked to reflect on their understanding and perceptions in various escalation/de-escalation moments during the first year of the war.

Interviews were on record where possible, and anonymised when this was requested by respondents. Since interviewing may have certain limitations due to human memory or positional bias, I triangulate the data with documentary evidence, speeches, press releases and news reports. I attempted to use a few diverse sources in support of my statements and did not claim my findings to be the only truth. As stressed above, the aim of this research is to show decision-makers' perceptions and not to offer a purely historical analysis of the studied events. These primary data are analysed thematically, with the themes based around four game theory elements and three time periods in the first year of the armed conflict. To this end, because of the amount of detail such a method requires, I only focus on major parties to the conflict from Europe — namely Russia, the EU and Ukraine. The book also uses secondary material to provide an overview of the history of EU-Ukraine-Russia relations and to offer the perspective of other scholars on some of my empirical findings.

The book is divided into an introduction, five chapters and a conclusion. The first chapter presents the literature overview, describes the gap my research aims to fill, introduces the game theory-based analytical framework, and explains how it will help to answer my research question. The second chapter discusses how Ukraine's independent foreign policy was developed by decision-makers in 1991-2014 and in particular focuses on the evolution of the country's relations with the EU and Russia. The next three chapters deal with the timeframe between February 2014 and February 2015 and present my original empirical findings from interviews and document analysis. I divide this year into three periods based on critical junctures and moments of escalation/de-escalation. My starting point is 21st February 2014, the day of the agreement between Yanukovych and the opposition leaders and of Yanukovych's evening departure from Kyiv (and the next day from the country). The following night, 22nd-23rd February, Putin held a meeting with a few advisors, during which the decision was apparently made to seize Crimea. The period of the annexation of Crimea, discussed in the third chapter, ended on 26th March, the date when Russia took over most Ukraine's possessions on the peninsula. The next period, the subject of my fourth chapter, lasts from 26th March until 5th September. It includes both the insurgency in Donbas in March-April, the start of the Anti-Terrorist Operation, and the open war which broke out in the summer. I end the chapter at the critical juncture of the Minsk I Agreement. This period was full of relevant events, and some scholars have highlighted the change in violence and shifts in Ukraine's politics after the presidential elections on 25th May (Alexseev 2016; Marples 2016). However, I study these five months in one chapter, since I consider the annexation of Crimea and the Minsk I and II Agreements to be more important critical junctures, and this was also recognised by many of my respondents. The fifth chapter looks at the period between the Minsk I and II Agreements. I decided to end my research timeframe on 12th February 2015, since the Minsk Agreements remained core documents for the solution of the conflict up until Russian invasion in February 2022 invalidated them, and I also see it as valuable in a scholarly sense to concentrate on this first year alone, since it was so rich in events and changes in actors' perceptions and interactions. At the end of each empirical chapter, I include a table of my core empirical findings for that period. The conclusion, apart from the summary of the research findings about 2014-2015, includes the section — "Lessons (Un)Learned", which connects events under study to 2022 and uses the same game theory analytical framework to reveal similarities and differences between Ukraine's foreign policy in 2014-2015 and during the full-scale Russian invasion in 2022. Now we will move on to a more nuanced discussion of the game theory framework, which will then enable me to develop my further analysis and to make sense of my novel empirical findings.

1 Framing the analysis: A review of key scholarship and a proposal for a game theory-based framework

Introduction

What shapes a country's foreign policy actions and reactions in times of conflict? This book studies Ukraine's foreign policy steps in the country's relations with the European Union (EU) and Russia during the first year of the conflict in Ukraine (February 2014 – February 2015). While it is often argued that global politics is determined for the most part by powerful players, others have suggested that international norms and interdependencies can also regulate international relations. Hence, when disagreement among major powers and/or flaws in the implementation of international agreements bring about conflicts, less influential states may still be able to navigate their foreign policy towards outcomes which are more positive to them. In my research, I use a framework inspired by game theory to explain crisis decision-making on the part of individual politicians in their relations with foreign interlocutors. I also tackle the broader puzzle of crisis decision-making in international politics. Specifically, my research question asks: *Which factors shaped the response of Ukrainian policy-makers in their relations with the EU and Russia during the first year of the conflict in Ukraine (February 2014 – February 2015)?*

This chapter presents a review of the literature, and in doing so it points to a literature gap that this research aims to fill, as well as providing a conceptual foundation for the empirical chapters of this book. Thus, the chapter is divided into: a) a review of relevant secondary literature regarding EU-Ukraine-Russia relations and the conflict in Ukraine; and b) the introduction of a game theory approach for foreign policy analysis. Looking at the literature written on the conflict in Ukraine, I found that one group of scholars sees the conflict as a product of the EU's incursion into Russia's traditional 'near abroad' (Mearsheimer 2014) and its misunderstanding of Russia's interests, which, in their eyes, pushed Russia into protecting its security (Charap and Colton 2017; Kissinger 2014; Mearsheimer 2014; Sakwa 2015). However, others stressed that it was Russia who acted outside the boundaries of international law (Allison 2014; Averre and Wolczuk 2016) and consequently damaged the security of the European continent (Gehring, Urbanski, and Oberthür 2017; Haukkala 2016). Underscoring these interpretations is the diversity through which key actors in the conflict viewed their own (and each other's) preferences and strategies, which is relevant for my approach. Thus, a precise look at policy-makers' analysis and decisions from a viewpoint of one country—Ukraine—will provide us with a more nuanced understanding of how crisis foreign policy decisions are made and how they develop over time during a war. In this research, I look at the armed conflict in Ukraine through the eyes of Ukrainian decision-makers, who perceived Russia and the EU to be direct participants in the conflict. For this reason, when I discuss Ukraine's foreign interactions with the EU and Russia, I take into account both Ukraine's actions on its territory (if these actions were guided by certain foreign policy perceptions, e.g., promised EU support, the presence of Russian troops in Donbas) and also relations with the EU and Russia (e.g., diplomatic discussions, official political statements, requests for the EU's help).

To explain what drives different foreign policy actors to act in a certain way and how a decision-maker can rationally analyse the environment before any action, I use a framework which rests on four core game theory concepts, which explicitly or implicitly permeate game theory literature, — information, trust, payoffs, and resources. Firstly, scholars highlighted the fact that having reliable information is crucial in relations between countries, and its absence may contribute to the development of wrong perceptions and even conflicts (Bennett 1995; Fearon 1995; Putnam 1988). Secondly, trust is vital for any cooperation between countries; scholars have argued that even with some common interests, states may fail to agree due to mistrust (Fearon 1995; Kydd 2000; Thompson 1995). Thirdly, the evaluation of each other's payoffs is part of every decision-making process and a mistake at this point may also lead to conflict (Fearon 1995). Lastly, available resources and a readiness to apply them may determine countries' projection of power in international relations (Clausewitz, Howard, and Paret 1976; Moravcsik 2010; G. H. Snyder 1971). I employ this four-pronged analytical framework to explain Ukrainian policy-makers' decision-making in their relations with the EU and Russia. This perspective will be useful not only for an understanding of Ukraine's foreign policy actions during the first year of the Russian-Ukrainian armed conflict, but also of foreign policy's strategic decision-making in any other country faced with a similarly complicated geopolitical environment. In the sections below, drawing on both area studies' focused research on the conflict and more specifically on game theory, I will outline my sub-questions as to what shaped Ukraine's foreign policy interactions with the EU and Russia from February 2014 to February 2015.

1.1. The conflict in Ukraine within a broader theoretical perspective

1.1.1. The EU-Ukraine-Russia relations

Before diving into a detailed discussion of game theory elements and how they can be employed to understand actors' decisions and interactions in international relations, we will first look at how other theoretical perspectives viewed relations between the EU, Ukraine, and Russia. In this way, I will place my research within the existing literature on European Area Studies and explain my scholarly contribution. To begin with, Ukraine's independence from the collapsed Union of Soviet Socialist Republics (USSR) attracted increased attention on the part of International Relations scholars. In 1991, some scholars called Ukraine a "critical strategic buffer" (Larrabee 1994, 14), a "frontier" (Moroney 2001), and a changer of the balance of power on the continent (Odushkin 2001, 374). D'Anieri (2019) explained how issues that contributed to the conflict in Ukraine were visible in West-Ukraine-Russia relations already from the 1990's. A realist scholar, Mearsheimer (1993), warned about likely Russian aggression against Ukraine if the latter were to give up its nuclear weapons arsenal (as it did in 1994). Some scholars described how in the 1990's EU officials connected Ukraine to Russia and lacked "a clear vision of Ukraine" (Moroney 2001, 20-21), whilst others mentioned Ukrainian-Russian sensitivity to each other's relations with the EU (Light, White, and Löwenhardt 2000, 88). According to Odushkin (2001), the EU was practical and quite careful not to irritate Russia, which would lead to the loss of valuable economic cooperation, energy security and stability inside the EU. Other scholars pointed out that the EU and NATO rejected Russia's requests for special treatment and the country was invited to wait in the queue together with other applicants (Charap and Colton 2017). Leshoukov (1998, 4) highlighted that the EU could also not fully understand either Russia's own self-perceptions or EU-Russia relations. Thus, I record that scholars saw Ukraine's independence as a game changer with regards to security in Europe and were contemplating how EU-Ukraine-Russia relations that could benefit stability on the continent would be developed.

Scholars were also well aware of Russia's determination to retain control over Ukraine and its disapproval of Ukraine's 'movement' to the West. Some scholars stressed in particular that after the launch of the Eastern Partnership[2] in May 2009, Russia expressed its concerns regarding the EU's actions in its "common neighbourhood" (Dragneva and Wolczuk 2014, 221; Gretskiy, Treshchenkov, and Golubev 2014; Haukkala 2015, 32; Sakwa 2015b, 562; Zagorski 2011). Others suggested that in terms of geopolitics, Ukraine may be more important for Russia than for the European Union (Dragneva-Lewers and Wolczuk 2015; Pastore 2014). Consequently, having a certain control over Ukraine was seen as vital for both Russia's perception of its security (Dragneva-Lewers and Wolczuk 2015, 2) and its aspiration to be a great power (Gehring, Urbanski, and Oberthür 2017). It is for this reason that it was crucial for Russia to include Ukraine in its integration

---

[2] Eastern Partnership is the EU's initiative to strengthen relations with Armenia, Azerbaijan, Belarus, Georgia, Moldova and Ukraine (The European Union's Eastern Partnership 2019).

projects (e.g., the Customs Union) (Maass 2019; Samokhvalov 2015). It was also pointed out that just as in the 1990's Russia supported the possibility of uniting the Commonwealth of Independent States (CIS) with the EU in a free economic zone (Leshoukov 1998, 6), its Eurasian Economic Union was not designed as an alternative, but as a complement to the EU (Sakwa 2015b, 561). Here, we see the importance of understanding actors' perceptions in decision-making, which is key to the approach offered in this book. Thus, a number of scholars were able to distinguish the importance of Ukraine in Russia's perception of its security.

Like the EU-Ukraine-Russia relations in general, Ukraine's possible integration with either side was viewed differently by scholars. Some of them noted competition between the EU's and Russia's integration projects in Ukraine in internal political practices, economics, foreign policy and ideology (Samokhvalov 2015), in geo-economics, geopolitics and geo-ideas (Charap and Colton 2017, 78), but also in regime promotion (N. R. Smith 2015). Maass (2019, 4) also suggested that both the EU and Russia were trying to increase their power via influence over Ukraine. On the one hand, Russia's objection to the EU-Ukraine Association Agreement was seen by Dragneva and Wolczuk (2014, 236) as "a strong mismatch between law and geopolitics", since Ukraine's free trade agreement with the CIS did not forbid participation in other regional projects (Dragneva and Wolczuk 2014, 227). Others argued that the AA was perceived as a threat to the Russian Customs Union (Samokhvalov 2015, 1380) and could also influence Russian-Ukrainian economic relations, which justified Russia's concerns (Sakwa 2015). However, Samokhvalov (2015, 1381) suggested that it could be that Russia was refused a role in the negotiations of the Agreement that hugely damaged the country's "great power identity". Thus, I can detect a diverse understanding by scholars of whether the EU-Ukraine Association Agreement was or was not a real or a perceived threat to Russia.

Now, let us see how the EU's foreign policy towards Ukraine was discussed in academia. In contrast to the perspectives presented above, some scholars did not consider that the EU exerted pressure on Ukraine regarding the AA (Burlyuk 2014, 35; Dragneva and Wolczuk 2014, 217; Gehring, Urbanski, and Oberthür 2017). On the contrary, there was mention of an "accommodative approach" on the part of the EU in dealing with Russia's interests in Ukraine (Natorski and Pomorska 2017, 59). Furthermore, Pastore (2014, 5) argued that the EU's compromise in delivering the AA occurred due to Russia's continuous pressure on Ukraine. However, it was stressed that in the absence of a membership perspective, the EU's conditionality could not work here in the way it did on those countries which joined the EU in 2004 (Burlyuk 2017; Lightfoot, Szent-Iványi, and Wolczuk 2016; Papadimitriou, Baltag, and Surubaru 2017). Additionally, the EU's policy regarding security in its Eastern Neighbourhood was blamed for the incompatibility of different approaches, when "a region-wide approach" was needed (Delcour 2010). The EU's strict conditionality, and its inability to give Ukraine more support during Russian trade wars in the summer of 2013 (Pastore 2014), showed "the limits of the EU's approach to regional economic integration" (Dragneva and Wolczuk 2014, 214). Moreover, some scholars attributed the EU's failure in its Eastern policy to the lack of stable economic development and democratic change in the region (Burlyuk and Shapovalova 2017; Lightfoot, Szent-Iványi, and Wolczuk 2016). The EU's democratization policy in Ukraine was criticized (Freyburg et al. 2011; Korosteleva 2013) and the effectiveness of the EU's promotion of the rule of law in Ukraine was also questioned (Burlyuk 2014, 2015). Scholars identified issues in the EU's policy towards Ukraine, then, which preceded the armed conflict of 2014, and one can argue that the EU's policy-makers overlooked some of the important parameters in dealing with the country. It would be interesting to carry out research on how crisis decisions are made by individual politicians and how their perceptions form relations between states. I offer such an analysis of the EU-Ukraine-Russia relations during the conflict in Ukraine from the perspective of Ukrainian policy-makers. In doing so, I use the game theory-based analytical framework, which will help us to understand in more nuanced fashion how actors misperceived each other's intentions in key crisis moments of escalation/de-escalation. Let us first see how this conflict was explained in the literature.

1.1.2. The armed conflict in Ukraine

Although Russia's strong interest in Ukraine and the EU's imperfect policy towards both Ukraine and Russia was already on the radar of scholars and policy-makers, the annexation of Crimea in March 2014 came to most observers as a shock. It could be argued that during the annexation, both the EU and Ukrainian policy-makers were operating in some kind of 'information vacuum', while their Russian counterparts had a better informational background. The armed conflict in Ukraine was considered by scholars to be both a challenge to security in Europe and to the EU's foreign policy in particular (Birchfield and Young 2018; Haukkala 2016, 653; Sobczyk 2015, 46). Scholars saw it as the result of the failure of the EU's soft power in its Eastern neighbourhood, of Russia's assertiveness in its 'traditional sphere of influence' (Flores, Alejandro, and Campoamor 2016) or of Ukraine's incompatible policies in relation to the East (Russia) and West (the EU and the US) (Dragneva and Wolczuk 2014; Dragneva-Lewers and Wolczuk 2015; Haukkala 2016). In regard to the EU, scholars highlighted the internal divide of its member-states during crucial developments in EU-Ukraine relations (Averre 2016; Pastore 2014; Sobczyk 2015), concentrated on the biggest supporters of Ukraine's road to the EU, such as Poland (Burlyuk 2017), looked at the role of the new Eastern and Central European member-states (Bossuyt and Panchuk 2017; Lightfoot, Szent-Iványi, and Wolczuk 2016), or studied German power in the EU's foreign policy during the conflict in Ukraine (Fix 2018).

In an attempt to explain the conflict, some scholars pointed to the EU's underestimation of Russian interest in Ukraine (Dragneva and Wolczuk 2014; Haukkala 2016; Pastore 2014). The following issues of the EU's foreign policy[3] were identified: the

---

3   Since in this book I mention concepts "EU's actorness" and "EU's foreign policy", it is important to define them. According to the EU's own definition, "The EU's joint foreign and security policy, designed to resolve conflicts and

lack of a strategic view (Averre 2016; Haukkala 2016), slowness in taking action, internal divisions, ambiguity, and difficulty in reaching compromise in implementing hard mechanisms of foreign policy (Sobczyk 2015, 49–50, 58). Some argued that Russia's aggressive policy in Ukraine turned the EU into a "passive bystander" (Maass 2019, 11), while others claimed that the EU lacked the capability to impact international security (Gehring, Urbanski, and Oberthür 2017, 731). Moreover, studying the EU's response to the war in Ukraine, scholars arrived at certain recommendations for the development of the EU's foreign policy in this regard (Averre 2016; Haukkala 2015, 2018; Rasmussen 2014; Sobczyk 2015). Thus, a number of scholars are in agreement that inconsistency and the 'weakness' of the EU's Eastern foreign policy could have been a trigger for the armed conflict in Ukraine (Averre and Wolczuk 2016; Dragneva and Wolczuk 2014; Dragneva-Lewers and Wolczuk 2015; Haukkala 2016, 2018). Yet while some saw the EU's policy regarding Ukraine as too soft, others saw it as too assertive.

On the other hand, it was argued that Russia perceived the EU's (and the West's) actions in Ukraine as a threat and that is why the country decided to counterattack. Some researchers blame the EU for its assertive policies in Ukraine (NATO/EU enlargement eastwards, the democratisation of Ukraine) and the EU's disregard for Russia's preference (i.e. influence over its 'near abroad') (Charap and Colton 2017; Kissinger 2014; Lukyanov 2016; Mearsheimer 2014; Sakwa 2015b). For instance, Mearsheimer (2014) put the core responsibility for the war on the West that was coming closer to "Russia's backyard and threatening its core strategic interests, a point Putin made emphatically and repeatedly". Other scholars also recognise that Russia was defending what it perceived as its sphere of influence (Åtland 2016; Flores,

---

foster international understanding, is based on diplomacy and respect for international rules" (Foreign and Security Policy 2022). One of the most widespread definitions of the European Union's actorness is proposed by Bretherton and Vogler, who define the EU's actorness through its external actions via opportunity (influence of external environment), presence (EU's ability to make influence abroad) and capability (internal justification of EU's foreign policy) (Bretherton and Vogler 2005).

Alejandro, and Campoamor 2016; Haukkala 2015; Tsygankov 2015). N. R. Smith (2015) found that both Russia and the EU contributed to the creation of a zero-sum game in Ukraine, which led to the armed conflict in 2014. In contrast, Robinson (2016) argued that Russia was reacting to the situation and tried to resolve the conflict in Donbas. The literature also mentioned that the EU took on the role of normative hegemon in relation to Russia, which angered the latter (Gretskiy, Treshchenkov, and Golubev 2014; Haukkala 2015, 2016; Lukyanov 2016; Wiegand and Schulz 2015). Thus, one group of scholars claimed that the EU's Ukrainian policy was too 'weak', while another group accused the EU of inattention to Russia's viewpoint and thus of provoking Russia via its attempts to integrate with Ukraine. In both cases, we notice misperceptions in the EU-Russia relations (the assertive EU from Russia's viewpoint and the EU not taking seriously Russia's geostrategic interests in Ukraine). I aim to contribute to this discussion on European Area Studies and fill in its gaps via a study of Ukrainian policy-makers' perceptions, decisions and interactions with the EU and Russia.

Another body of literature, focusing on international law and norms, blames Russia for breaking international law due to its annexation of Crimea and its support for pro-Russian insurgents in Donbas[4]. Some referred to the war in Ukraine as "the collapse of the post-Cold War regional order in the wider Europe" (Averre

---

[4] This is not the aim of this research to investigate the application of different terms, but I would like to clarify my position here. Due to the substantial increase of violence in Donbas region following the presidential elections in Ukraine on 25th May (Alexseev 2016; Marples 2016), I refer to events in spring as "insurgencies" and starting from June as "an open warfare". Although I mention local residents, who rebelled against the new Ukrainian government, I do not name these events "a civil war", since the role of Russia was decisive due to the presence of its curators, militants and weapon. This Russian involvement was confirmed not only by Ukrainian and Western sources, but also by Russian leaks, e.g., Glazyev tapes and Surkov leaks (Censor.net 2018; Surkov leaks 2016). Discussing events of 2014-2015, I use terms "war in Donbas", "conflict in Ukraine", "armed Russian-Ukrainian conflict" interchangeably. I name residents in Donbas, who rebelled against the Ukrainian government, "rebels", "insurgents" and "separatists / Russian-backed separatists". Ukrainian authorities named them "separatists" as well (Turchynov 2014).

and Wolczuk 2016, 551). Others stressed that with the annexation of Crimea, Russia had forcibly changed the borders in post-Cold War Europe and consequently damaged the security situation on the European continent (Gehring, Urbanski, and Oberthür 2017; Haukkala 2016). Allison (2014) and Dubinsky with Rutland (2019) also explained how Russia tried, to a certain extent successfully, to employ international law to justify its actions in Ukraine. In addition to considering Russian actions to be illegal, scholars also see as another possible reason for the war Ukraine's own incompatible policy of integration with both Russia and the EU (Dragneva and Wolczuk 2014; Dragneva-Lewers and Wolczuk 2015; Haukkala 2016). Although all the perspectives I have referred to recognise the existence of misunderstanding, misleading signals, and misperceptions in EU-Ukraine-Russia relations, it would be beneficial to look deeper into Ukrainian policy-makers' analysis of the situation and their interactions with their EU and Russian counterparts. The nuanced analysis of Ukrainian leaders' decision-making and interactions with their interlocutors in the EU and Russia in respect to this war will fill the gap of a relatively understudied section of the literature on foreign policy analysis and area studies — individual policy-makers' impact on foreign relations during crisis situations.

Another point which needs mentioning is that there is a considerable amount of research with a primary focus on West (or EU)-Russia relations regarding Ukraine[5] (Alcaro 2015; Birchfield and Young 2018; Charap and Colton 2017; Ericson and Zeager 2015; Haukkala 2015, 2016; Kudelia 2019; Sakwa 2015a), but comparatively limited research on Ukraine's own foreign interactions with the EU and Russia (Averre and Wolczuk 2016; D'Anieri 2019; Dragneva-Lewers and Wolczuk 2015; Samokhvalov 2015; Shyrokykh 2018) or on internal sources of the conflict (Katchanovski 2017; Kudelia 2014, 2016; Wilson 2016). This leaves Ukraine's foreign policy during the armed conflict in Ukraine relatively understudied. In this book, we will look at the war in Ukraine

---

5   Apart from this, Freedman (2019) analysed Russia's strategic decision-making in relations with the EU and Ukraine in respect to the conflict in Ukraine.

from the perspective of the country's involvement in a 'geopolitical game' of sorts, which developed between Ukraine, Russia and the EU. I concentrate in particular on perceptions, analysis and interactions on the part of Ukrainian decision-makers with their EU and Russian counterparts (focusing solely on core actors in Europe) during moments of escalation and de-escalation in February 2014 – February 2015.

This section has shown that some scholars are aware of the importance of Russia's aim to exert influence over Ukraine, and thus they suggested that the West's misunderstanding of this, and in particular the EU's attempts to integrate with Ukraine, might be the core reason for this conflict. Another body of literature put the responsibility for the conflict on Russia's illegal actions in Crimea and Donbas. Others refer to Ukraine's incompatible East-West policy, and the fact that the EU was not prepared to take appropriate actions over threats near its borders as possible triggers for the war. While scholars did mention the EU's, Ukraine's and Russia's limited awareness of each other's preferences, different under-standings of the environment and of the other sides' capabilities, I have identified a relatively understudied section of the literature — individual policy-makers' analysis of the environment, their interactions with foreign interlocutors and consequent decision-making in international relations. Thus, my research aims to address this gap by providing a deep analysis of actors' perceptions and interactions in foreign relations via the employment of the game theory-inspired framework for decision-making. Game theory highlights the importance for decision-makers to have information about the preferences of other countries, to be able to assess trust in their strategies, to understand the payoff structure and the resources of all sides involved. In what follows, I combine these elements into a four-dimensional analytical framework, which will help to structure my analysis of actors' foreign policy decision-making. Moreover, the literature disagrees on responsibility, but agrees that both the West and Russia were trying to gain influence over Ukraine. The key question that remains understudied, especially in the crucial months after February 2014, is how Ukraine tried to navigate a path between them. Thus, in this book, I look at Ukrainian leaders' decision-making in their relations with their interlocutors in Russia and the EU during different moments of escalation/de-escalation in the first year of the armed conflict in Ukraine.

1.2. Foreign policy decision-making through a game theoretical toolkit: Information, trust, payoffs, and resources

We have already discussed diverse scholarly approaches to EU-Ukraine-Russia relations and the armed conflict in Ukraine. Building on existing literature on area studies and foreign policy analysis, I pay particular attention to how, in different contexts, different actors with various capacities and/or tools at their disposal, ultimately make different strategic calculi. Although literature on foreign policy analysis is broad and well-developed (Hill 2002; Hudson 2020; S. Smith, Hadfield, and Dunne 2016), in my research I focus mostly on the literature on game theory, its application to international relations and develop my game theory-based analytical framework for foreign policy analysis. In this way, I borrow certain elements from the toolbox of game theory perspectives and place my focus on Ukrainian decision-makers' interactions with their EU and Russian counterparts in 2014-2015. According to Brams (1985, xi), "games in game theory — whether serious or frivolous — are situations of interdependent decision-making, in which outcomes depend on the choices all players make". Game theory has been widely used to explain conflicts around the world (Brams 1985; Gates and Humes 1997; Hipel and Fraser 1988; Lynn 2005; Moore 1995; Prosch 2007; Snidal 1985; Snyder 1971). The best known example is the use of models — the rational actor, organizational process and governmental politics — to explain US-USSR interactions during the Cuban missile crisis (G. Allison 1971). Surprisingly, game theory approaches have not been consistently applied to the study of the conflict in Ukraine (but see the analysis of the West-Russia relations in this respect by Ericson and Zeager 2015; Veebel and Markus 2016).

The book enriches the literature on foreign policy analysis and area studies by offering a novel angle of study of individual policy-makers' crisis management, employment of a game theory-inspired analytical framework to the war in Ukraine, and also a focus on Ukrainian leaders' actions in their relations with the EU and Russia in February 2014 – February 2015 (instead of only a discussion of the EU-Russia relations). I would like to clarify a few points regarding my approach. Firstly, I study the actions of Ukrainian decision-makers in connection with the armed conflict in Ukraine both in the country's territory (e.g., military operations) and in their interactions with the EU and Russia (e.g., negotiations, requests for support, official political statements). The inclusion of the former is justified by the fact that Ukraine's response to the events in Crimea and Donbas were by and large directed by the perceived or actual involvement of the EU and Russia (e.g., the actions of the Russian military and advisors, the EU's verbal and financial support and also the fight to choose the EU over Russia). Secondly, by actors' perceptions I understand actors' understanding, analysis of their interlocutors and the broader environment within which they operated; I also show the difference between these perceptions both among different actors, and from reality. Thirdly, I do not theorise the conflict as a 'game' and do not apply formal game theoretic modelling, but instead I analyse the decisions of Ukrainian decision-makers by utilising four key game theoretic elements: 'information', 'trust', 'payoffs' and 'resources'. In my discussion, we will discover why scholars see these elements as relevant to a country's decision-makers in their foreign policy analysis. Based on these four elements, I build an ideal analytical framework for decision-making in foreign policy relations. Then, I apply this framework to Ukraine's decision-making in the country's relations with the EU and Russia in 2014-2015 and detail empirically the ways in which Ukraine deviated from that ideal/rational type of decision-making. Looking at Snidal's (1985) classification of application of game theory to empirical cases (metaphor, analogy, model, and theory), I would situate my interaction with the theory between analogy and model. The developed here game theory-inspired analytical framework could be named a model of a rational decision-making in foreign policy and policy-makers could strive to follow this model. However, deviations from the model in the real world turn it into analogy when we do not observe all the characteristics of the framework on our empirical case.

1.2.1. The role of information in foreign policy decision-making

We will begin our acquaintanceship with the proposed game theory-based framework for analysis of state decision-making with the role of information about interlocutors' preferences. While being a core requirement of both rational choice and game theory (Bennett 1995; Fearon 1995), information is considered to be a precious asset in international relations (Bennett 1995; Fearon 1995; Khumalo and Baloyi 2018; Michel 2013; Milner 1997; Mock 1992). That is why scholars emphasize the theory's assumption of opponents having "common knowledge" about the others' preferences, rationality, and the rules of the game (Gates and Humes 1997, 8). However, we already know that in EU-Ukraine-Russia relations, scholars have observed diverse perceptions on the part of participants rather than this common knowledge. It was also noted that sometimes game theory assumes more information than can actually be achieved (Snidal 1985, 26), and the inability to access proper information in the real world is one of the main critiques of rational decision-making (Sen 1977). For this reason scholars have discussed whether fully rational decision-making is possible, due to both restrictions in human intellectual abilities and unavailable information (Lindblom 1959, 84; Tingley and Walter 2011). Thus, decision-makers with the most wide-ranging access to information would have an advantage over their interlocutors in other countries. That is why it is important to obtain reliable information.

On the other hand, if a state has difficulty acquiring information, or acquires flawed information, this can result in worse outcomes. Due to a shortage of coherent information in international relations, scholars have highlighted the competition for information between states (Khumalo and Baloyi 2018; Moore 1995; Posner and Goldsmith 2003). Where there is an information vacuum (as in EU-Ukraine-Russia relations during the unfolding of the conflict), actors rely on observation of their opponents' reputations and the history of their interactions with others (Axelrod 1985, 12, 146, 150). Scholarship shows that in interactions based on imperfect information, actors are cautious about revealing any information to opponents (e.g., concerning a choice of strategies) (Tsebelis 1990, 143). Flawed information may lead to inaccurate and differing perceptions, which results in participants behaving in accordance with diverse understandings of the situation (Bennett 1995, 27). In the same vein, Taber (1992, 888–89) argued that due to biased perceptions, interpretation of information is crucial in foreign policy-making, while Thompson (1995) showed how opponents may come to contradictory conclusions from similar information due to their bias (e.g., "us versus them") in interpretation. Thus, the correct estimation of an environment and opponents' strategies increases the possibility of getting the desired outcome in IR (Thompson 1995, 851). Consequently, wrong perceptions and beliefs in international politics may lead either to unwanted cooperation (Gates and Humes 1997, 161) or a non-cooperative worth outcome for the parties involved, for example in the form of "an unnecessary power competition" (G. H. Snyder 1971, 80) or a failure of international agreements (Milner 1997, 21). Additionally, Bennett (1995, 30-31) stated that an actor may see various games, while believing that his perception is a common view. For instance, World War I was called "a war which nobody wanted", yet it might have started due to various perceptions of the situation by the powers involved (G. H. Snyder 1971, 71). Therefore, in such contexts, countries may enter conflict because of a mismatch between their perceptions and reality. It is also highly likely that in the case of the first year of the conflict in Crimea and Donbas, Russia, Ukraine, and the EU had vastly divergent perceptions of each other's preferences, strategies and the environment. In the chapters that follow, we will discover how Ukrainian leaders' perceptions were guiding their decisions.

What kind of information is relevant and how do perceptions about other actors shape international relations? Scholars have noted the importance of knowledge about other players' preferences and payoffs for strategic decisions in international relations (Fearon 1995; Gates and Humes 1997, 4; Powell 2002, 17). Firstly, some scholars have argued that incomplete information about actors' preferences may contribute to flawed expectations about the trajectory (escalation/de-escalation) of a conflict (Ericson and Zeager 2015, 153). Secondly, scholars have also highlighted the risk that actors' preferences are connected to their flawed understandings of a particular issue, and therefore their perceptions and information processing may result in erroneous calculations about the other actors' possible payoffs (Snidal 1985, 42). Although the literature on misperception and on incomplete information are often seen as competing perspectives, they are both helpful in creating of my ideal decision-making framework and testing it on Ukraine's foreign policy. On the other hand, scholars have pointed out the importance of analysis of leaders' preferences, due to their core role in crisis decision-making (Kydd 2000, 352; Morrow 1986, 1133; Nye 2005) and a possible diversity between theirs and their populations' interests (De Mesquita 2006, 638; Kydd 2000, 352; Majeski and Fricks 1995, 626). My empirical data will also show that, for instance, Putin's preferences were important in Russia's actions, but this was not fully understood by Ukrainian decision-makers. Therefore, both countries' and their leaders' preferences are important elements in strategic foreign policy decision-making.

The consequence of flawed knowledge about other actors' preferences could lead to a worse outcome for a country. For instance, security dilemmas in inter-state relations is a good example of a prisoner's dilemma (Brams 1985, xii; Snyder 1971, 73), when every country believes in defensive arming (mirror theory) (Snyder 1971, 78). Countries often cannot reach agreement even with common preferences, which is due to wrong estimations of opponents' preferences (Larson 1997, 701). Scholars have also shown that complete information would render impossible exhaustive arms races (Powell 2002; Schelling 2005; G. H. Snyder 1971) and multilateral wars (Werner 2000). Even more importantly, the balance of power may not prevent the avoidance of conflicts due to wrong estimations of perceptions of intention, but not perceptions of capabilities (G. H. Snyder 1971, 98). In this way, scholars have described conflicts evolving from miscalculations of someone's commitment to fight (Bennett 1995, 32; Fearon 1995, 393–94; Snyder 1971, 100). The EU and Ukraine could have also misunderstood Russia's commitment to maintaining its influence over Ukraine even at the cost of international sanctions[6]. Interstate sanctions would also not be possible, while the risk of their imposition is sufficient to change states' behaviour (Lacy and Niou 2004, 27). For example, EU-Russian sanctions during the war in Ukraine were analysed as a chicken game, where both opponents prefer to lift sanctions, but because they lack knowledge of their opponent's strategy, they keep them and destroy each other's economies (Veebel and Markus 2016, 468). Thus, failure in the assessment of others' preferences may lead to negative results in foreign relations. For this reason, I will look further into Ukrainian leaders' knowledge about their interlocutors' preferences.

In addition to information about a country and its leaders' preferences, rational decision-making also includes analysis of various levels of games and their nature. In spite of classical rationalist assumptions of a unitary state, my analytical framework recognises research on the impact of domestic politics on international decision-making. In the same way as Tsebelis (1990, 166) described games in multiple arenas in domestic politics, both electoral and parliamentary[7], IR scholars discussed domestic and international arenas in international politics (Bennett 1995; De Mesquita 2006; Pahre and Papayoanou 1997; Powell 2002; Putnam 1988). Scholars have suggested that lack of understanding of the other state's internal power dynamics and interactions may lead to miscalculations in the international arena (Bueno de Mesquita 2006; Pahre and Papayoanou 1997; Putnam 1988; G. H. Snyder and Diesing 1977), while state leaders need "to play simultaneous games at two separate tables" (Bennett 1995, 38). That is why

---

6   In the same way, before 2022 Russia's full-scale invasion of Ukraine, both EU and Ukrainian politicians could not believe that Russia would go that far.

7   Tsebelis (1990) explained how politicians are involved in two simultaneous games, electoral and parliamentary, which consequently determine their re-election and career development.

thorough analysis of other countries' internal political situation is crucial for successful cooperation in international relations (G. H. Snyder and Diesing 1977, 522). In addition to multiple arenas, uncertainty about the type of game (e.g., a chicken or a prisoner's dilemma) in which the opposite party is involved exists in international politics, and the strategies applicable for one game may be wrong for others (G. H. Snyder 1971, 92). For instance, a game may start as a 'chicken' due to the high costs of war, but after a defender experiences substantial losses, the game may turn into a prisoner's dilemma[8] (G. H. Snyder 1971, 96). The conflict in Ukraine might have started in 2014 as a chicken game due to the lack of information about the intentions of the opponents and evolved into a dollar action game with a point of "irrational bid"[9] (Veebel and Markus 2016, 467). Thus, an understanding of levels (international and domestic) and types of games (e.g., a prisoner's dilemma or a chicken game) contributes to a more successful crisis management.

Therefore, information about countries' and their leaders' preferences and all of the games (interactions) they are involved in is one of the core elements in foreign policy decision-making (Fearon 1995; Putnam 1988). As scholars have argued, uncertainty due to asymmetric information leads to deviations from an equilibrium (negative outcomes) and possible conflicts in international relations (Bennett 1995; Milner 1997; Powell 2002; Schelling 2005; G. H. Snyder 1971). The literature outlines the expectation that countries which have a better framework for analysis of their opponents' preferences, domestic politics, and leaders' interests, have a better chance of achieving their interests in inter-state relations. Based on this, my first sub-question is: *What was the type and quality of information available to Ukrainian policy-makers regarding the preferences of the EU and Russia at different points of escalation/de-*

---

8   In a chicken game, the defect-defect outcome is the least desirable; thus, when one actor defects, it is better for another one to cooperate. In a prisoner's dilemma, it is better to defect when the opponent defects.
9   Irrational bid is seen as a moment, in which players are ready to pay more for a smaller value (to pay 5 dollars for 1 dollar), when "the choice is between losing everything or raising the bid" (Veebel and Markus 2016, 469).

escalation of the conflict? Yet apart from information, game theory requires that we analyse other elements of decision-making: trust in interlocutors, their payoffs, and resources. Thus, I will focus now on the importance of trust in relations between countries.

1.2.2. Trust in interstate relations

Definition of trust

Since we already know the relevance of information about interlocutors' preferences in foreign policy decision-making, we will now see how trust in other's strategies impacts these decisions. It can be argued that trust reduces information asymmetry by allowing one side to believe what the other says about its intentions and strategies. Whilst some scholars have argued that trust comes into play when information is limited (Hoffman 2002, 881; Natorski and Pomorska 2017, 57), others have stated that countries also need to judge if they can trust information received from opponents (Müller 2004, 394). How do scholars define trust in IR? According to Hoffman (2002, 378, 394), trust is the readiness to put someone's interests under another's control, anticipating an opponent's respect of previous agreements. While trust is connected with uncertainty and involves "a leap of faith" (Booth and Wheeler 2008), it can be also viewed as "a willingness to take risks on the behaviour of others based on the belief that potential trustees will 'do what is right'" (Hoffman 2002, 375). Scholars have argued that the probability of your opponent keeping his/her word should be above a certain threshold, which, in combination with the history of your previous interactions, contributes to the emergence of trust (Kydd 2000; Larson 1997; Luhmann 1979). On the other hand, scholars have contemplated whether "threat-based relationships", like 'the balance of terror' during the Cold War, can also be called trust (Hoffman 2002, 380). For instance, in a chicken game, opponents challenge each other, trying to establish commitment to a chosen strategy (Bennett 1995; G. H. Snyder 1971). Some see such 'negative' trust as power, thus assuming that trust emerges when an actor believes his opponent will behave in his favour, while power appears when an actor threatens revenge in response to an opponent's unacceptable behaviour (Bachmann 2001, 350). Although Larson (1997, 714) sees "good intentions" as part of trust, he admits that force may be a way of establishing commitment in international relations (Larson 1997, 710). In the same way viewing trust as a positive expectation, Booth and Wheeler (2008, 229) connect it with confidence and predictability. Thus, in this research, I define trust as a belief in certain words, strategies, and signals on the part of interlocutors (both positive and negative) — an assumption that they will behave as anticipated.

Because the notion of 'a fight of all against all' prevails in international relations, trust could be seen as irrational in interstate relations. For instance, Michel (2013, 872) sees trust and cooperative strategies as irrational, because it is "irrational to trust actors that act rationally". A trusting actor is vulnerable due to the risk of opportunism or default on the part of his opponent (Larson 1997, 709). Others have claimed that countries acting in a trustworthy way and against their self-interests are irresponsible and hard to cooperate with (Lieberman 1964, 271). However, states may sacrifice their "immediate self-interest" and keep commitments for the sake of a coalition, which, in turn, may be in their strategic interest in an uncertain future (Lieberman 1964, 272, 279). It was also shown that in spite of assumptions of rationality, actors do trust each other often (Bachmann 2001; Luhmann 1979; Müller 2004, 400) and trust can be seen as a rational strategy to reduce uncertainty (Bachmann 2001; Coleman 1990; Keohane 1986). It was also argued that in an anarchic world, countries cooperate if they prove their commitments to opponents and evolve mechanisms to monitor cheating, thus creating reciprocal relationships (Larson 1997, 703). Wheeler (2018) also explained that personal trust between state leaders is relevant for the right interpretation of "signals of peaceful intent" and without such trust even costly signals could be misinterpreted. Hence a conflict develops when there is a certain high level of mistrust, which means that cooperation is not considered rational, and defection is a preferred strategy (Kydd 2000, 333). Consequently, in time, trust may appear to be following a series of reciprocal cooperative moves initially based on the self-interest of states (Keohane 1986, 21; Larson 1997, 707). Moreover, Axelrod's (1985) experiments proved a Tit for Tat strategy[10] to be the most successful in interactions. Although there are certainly situations in which mutual trust benefits cooperation, the start of the conflict in Ukraine in 2014 could be seen as an example of irrational trust in Russia's respect for international laws. Whilst Russia is often blamed (and in my view rightly) for the war in 2014 (Averre and Wolczuk 2016; Gehring, Urbanski, and Oberthür 2017; Haukkala 2016; Sobczyk 2015), it might still be possible that the EU's and Ukrainian leaders' blind trust in the fact that there was a very low likelihood of Russian aggression also played a role in the development of this conflict (otherwise, this may be due to a wrong assessment of Russia's interests/capabilities). Thus, too much trust in the *status quo* might be as dangerous in driving actors' perceptions of possible outcomes as low levels of trust might be.

Mistrust, trust-building and misleading

What are the potential outcomes of *mistrust* among countries? As noted in the section on information, one of the most vivid situations in which the prisoner's dilemma is applied in international relations is disarmament (Snyder 1971, 68), where "states are trapped in the double-defection box of a prisoner's dilemma" (Kydd 2000; Snyder 1971, 69). It was proven that actors may actually prefer to undertake disarmament, but do not trust opponents to do the same, which leads to lack of cooperation due to the so-called "perceptual dilemma" (Bennett 1995, 31; Kydd 2000; Wheeler 2018). Scholars have suggested that it is not primarily the conflicting preferences which lead to hostile behaviour, but more likely uncertainty due to lack of knowledge about and mistrust in their opponent's real intentions (Devetak, George, and Percy 2017, 42; Fearon 1995, 401; Lieberman 1964, 272; Michel 2013, 884). In-

---

10 Tit for Tat strategy stands for a first cooperative move in a prisoner's dilemma and a sequential response with a strategy used by an opponent in the previous move.

terestingly, experiments have shown that opponents in a conflict situation often view each other's preferences as more incompatible than they are in reality, which Thompson (1995) termed "incompatibility perception". It may result in a "premature compromise" — a situation in which an actor is sure that his opponent has different interests and proposes concessions even before presenting his favoured resolution (L. Thompson 1995, 844). Perceptions of good 'us' and bad 'them' (G. H. Snyder 1971; L. Thompson 1995), or the belief that the other party "cheated first", further decrease trust (Larson 1997, 718). However, sometimes leaders who do not bear the cost of conflicts exploit the erroneous beliefs and fears of their nations in order to retain their positions at home (Kydd 2000, 352). Scholars have also argued that countries can fail to reach cooperation due to a mistaken estimation of "the other side's motives and intentions" (Fearon 1995, 401–2; Larson 1997, 703) or belief that its real interests may stay hidden even after proper calculations (Müller 2004, 400). This could explain the deadlock in the Minsk Agreements, which (as my respondents explained) were not implemented mainly due to the eroded trust in Ukraine-Russia relations. That is why, during the decision-making process, states carefully analyse others' interests, intentions, and also trustworthiness (Booth Wheeler 2008; Larson 1997; Müller 2004; Wheeler 2018).

One might ask how inter-state trust can be built, nurtured, and reproduced over time. As past interactions are important for trust-building (Snidal 1985, 49), according to game theory, a player may choose a non-opportunistic strategy to establish reputation (Larson 1997, 710). Scholars see the possibility of building trust by means of small agreements (for examples, see: Kydd (2000, 334) and Axelrod (1985, 132)), which allows the testing of each other's credibility with only small risks (Axelrod 1985, 132; Kydd 2000, 333; Larson 1997, 703; Snidal 1985, 51). On the other hand, costly concessions by one opponent, which make him/her vulnerable to the other, might more rapidly build trust among the adversaries[11]

---

11   Kydd (2000) explained how the Soviet Union was building trust with the West via such signals at the end of the Cold War, and Natorski and Pomorska (2017,

(Booth Wheeler 2008; Kydd 2000; Larson 1997, 713; Wheeler 2018). Building trust should be consistent across various spheres, as it is believed to show a state's deep motivations (Larson 1997, 704), and developed over time, while previous hostile interactions may prevent future trust relations (Kydd 2000, 331). Scholars have argued that even in an anarchical world system, states may arrive at cooperation which involves the application of appropriate alternative strategies, international regimes with institutions created and reciprocal interactions (Booth and Wheeler 2008; Keohane 1986, 27). While ideological views such as "us against them" contribute to mistrust among nations (Larson 1997, 713; Thompson 1995), empathy with others and distancing oneself from a situation may make it possible to view a conflict as an outsider which helps to foster its solution (Larson 1997, 718; Thompson 1995, 851). However, while there are ways to establish trust among countries, it is also possible to influence others by means of fake signals.

In addition to attempting to establish trustworthy relationships, countries may also attempt to purposefully mislead their foreign interlocutors. Scholars have explained that incomplete information pushes actors into using bluffing (Gates and Humes 1997, 161), deceit and mutual threats (Bennett 1995, 20-21; Müller 2004, 398) or bargaining strategies, with the aim of changing the other player's perceptions (Fearon 1995; Powell 2002; Snyder 1971). These strategies are particularly relevant in a game of chicken, where each player rationally tries to convince his opponent that he is not going to surrender, thus "to establish commitment" (Bennett 1995, 24). Consequently, opponents reach a compromise due to "mutual perceptions of each other's 'toughness'" (G. H. Snyder 1971, 86). In addition, viewing others as strategic decision-makers contributes to the fear "that apparently innocent and useful information is untrue" (Müller 2004, 398). The importance of perceptions leads to a prediction that states which are better able to form the desired perceptions of their opponents (e.g., wrong beliefs), could achieve better results in international

---

62) described a similar tactic in trust-building by EU member-states during the response to Russian actions in Ukraine.

politics. We will see how Russia's behaviour in Crimea and Donbas confirmed this — 'green men', a rapidly conducted referendum, deception about its military in Donbas and about the downing of MH17, — all created wrong perceptions about Russia's actions in Ukraine and complicated other actors' response to them.

Thus, we have seen the relevance of trust in cooperation between countries: actors with similar preferences may fail to agree due to mistrust and actors with opposite preferences may fail to avoid conflict due to trust in the *status quo*. It has been proven that conflicts may happen when opponents' interests are in opposition; however, they are usually not so different, and cooperation fails only due to mutual distrust (Booth and Wheeler 2008; Fearon 1995; Kydd 2000; Thompson 1995). Conflicts are still possible with certain trust (e.g., trusting some colleagues but not others, as in the case of terrorism) (Hoffman 2002, 395; Larson 1997, 727) and some cooperation is possible without trust (Axelrod 1985). I have also shown that wrong trust (i.e. both trust in opponent's 'good' intentions, when his intentions are 'bad', and trust in his 'bad' intentions, when they are 'good') can lead to negative outcomes and conflicts. This brings me to my second sub-question: *To what extent was trust towards their interlocutors in the EU and Russia important in determining the strategy of Ukrainian policy-makers during different moments of the escalation/de-escalation of the conflict?* However, to fully explain countries' strategic decision-making, in my view we must combine our analysis of the role of trust with that of other concepts of game theory — payoffs and resources.

1.2.3. Analysis of payoffs in international interactions

The previous analysis of trust still leaves questions that can only be answered by an incorporation of an analysis of aims for the achievement of which actors assess information about their interlocutors and estimate the appropriateness of trust in their strategies. In this way, we now switch to the role of expected payoffs, their formation and variation in strategic decision-making in state interactions. In this research, I define preferences as actors' most desired goals which influence payoffs, a payoff being the value associated with the possible outcome of a game (Barkley 2016, 120). While states rationally follow their chosen goals and aim to maximize their utilities when making decisions (Luce and Adams 1956, 159), the game-theory analysis needs to reveal how states' preferences are reflected in their payoffs (Snidal 1985, 40). It was suggested that preferences and payoffs can be uncovered through the analysis of states' decisions in previous similar situations, leaders' speeches, or information on vital interests from archives and other official documents (taking into account their possible biases) (Snidal 1985, 41). Scholars have shown that different perceptions due to information processing and states' bureaucracies may lead to misperceived payoffs in the course of decision-making (Bennett 1995, 30–31; Luce and Adams 1956; Snidal 1985, 42), which may in turn produce worse outcomes for all actors involved (G. H. Snyder 1971, 80). Thus, the decision-making process should include careful analysis of everyone's payoffs. Further, we will see different kinds of payoffs, consider how they are determined, and contemplate the role of actors' payoffs in Ukraine's decision-making during the war.

We must first address the diversity of payoffs that actors might perceive. Axelrod (1985, 17) pointed out that payoffs do not need to be comparable, symmetrical or "measured on an absolute scale"; they just need to be ordered according to game theoretic requirements and to be relative to opponents' payoffs. For instance, considering the war in Ukraine, Russia might have viewed the preservation of its traditional values as a desired payoff (Kissinger 2014; Sakwa 2015b). Moreover, ideology may be used by leaders to ground their preferred policies on, or the image of an adversary may become an authorization of leaders' domestic use of power[12] (Larson 1997, 711). On the other hand, there is a scholarly discussion on whether states' gains are to be measured on an absolute or a relative scale. Some scholars perceive states as if they were firms in an oligopolistic market, where they struggle to get

---

12 For examples within both authoritarian and democratic states see: Larson (1997).

more asymmetric and relative victories instead of absolute gains for all participants (Michel 2013, 884). Powell (1991) also claimed that a state's concentration on relative gains (like power) can lead to conflict, and that aspiration for a common absolute gain is a precondition of cooperation. He concluded that states aim for relative gains when there is an option to use force, but value absolute gains more highly when there is no such option and cooperation is possible (Powell 1991). Therefore, I would expect that a state's careful analysis of its own and its opponent's payoffs in the process of strategic decision-making would help it get the best outcome from any interaction. For instance, what has been described by scholars as Ukraine's policy of simultaneous integration with Russia and the EU (Dragneva and Wolczuk 2014; Dragneva-Lewers and Wolczuk 2015; Haukkala 2016) might have failed because of the lack of analysis of both the EU's and Russia's payoffs, which I am going to discuss in my empirical chapters.

Despite all the critiques of rational decision-making in international relations, scholars have shown that countries pursue rational self-interest in different kinds of political games and use international law to get the best payoffs (Guzman 2008; Moore 1995; Posner and Goldsmith 2003; Thompson 1995). However, what at first sight seems to be irrational behaviour might instead be a sign of 'nested games' played in multiple arenas (Tsebelis 1990). For example, as I described earlier, elites engage in two different games (a chicken and a prisoner's dilemma) in electoral and parliamentary arenas, and they are interested in the best combination of payoffs in the two arenas (Tsebelis 1990, 166). On the other hand, while a rejection strategy with worse payoffs provides the only equilibrium in a prisoner's dilemma (Bennett 1995, 24), this creates "a dilemma for rational choice" (Bennett 1995, 25). Nevertheless, Axelrod (1985) showed that cooperation is possible with 'conditional strategies' applied in different real-life situations structured as an iterated prisoner's dilemma. Moreover, Snyder (1971, 69) pointed to the existence of a time lag between a decision and a payoff in real-life situations of the prisoner's dilemma, which decreases motivation to defect due to the possibility of calculating the need for pre-emptive defection. After a few cooperative moves, the changed nature of interactions may make actors care about each other's welfare, thus increasing payoffs for mutual cooperation (Axelrod 1985, 85). Therefore, rationally aiming at the highest payoffs, actors are able to reach cooperation. We will now explore the measurement of actors' payoffs.

Let us see which factors influence the formation of payoffs. First of all, perceptions of payoffs in time are relevant. Scholars stressed that present payoffs are for the most part more important than future ones due to uncertainty about future, internal and external factors; therefore, cooperation may emerge only when the cumulative sum of the next discounted payoffs is high enough (Axelrod 1985, 12–13; Keohane 1986, 9; Snidal 1985, 50-51). In the same way, even during a conflict between nuclear superpowers, present gains may be more relevant, and a nuclear war may be an unrealistic outcome in a chicken game (Snyder 1971, 93). When 'the shadow of the future' is small, it is sensible to defect (Axelrod 1985, 59), which may be the case for individual leaders following their preferences to win the next election (e.g., this could be the case for Yanukovych and Putin). On the other hand, when 'the shadow of the future' is substantial, even egoistic states may arrive at cooperation due to the threat of retaliation (which will decrease their payoffs) by their opponents for non-cooperative behaviour (Powell 1991, 1306). Secondly, scholars have argued that states' payoffs are influenced by promises, threats (Reynolds 1994, 130) and costly signals (troop mobilisation, side payments), while "cheap talks" do not affect them, although they greatly increase cooperation (Majeski and Fricks 1995, 625). In addition, scholars have shown that actors may change conflicts from a chicken game to a prisoner's dilemma when one party promotes its structure of payoffs (e.g., by threats and provocations) (Snyder 1971, 92). At that moment, war is probable, unless the game turns back into a chicken one again (Snyder 1971, 93)[13]. In the same vein, Wagner (2000) stressed that wars may develop not out of a mis-

---

13   In a chicken game, war is a mutually negative scenario. However, after one side's provocations and pressure, the payoff for cooperation drops for the other side and it prefers defection, ending up in the defect-defect box of a prisoner's dilemma game.

take, but out of a well-thought-out deliberate decision with the aim of changing the payoffs of the game. This view is supported by Fearon (1995), who explained the rationality of wars when leaders' cost/benefit analysis favours conflict gambling over the pre-war alignment of forces. Therefore, an actor may start a war (either an open-scale or a limited) with the goal to improve his/her relative power and thus expected payoffs in negotiations (Wagner 2000, 470). This is likely to be the case with Russia's gambling over Crimea and Donbas; some of my respondents explained Russia's involvement in Donbas as Putin's desire to use it as 'a bargaining chip' over Crimea.

Based on the above arguments, I assume that good estimation of both one's own and one's opponent's payoffs is another core factor in getting the most in international relations. Countries may be focused on their absolute gains, which makes cooperation possible, or struggle for relative gains, which increases the probability of a conflict. Being involved in various games in different arenas, actors want to get the best combined payoffs from all of them. Present payoffs are mostly valued more highly than future ones, which requires discounting future gains due to uncertainty. Moreover, an actor may start a war with the aim of improving his/her payoffs. Based on this, I form my third sub-question: *How did Ukrainian policy-makers perceive Ukraine's, Russia's, and the EU's payoffs in different periods during the first year of the conflict in Ukraine?* For the whole picture of decision-making in foreign policy, I present below one more aspect of game theory — the resources of actors and their readiness to use them in a particular interaction.

1.2.4. The importance of resources in international relations

Whilst above I have explained the concept of payoffs and the way anticipated payoffs determine interactions between countries, there is still the remaining gap in understanding of the tools which actors use to reach their payoffs. To explain this, now I concentrate on the role of various resources in international relations. Scholars have confirmed that a state's power is "based on capabilities" (Holsti 1964, 182), and this is often measured in resource provisions, such as population, GDP and strength of the army (Hart 1976, 289). Hart (1976) distinguished three types of power: control over resources, actors or outcomes, with the last of these (the ability to reach certain outcomes) being superior and comprising the former ones (Hart 1976, 296). It was also argued that weaker resource-provision (in comparison to resource-abundancy) imposes constraints on a country's foreign policy (Clark, Nordstrom, and Reed 2008, 763). Beitz (1975, 368) highlighted the uneven and unjust distribution of natural resources between countries, which makes some of them heavily disadvantaged and hence willing to struggle for more equal shares. The fight for such redistribution of resources, specifically strategic ones, such as oil, was the reason for many wars in the course of history (Dannreuther 2013). While aiming at the maximisation of one's own share may cause conflict, cooperation can increase the 'pie' and leaves other resources undestroyed (Powell 2002, 2). One of history's greatest economists, Adam Smith, believed that cooperation between nations which specialised in carrying out economic activities connected with their unique resources was a panacea for everyone's welfare (A. Smith 1776). However, having abundant resources may bring negative consequences for a country in the form of authoritarianism, inequality or low economic development (Le Billon 2001; Shaffer and Ziyadov 2012). Moreover, Soltanov (2012, 314) showed that resource-rich nations were more likely to involve themselves in international conflicts if they had domestic instabilities. On the other hand, the international community is less eager to solve conflicts which involve resource-rich countries, due to their own commercial interests in those countries (Le Billon 2001, 578–79). Therefore, the resources of countries impact their involvement in foreign relations.

Scholars have confirmed the necessity of proper resources for countries to secure the best deal in interstate bargaining. For example, Bachmann (2001) argued that when instead of trust a country uses power, in most cases it needs to secure this with available resources. Moreover, some scholars understand power as the ability of countries to employ resources with the aim of forcing others to behave in ways that they would not otherwise do (Barnett and Duvall 2005, 40). Economically stronger states have a higher probability of winning a war (Powell 1991, 1312). Additionally, one resource—nuclear weapons—has a special role in modern international relations. Scholars have observed that possession of nuclear weapons contributes highly to a country's success in international bargaining (Horowitz 2009; M. Simon 2004) and makes concessions to others in international disputes unlikely (Horowitz 2009). Consequently, Holsti (1964, 184) argued that countries invest in intelligence to find out about "other states' capabilities and intentions". In my subsequent discussion, it will become clear how Russia's vast resources, specifically in terms of energy, helped in its operation in Ukraine, but also in maintaining a certain influence over the EU (due to their economic interdependency). Thus, opponents' resources are an important part of the foreign policy-making analysis, that helps to estimate if an opponent has the means to back its goals.

However, it is not only the absolute estimation of resources which influences foreign relations; countries' readiness to use their resources in a particular interaction can also be decisive. It was argued that "while technology determines what is possible, states choose what sorts of wars to fight within those constraints, and an understanding of the relationship between fighting and bargaining helps to explain those choices" (Wagner 2000, 470). A country's deployment of resources can also reveal its intentions (Schelling 2005, 109). Scholars have pointed out that countries are rarely ready to invest all of their economic and military resources in a particular war, and so the outcome might depend not on the absolute comparison of adversaries' resources, but on the extent to which they engage in a war (Clausewitz, Howard, and Paret 1976; Moravcsik 2010; G. H. Snyder 1971). In this vein, weaker countries may prevail in wars if their "preferences at stake" are higher (Moravcsik 2010, 5). This might explain the EU's not using all of its resources to deter Russia, since in its "hierarchy of interests" (G. H. Snyder 1971, 100), the resolution of the conflict in Ukraine was not a priority. Moreover, scholars have argued that while some countries have the ability to employ their resources to influence others, like the USA, others do not possess such an ability (Barnett and Duvall 2005, 41). Hence, I expect that readiness of different countries to use their resources in Ukraine also played an important role in the development of the conflict, and so it is crucial to assess Ukrainian leaders' analysis of this aspect. Countries may also start wars deliberately to decrease others' capabilities.

Although wars are often seen as negative outcomes, there are situations when a conflict is seen as the best option in international relations. For instance, Wagner (2000, 473) argued that military fighting can pursue two different goals: to uncover information about adversaries' relative capabilities, or to change them. This change in opponents' relative powers will change "the terms of any negotiated settlement they might reach" (Wagner 2000, 471). Both winners and losers have their resources destroyed, but differentially; thus a conflict lasts either until the states involved reach an acceptable agreement, one of them is completely eliminated (Powell 2002, 22), or one of them "concedes the stakes to the other by quitting" (Morrow 2002, S44). Reducing the enemy's resources might be another motivation, if defeating him/her is impossible (Clausewitz, Howard, and Paret 1976, 611). On the other hand, governments need to achieve a balance between costly domestic programmes and improvement of their military strength in the allocation of their countries' resources (Bennett 1995, 39). Thus, higher domestic accountability might be a reason for democracies to be more selective in the wars they enter: they prefer wars with minimised costs (De Mesquita 2006; Moravcsik 2010, 5). Although democracies are able to invest more resources in conflicts than autocracies are (Powell 2002, 19), they prefer to resolve conflicts peacefully and get involved in wars only when there is a high probability of victory, whilst autocracies are ready to fight even with a low chance of victory (De Mesquita 2006, 640). Thus, there might be sensible reasons for countries to start wars, but autocracies do this more frequently than democracies.

Scholars have argued that starting a war can be a bargaining strategy for a state; however, democracies do not enter wars as readily as autocracies due to higher accountability to their people. It was also shown that nuclear weapon is a unique resource which substantially increases a state's bargaining power in foreign policy. Moreover, it is important to analyse the extent to which a country is ready to apply its resources to a particular foreign interaction, since states with bigger capabilities may have less motivation to get involved, and so weaker ones may prevail in a conflict due to the fact that they have higher preferences at stake. From this, I form my fourth sub-question: *How aware were Ukrainian leaders of Ukraine's (and others') resources and readiness to use them at different points of escalation/de-escalation of the conflict?*

Conclusion

This chapter has introduced the theoretical framework of my book. I first provided an overview of IR and area studies literature dealing with EU-Ukraine-Russia relations and the armed conflict in Ukraine. After that, I introduced certain insights from game theory, which form the parameters of my foreign policy analysis of Ukraine's strategic decision-making in February 2014 – February 2015. Despite its extensive engagement with the war in Ukraine, the existing literature has not yet fully explored internal decision-making dynamics of the key protagonists, and this is very much the case for Ukraine. For instance, some sections of the literature blame the West for aggravating the crisis through pressure on democratisation, integration offers and support for the Euromaidan, which pushed Russia to protect its vital interests in Ukraine. These scholars recognise the West's misunderstanding of Russia's preferences and capabilities, which is also part of the approach I offer. Another group of scholars underlined the illegality of Russia's actions in Crimea and Donbas, while others discussed Russia's own perception of international law in the Ukrainian context. A different body of literature has shed light on the failure of Ukraine's 'sitting on two chairs' East-West policy, or the EU's flawed (too indecisive and weak) policy in its relations with Ukraine and Russia, as triggers for the conflict. These perspectives also touch upon diverse perceptions of the actors involved and the lack of strategic insight into some of their foreign policy articulation.

It is in this area of internal crisis-management dynamics that my book seeks to complement existing research on the war in Ukraine. The literature on foreign policy analysis would benefit from a thorough study of decision-makers' perceptions, their analysis of the situation and foreign policy interactions. In my research, I look at Ukrainian leaders' response to the conflict in Crimea and Donbas (troop mobilisation, the use of the military against pro-Russian rebels), as well as interactions with the EU and Russia (diplomatic communication, requests for the EU's help, peace negotiations). All of these actions on the part of the Ukrainian state are included in my foreign policy analysis, since they involved the EU or Russia in one way or another, e.g., the presence of Russian military and advisors in Crimea and Donbas, Ukrainian decision-makers' consultations with the EU before taking certain war decisions, the EU's sanctions against Russia due to its actions in Ukraine, etc. The game theoretic toolkit employed here offers an analytical depth and a systematic way of analysing continuity and change in the thinking of Ukrainian decision-makers in their relations with EU and Russian interlocutors. Against this background, my main RQ is: *Which factors shaped the response of Ukrainian policy-makers in their interactions with the EU and Russia during the first year of the conflict in Ukraine (February 2014 – February 2015)?*

In the second part of the chapter, I reviewed game theory literature dealing with international relations and foreign policy analysis in particular and contemplated how it could help me to explain Ukrainian leaders' decision-making during the war. Going through these sets of literature, I have uncovered four elements, which have been elaborated, both explicitly or implicitly, by game theory scholars and which could serve as a basis for analysis during the decision-making process: information about interlocutors' preferences, trust in their strategies, anticipated payoffs, and the resources available for any particular interaction. Firstly, scholars comprehensively explained the relevance of information about opponents' preferences in international relations and how inadequate information can lead to misguided decisions. Based on this, my first sub-question is: *What was the type and quality of information available to Ukrainian policy-makers regarding the preferences of the EU and Russia during different points of escalation/de-escalation of the conflict?*

Secondly, scholars highlighted the importance of trust in relations between countries, explained how cooperation might break down due to mistrust (even when preferences are compatible) and discussed the bluffing strategies used by actors to change others' perceptions. Therefore, my second sub-question is: *To what extent was trust towards their interlocutors in Russia and the EU important in determining the strategy of Ukrainian policy-makers during different moments of the escalation/de-escalation of the conflict?* Moreover, scholars have demonstrated that an understanding of how countries' preferences reflect in their payoffs was an important factor in foreign policy decision-making. This forms my third sub-question: *How did Ukrainian policy-makers perceive Ukraine's, Russia's, and the EU's payoffs in different periods during the first year of the conflict in Ukraine?* Lastly, the resources which actors are ready to use in a particular interaction is another crucial element in decision-making. Thus, my fourth sub-question is: *How aware were Ukrainian leaders of Ukraine's (and others') resources and readiness to use them at different points of the escalation/de-escalation of the conflict?* These four questions will help me to operationalise my game theory-inspired analytical framework, structuring my analysis and my consequent explanation of Ukrainian policy-makers' decisions in their relations with the EU and Russia in respect to this war.

It is important to stress that it is not the objective of this book to explain the outcome of this conflict, a task that involves a much broader set of issues and actors (e.g., the inclusion of the role of the US in this war). Instead, the main focus of my analysis is Ukraine's strategic decision-making during the first year of the armed conflict. In this sense, Ukrainian policy-makers are the subjects of my investigation, whereas their perceptions, decision-making and interactions with the EU and Russia regarding this conflict are the objects of my study. In the discussion that follows, I firstly contextualise the events of 2014 by looking at the history of Ukraine's foreign policy in its relations with the EU and Russia since 1991. After this, I move to the three empirical chapters, which offer an in-depth, nuanced analysis of Ukrainian leaders' decision-making during different moments of the escalation/de-escalation of the Russian-Ukrainian war in 2014-2015. Insights from game theory will help me to uncover the thinking and perceptions of Ukrainian decision-makers before they took crucial state decisions in their interactions with the EU and Russia and in their response to the war on Ukrainian territory. In addition, I will also elaborate on the EU's and Russia's approach to the conflict as a way of providing a fuller context to the constraints and dilemmas facing officials in Ukraine. In this work, I use rich primary data, collected via 38 elite interviews with EU, Ukrainian and Russian policy-makers, analysis of official documents, transcripts of meetings and media outlets from all three sides. Before the analysis of the armed conflict itself, however, let us first offer a retrospective of relations between Ukraine and its two key interlocutors in Europe — the European Union and Russia.

2 A backward look: Ukraine's relations with the European Union and Russia in 1991-2014

Introduction

History can provide us with vivid insights into the present; accordingly, Ukraine's history is important for our understanding of the 2014 war. Although the events of 2014 took some scholars and policy-makers by surprise (Åtland 2016; Averre and Wolczuk 2016, 551; Dubinsky and Rutland 2019, 46), it can be argued that they did not come out of nowhere, but were dependent on, and perhaps the product of past processes, relationships and interactions. It is for this reason that some scholars describe Russia's role in the conflict as constituting "both change and continuity in Russia's foreign policy" (Tsygankov 2015, 271). Others have argued that many of the elements of the 2014 armed conflict existed already in 1993 (D'Anieri 2019, 29). Thus, a look back at the history of Ukraine's independent domestic and foreign policy will be particularly useful in our later understanding of the preconditions of the armed conflict under study. In my discussion of each period, I demonstrate how the game theory-based analytical framework proposed in the previous chapter helps us assess the history of Ukraine's decision-making in relations with Russia and the EU. However, the framework does not penetrate the whole of this chapter, as it does with subsequent ones. My historically contextualized analysis will specifically look at the formation of Ukraine's independent public and foreign policy over time and will demonstrate that there was a discernible pattern of repeated misconceptions in EU-Ukraine relations and moments of tensions in Ukraine-Russia relations. I stress that such events, like confrontations over Crimea in 1993-94 or tensions regarding Tuzla Island in 2003, each had the potential to develop into an open war between the countries. While the particular combination of factors which were present in 2014 and which made the military conflict possible were not present during these previous moments, these events did act as a foundation for the relationships and interactions between EU, Ukrainian and Russian policy-makers in 2014.

In what follows, I outline the historical geopolitical context in which Ukraine had to operate since its independence, and which gradually developed into the armed conflict in Ukraine[14]. Analysis of secondary scholarly literature, official documents, speeches and press releases, and my original interview data, will serve as the main sources for this chapter. The game theory framework which I previously introduced — information, trust, payoffs, and resources — will help me to assess Ukraine's decision-making process in its interactions with Russia and the EU. Nevertheless, the analysis I offer in this chapter is not a purely historical explanation of Ukraine's relations with Russia and the European Union since 1991. My aim is not only to list events, which can be found in other literature, but rather to mention core moments, to connect the dots and to develop analytical conclusions. This 'journey into history' will provide the foundations and boundaries of my analysis in the chapters to come.

The chapter is divided into key historical periods, which combine patterns of actions and reactions in Ukrainian foreign policy in the country's relations with Russia and the EU. Knowing the historical patterns and trends in terms of the relationship between these three actors will help us to better understand how and why they behaved as they did in 2014. The core moments of EU-Ukraine and Ukraine-Russia relations are shown in Table 1 and Table 2. The way the chapter is divided up coincides with the presidential terms in Ukraine for two core reasons. Firstly, the Ukrainian Constitution provides the president with the main responsibilities regarding the country's foreign relations (Verkhovna Rada of Ukraine 1996). Both when Ukraine was a

---

14 In my work, I define the armed conflict in Ukraine as the annexation of the Crimean Peninsula by the Russian Federation, the war in Donbas, and consequent political and economic confrontations between Russia and other countries (in particular Ukraine, the EU, US), which developed out of Ukraine's prospective geopolitical choice. As previously explained, I focus on events of 2014-2015 and touch upon 2022 Russian invasion of Ukraine only in the end of the book.

parliamentary-presidential and a presidential-parliamentary republic[15], every president retained an influence over the country which went far beyond his constitutional obligations and was the centre of power in the country (Dragneva and Wolczuk 2016, 681). Secondly, some changes within the EU and Russia coincided with presidential rules in Ukraine. For example, 2004 was not only the year of the Orange Revolution in Ukraine, but also of the EU's largest enlargement and the introduction of the European Neighbourhood Policy. This was also a turning point in the worsening of Ukraine-Russia relations, caused not only by the 'colour revolutions' but also by high energy prices and Russia's more assertive foreign policy (Pifer 2009, 394). The following years, of Yushchenko's pro-EU policy, saw the introduction of the EU's Eastern Partnership in 2008 and Russia's reactions to this. The Yanukovych presidency overlapped with Putin's preparation for and return to power in 2012 and the introduction of Russia's new integration projects, which also influenced Ukraine-Russia relations substantially. That is why I see it as reasonable to divide the chapter into three periods: the years from independence to the Orange Revolution (1991-2004), Yushchenko's presidency (2005-2010), and Yanukovych's presidency (2010-2014).

2.1. Ukraine's independence and its foreign policy in 1991-2004

2.1.1. International recognition and territorial disputes with Russia

In their struggle for independence, Ukrainians had to fight with their neighbours for centuries, yet often became part of foreign empires such as Russian, Ottoman and Austro-Hungarian, or the Polish Kingdom (Friedman 2013). The country's geostrategic posi-

---

15   The Ukrainian Constitution of 1996 defined Ukraine as a presidential-parliamentary republic. In 2004, the Verkhovna Rada of Ukraine changed the Constitution, and the country became parliamentary-presidential; this change was cancelled in 2010 but reinstated in February 2014. During each period, conflicts over power sharing between a president and each parliament were 'a norm' in Ukrainian political life.

tion between 'East and West', 'South and North'[16], access to two seas (the Black Sea and the Sea of Azov), reserves of natural resources (iron ore, coal, manganese, salt and many others), fertile black soil (1/3 of the world's reserves), the Ukrainian workforce, agriculture and industries — all were attracting conquests (Canadian Institute of Ukrainian Studies 2001). Despite this, Ukraine had periods of independence, such as Kievan Rus (9th-13th century), Cossack Hetmanate (17th-18th century) and the Ukrainian State in 1918. Currently, being the second biggest country in Europe (after Russia) and, in addition to the above mentioned resources, also having a certain industrial potential (including military and air-space complexes), Ukraine attracts the interest of major powers (Mroz and Pavliuk 1996; Odushkin 2001; Taylor 2014). In this section, I explain the formation of Ukraine's foreign policy from the country's independence up to 2004. I discuss international recognition of the country, its 'controllably turbulent' relations with Russia and its attempts to get closer to the European Union. Finally, I analyse the strategic decision-making of the country's leadership of that time using the game theory analytical framework.

To begin with, Ukraine accepted the historic Act of Independence of Ukraine on 24 August 1991 (Verkhovna Rada of Ukraine 1991). On 1 December 1991, in the independence referendum, 90% of Ukrainians supported the independence of the country (Encyclopedia of Ukrainian history 2020). On the same day, in the presidential elections, Leonid Kravchuk was elected the first president of independent Ukraine. Poland and Canada were the first countries to recognise Ukraine's independence on 2 December 1991. Most European countries recognised Ukraine in the following days, but for some countries across the world it took several years. As an independent country, Ukraine had to form its foreign policy. To the West, a substantial part of Europe was united in the European Community. Yet between Ukraine and the

---

16 In the Middle Ages, an important trade route 'from the Varangians to the Greeks' went through Ukraine and was connecting Scandinavia with the Byzantine Empire (thus, North with South) (Varangian route 1993).

European Community, there were other post-communist countries, that, together with Ukraine, were creating a kind of buffer in relation to Russia. In this way, in the 1990's Ukraine was not so geopolitically important as it would become after 2004 (when it already bordered the European Union). Policy-makers and scholars agree that EU-Ukraine relations started when the European Community officially recognized Ukraine as a sovereign state in 1991 (European Union— EEAS 2019; Tenerowicz 2012, 159). When this new kind of Ukrainian state was forming, crucial changes were also happening in Europe—on 7th February 1992 the Maastricht Treaty was signed and the European Union was established (Treaty on European Union 1992). The Treaty, being one of the two basic treaties of the EU, brought member-countries closer and also developed their more coordinated foreign policy (Haukkala 2015, 26). So, Europe of 1992 was comprised of several newly independent countries which had been part of the former USSR and the Warsaw Pact in the East, and a union of developed European countries in the West. Ukraine had to navigate in this new geopolitical reality.

It was not only a cooperative environment that awaited Ukraine, but at the same time the first issues arose in its relations with Russia. The partitioning of the USSR led to substantial difficulties in Ukraine-Russia relations due to "the large number of historical, religious, economic, political and security legacies involved" (Dragneva-Lewers and Wolczuk 2015, 14). The newly independent countries were taking possession of Soviet military stationing on their territory, but the ownership of the Black Sea Fleet[17] in Crimea, which was an operationally strategic military association, caused disagreement between Ukraine and Russia (D'Anieri 2019, 39–40; Fedorovyh 2007; Wood et al. 2015, 7). Firstly, Ukraine included the Black Sea Fleet in its Army; later Russia did the same, which heated up the conflict (Fedorovyh 2007; Vynogradova and Chervonenko 2017). In 1993, Russia tried to

---

17   The Black Sea Fleet consisted of 440 ships, 18 submarines, 200 support vessels, 300 planes and 70 000 personnel, and was equipped with nuclear weapon (Pryidun 2018, 114).

bargain gas supplies in exchange for the whole of the Black Sea Fleet in Crimea (D'Anieri 2019, 41; Dragneva-Lewers and Wolczuk 2015a, 18; Pryidun 2018, 116). It is important to note that this was the first, but not the last, time when Russia used Ukraine's energy dependency as strategic leverage. On the other hand, Russia was attempting to gain control over Crimea through the Black Sea Fleet (Pryidun 2018, 115), e.g., via the declaration of Sevastopol as a Russian city in 1993, and by acts of disobedience in relation to the Ukrainian authorities in 1994 (Sasse 1996, 92–94; Vynogradova and Chervonenko 2017). In those years, conflictual moments were taking place both in official Ukraine-Russia interactions, and between ordinary Black Sea Fleet sailors and Crimean citizens (for examples see: Mezentsev 2008). According to some scholars, this could potentially have led to war (Kapsamun 2014) or secession of the peninsula (Larrabee 1994, 14; Sasse 1996). Such instability (with potential separatism) on the peninsula was regulated by Ukraine's acceptance of the law "On the Autonomous Republic of Crimea" in 1995 (Verkhovna Rada of Ukraine 1995). And the signature of the Ukraine-Russia agreement "On a Phased Settlement of the Black Sea Fleet Issue" solved the fleet issue: Ukraine received its 15-20%[18], Russia – all the rest, and Sevastopol's bay was divided for the stationing of both fleets (Ukraine, Russian Federation 1994). The issues I have described prove the importance of Crimea for Russia and the latter's potential to inflame the peninsula's political situation.

Despite difficulties in relations with some countries, the first governments of independent Ukraine seemed to trust in the peaceful intentions of its foreign partners. Firstly, in 1991-1992, Ukraine's President Kravchuk refused participation in all of the security and military cooperation offered by Russia under the Commonwealth of Independent States coordination (D'Anieri 2019, 36). Later, in the 1993 Military Doctrine, Ukraine proclaimed its neutrality and rejection of nuclear weapon proliferation (Verkhovna Rada of Ukraine 1993). On 10 July 1994, Leonid

---

18 Initially, Ukraine received half of the Fleet, but sold „all but 15 to 20 percent of its half to Russia in return for debt relief" (Larrabee 1994, 17).

Kuchma was elected the President of Ukraine and on 5 December 1994, following discussions with foreign interlocutors, he signed the Budapest Memorandum[19] (Ukraine, the Russian Federation, the United Kingdom of Great Britain and Northern Ireland, the United States of America 1994). Although relinquishing Ukraine's nuclear weapons was not an easy decision and the country needed financial assistance (which it received in due course), the Budapest Memorandum was still a rather controversial step[20] (D'Anieri 2019; Larrabee 1994; Mroz and Pavliuk 1996). On the one hand, Ukraine declared itself to be a peaceful country, while on the other, its security rested on the willingness of the signatories to respect the territorial integrity of Ukraine. At that time, a famous proponent of realism in world politics—John Mearsheimer (1993)—advised Ukraine not to become a non-nuclear country and predicted Russian aggression if it did. However, cooperative relations between the two countries were established at least on paper in 1997, when the Treaty on Friendship, Cooperation and Partnership was signed, and confirmed, among other things, Russia's acceptance of the territorial integrity of Ukraine[21] (Ukraine, Russian Federation 1998). A number of other agreements were also signed between Ukraine and Russia and the final division of the Black Sea Fleet was ended by the 2000's[22]. As an outcome, the Russian Black Sea Fleet (338 ships and 25 thousand soldiers) re-

---

19   According to the Budapest Memorandum, Ukraine gave up its nuclear weapons and transferred them to Russia in exchange for financial compensation and guarantees to respect its territorial integrity by the Russian Federation, the United Kingdom and the USA (Ukraine, Russian Federation, the United Kingdom of Great Britain and Northern Ireland, the United States of America 1994).
20   For discussion about Ukraine's complicated bargaining with Russia and the US regarding the surrender of its nuclear weapons, compensation and security guarantees for Ukraine, see: (D'Anieri 2019, 47–53).
21   The Agreement was criticised in Ukraine due to the obstacle the Russian Black Sea Fleet might create for Ukraine's desire to join NATO, and in Russia due to the recognition of Crimea and Donbas as parts of Ukraine (some Russians saw these as „natively Russian lands") (High relations 2013).
22   For the description of the phases and conditions of the partitioning of the Black Sea Fleet, see: (Fedorovyh 2007; High relations 2013; Kapsamun 2014); for details about the related complications in Ukraine-Russia relations see: (Levyk 2014; Pryidun 2018; Tsitsuashvili 2009).

ceived the right to reside in Sevastopol[23](Vynogradova and Chervonenko 2017). Hence, the Ukrainian state compromised on its security by leaving its sovereignty to the goodwill of other countries — it gave away its nuclear arsenal and let a foreign fleet station in its bays. As we will later see, this trust in the good intentions of foreign interlocutors proved to be unjustified.

In spite of a legally reached agreement regarding Crimea, Russia did not stop its attempts to destabilise the situation in the region. For instance, the Russian consulate in Crimea, which was opened in 1999, gave Russian passports to Crimeans (Russian Consulate General is opened in Simferopol 1999), which scholars saw as part of Vladimir Putin's presidential campaign (Wood et al. 2015, 8). Russian (and Russian-sponsored) NGOs, initiatives and youth organisations existed in Crimea and since Ukraine's independence had promoted joining Russia (Wood 2015b, 8–10). The role of the Black Sea Fleet (its personnel and their families, its cultural and military events etc.) in the pro-Russian movement was also substantial (Tsitsuashvili 2009). Moreover, a crucial event, which could have led to a Russian-Ukrainian war, took place in autumn 2003 — Russia started building a dam to the Ukrainian island Tuzla[24]. The Chief of the Border Guard Service of Ukraine explained that during the Tuzla incident, Ukraine "got into a system of hybrid relations [with Russia]" for the first time (Int-10 2020). In his view, in spite of Russia's provocations (in the Russian media, putting a Russian sign on Tuzla, building a dam close to the island and the lack of communication from Russia), there were no instructions from the Ukrainian authorities for a long time, and according to Lytvyn's sources, President Kuchma somehow knew about Russia's desire to annex this territory (Lytvyn 2019, 44–66). After a certain time, President Kuchma discussed the situation with President Putin personally and Russia stopped the construc-

---

23 Ukraine included its part of the Black Sea Fleet into its Military Forces, and the Russian part kept the name — the Black Sea Fleet of the Russian Federation. For its lease in Sevastopol, Russia paid $98 million every year, which went to repay Ukraine's debt for the import of Russian fuel (Balmaceda 1998, 265).
24 The tiny island of Tuzla (3 km²) is situated between the Ukrainian Crimean and the Russian Taman peninsulas.

tion (Kuchma on Tuzla and after Tuzla 2003). These incidents with the Black Sea Fleet and Tuzla could be seen as Russia's first dangerous alarm bells, the solving of which required much effort on the part of Ukrainian decision-makers[25], and also exposed Russia's constant preference regarding Ukraine — to maintain a certain influence on the country. Apart from this, Russia was also trying to re-integrate with Ukraine, which is discussed below.

2.1.2. Integration options for Ukraine

Although post-Cold War Europe was driven by the spirit of partnership and integration, not all doors were open to Ukraine. On the one hand, Russian officials could not accept Ukraine's independence, which they were publicly acknowledging in the 1990's (Charap and Colton 2017, 56) or even in the 2000's (Malek 2009, 534). On the other hand, scholars noted that although in the 1990's the European Union was also not sure if Ukraine would preserve its independence (Larrabee 1994), its cooperation was limited (Dragneva-Lewers and Wolczuk 2015). Since the signature of the Partnership and Co-operation Agreement in 1994 (98/149/EC, ECSC, Euratom 1998), there were many ups and downs in EU-Ukraine relations. In 1998, President Leonid Kuchma confirmed that integrating with the EU was a strategic course for Ukraine (Verkhovna Rada of Ukraine 1998) and in a certain way 'introduced' the feeling of European identity in Ukrainians (Shulman 2005). Although the political elite in Ukraine since independence was quite in favour of EU integration, no substantial 'homework' was done to bring the country closer to the EU standards in various areas (Kuzio 2005b, 61; Pifer 2009, 388–89; Tenerowicz 2012, 158). Due to Ukraine's slow implementation of reforms and the EU's domestic situation[26], the EU was neither ready to offer a more comprehensive agreement, nor the prospect of membership which Ukraine was seeking (Dragneva-Lewers and Wolczuk 2015, 38–39, 41; Kuzio 2005b, 62). Thus, the EU-Ukraine relations of that

---

25 Kuchma confessed that the Tuzla incident was one of the hardest moments in his presidency (Lytvyn 2019, 66).
26 The EU was preparing for the acceptance of 10 new members in 2004, which left almost no capacity for any further enlargement in the near future.

time were trapped in mutual misunderstanding: Ukraine wanted to have a membership perspective and the EU was concentrated on reforms in the country (Moroney 2001). At the same time, EU-Russia relations were also not moving forward easily and even the signature of the Partnership and Cooperation Agreement took much longer than expected and showed substantial differences in the two parties' views of their relations (Haukkala 2015, 26–27). Thus, certain difficulties in relations between the EU and its Eastern neighbours could be noticed already in the 1990's.

Although the EU did have an interest in Eastern Europe, the EU's inconsistency, a flawed analysis of others' preferences and a variety of domestic interests contributed to the first issues in these relations. Firstly, the way in which NATO and the EU were coming closer to Russia geopolitically via their enlargements did not always take into account the strong ties of these countries with Russia, which produced hostile emotions in the country. On the other hand, some scholars argued that the West lost its opportunity in Russia in the 1990's, when the country was willing to integrate with it (Charap and Colton 2017). The view has been expressed that the West either did too much or too little (Stoner and Mcfaul 2015, 167–68). Secondly, scholars have pointed out that the EU's behaviour as a normative hegemon for its neighbours, including Russia, presupposed unequal relationships (Haukkala 2015, 36) and for that reason Russia disapproved it (Charap and Colton 2017, 78). Some scholars argued that for Ukraine, the EU was seen as a civilizational choice and a salvation from dependence on Russia (Dragneva-Lewers and Wolczuk 2015, 32; Mroz and Pavliuk 1996). Others noted that there was no Russian objection to the general idea of the EU's enlargement eastward in the 2000's (Light, White, and Löwenhardt 2000, 77), which might be due to Russia's perception of the EU enlargement "as an acceptable alternative to NATO expansion" (Light, White, and Löwenhardt 2000, 81). According to a Russian scholar, Russian decision-makers always knew about Ukraine's goal to integrate with the EU; however, they accepted this as long as Kuchma publicly argued for close ties with Russia, which helped Russian politicians to retain domestic support (Int-26 2020). Thirdly, Russians also sensed certain issues in the integrity of the EU's foreign policy. For example, scholars argued that in the time of the Chechen wars, Putin learned that the EU could 'close its eyes' to human rights' violations if some of its members were eager to follow their pragmatic interests, which consequently made him favour county-to-country relations (Haukkala 2015, 29–30). Similar issues in the EU's foreign policy (inconsistency, inattention to Russia's preferences and lack of integrity) would contribute to the development of the war in Ukraine in 2014. For its part, Russia attempted to reconnect former Soviet republics into new integration unions already from the 1990's.

Scholars have argued that Russia aimed to bind Ukraine to itself via its integration projects and perceived integration as a way to solve all sensitive issues (e.g., Crimea) in Ukraine-Russia relations (Dragneva-Lewers and Wolczuk 2015, 11). This was not something independent Ukraine would agree to; as a way of leaving the Soviet past behind, Ukraine was trying to get closer to the West via cooperation with the US and integration with the EU (Mroz and Pavliuk 1996). However, it has been argued that Ukraine met with "Russia's refusal to let Ukraine 'go' and the EU's reluctance to let Ukraine 'in'" (Dragneva-Lewers and Wolczuk 2015, 7). One view is that Russia aimed to integrate its projects with the EU sometime later via the negotiations of the EU's enlargement by the whole integration block (Leshoukov 1998). In spite of this, Ukraine under Kravchuk and Kuchma was carefully avoiding too close ties with Russian integration projects. Ukraine did not sign the Decision on the adoption of the CIS Charter and maintained observer status (Ministry of Justice of Ukraine 2020), which, according to scholars, was not effective in achieving economic benefits, such as free trade (Dragneva-Lewers and Wolczuk 2015, 17; Shmelova 2008, 37). Furthermore, already in the 1990's Russia had started to connect Ukraine's integration choices and the solution of the Black Sea Fleet issues with gas prices (Balmaceda 1998, 260). Therefore, it can be observed that Russia viewed Ukraine as a crucial member in its integration unions and was ready to make the country join them even by using some kind of political and economic force.

The year 2000 marked Vladimir Putin's rise to power and consequent shift in Russia's foreign policy, which became even more assertive than it had previously been. In the same year, the Eurasian Economic Community (EEC) was established and it aimed at the integration of post-Soviet countries (Eurasian Economic Community 2000). At the same time, Putin was developing cooperative relations with the EU and the four Common Spaces were created in 2003 (European Commission 2005; Haukkala 2015, 30–31). An EU official directly involved in EU-Russia relations mentioned that in the early Putin years, "Russia was interested in ever closer relations with the EU ... and wanted to be recognised as an equal partner" (Int-35 2021). However, Russia continued its strategy of subsidising gas exports in return for good relations with Ukraine (Dragneva-Lewers and Wolczuk 2015, 14), and the highest price would apply if Ukraine chose to turn from 'East to West' (Dragneva-Lewers and Wolczuk 2015, 21). Ukrainian decision-makers had to respond to these foreign policy challenges.

In respect to Ukraine's policy-making, it is important to acknowledge that Ukraine was not yet a full democracy and the majority of Ukrainians had no influence on the country's foreign policy. Thus, the country's preferences and payoffs in foreign policy were often dependent on the interests of the most powerful oligarchs (Kuzio 2005b), who also possessed tools[27] to reach their goals (Szeptycki 2008). Most of these oligarchs resisted the economic reforms required by the EU, since they preferred to preserve their power and rent-seeking incomes, with their substantial part coming from business with Russia (Meister 2019, 309), and primarily from trade in gas (Dragneva and Wolczuk 2016, 681–82; Szeptycki 2008). However, Ukraine's ruling elites were against both losing their sovereignty and resources to Russia, and developing excessively close ties with the EU, which would mean losing their power because of anti-corruption laws and the development of "competition, transparency, and rule of

---

27 These oligarchic tools of influence included: possession of core Ukrainian media, and connections to Ukrainian, EU and Russian policy-makers (Szeptycki 2008, 64).

law" (Kuzio 2005b; Meister 2019, 309–10). Thus, Kuchma's multi-vector foreign policy provided an acceptable equilibrium for the leading oligarchs.

Dissatisfaction on the part of some of the Ukrainian population with the wide-spread corruption, poverty and dependence on Russia was reflected in popular protests, e.g., "Ukraine without Kuchma", which followed the murder of journalist Georgiy Gongadze in 2000 (Shmelova 2008, 30), and the victory of the opposition party "Our Ukraine" in the 2002 parliamentary elections (Kuzio 2005a; Onuch 2014a). The complicated domestic situation pushed the Ukrainian President to search for certain economic benefits in cooperation with Russia. In 2003, Kuchma signed the agreement on the Single Economic Space with Russia, Kazakhstan and Belarus, which was ratified by the Ukrainian government in 2004 (Martynov 2005). However, the oligarchs, who preferred the country's sovereignty and its partnership with the West, were annoyed with this step (Zon 2005, 15). Moreover, the majority of Ukrainians refused to accept Kuchma or his appointee as the next president[28] (Kuzio 2005a, 2005c). According to the Democratic Initiatives Fund, in 2004, 87.7% of Ukrainians evaluated Kuchma's presidency "5" or lower on a 10-point scale, with 27.7% giving the lowest "1" grade (Democratic Initiatives Fund 2004). The Ukrainian population's dissatisfaction with the country's overall poverty and its oligarchy, fuelled by the fraudulent victory of Viktor Yanukovych in the 2004 presidential elections, developed into the Orange Revolution (Onuch 2014a; Wilson 2015). The protests brought about new elections and the subsequent victory of Viktor Yushchenko—a more pro-EU candidate, who also promised to eradicate corruption (Kuzio 2005a). However, not only oligarchic interests, but also Ukraine's economic and social difficulties had their influence on the country's foreign policy, which we will study in the next section.

---

28 A public opinion poll showed that Kuchma's appointee Yanukovych would lose in the first and the second round of the presidential elections in 2004 (Public opinion poll in Ukraine 2004).

2.1.3. The impact of Ukraine's domestic situation on its foreign policy

Ukraine's domestic economic and social situation had a certain impact on the country's foreign policy and so it is worth looking at this. In the 20th century, Ukraine had various economic advantages: for instance, it was known as the breadbasket of Europe, and it contained a substantial part of Soviet heavy industry (Dean 2000, 94), and in particular an important part of its military complex (Odushkin 2001, 375–76). However, after becoming independent, the country was unable to develop quickly. High inflation, the transition to a market economy and near economic collapse were the country's domestic threats in the 1990's (Mroz and Pavliuk 1996, 54). This combination of misfortunes created economic difficulties and Ukraine's performance was much lower than that of other East European or post-Soviet countries (Dean 2000). Firstly, unlike the Baltic and East European countries, Ukraine did not quickly develop a market economy but was stuck with a hybrid, half state half private (Davis 2016, 168). Secondly, the country received less FDI than those other countries (Shmelova 2008, 41), which made Ukraine dependent on foreign consulting and financial help (Dean 2000, 101; Mroz and Pavliuk 1996, 59). The EU was also sending substantial aid to Ukraine via programmes dealing mostly with national, regional, border and nuclear security issues (Tenerowicz 2012, 165). Thus, economic hardship made Ukraine dependent on financial support from the West. In addition to this, the country was economically bound up with Russia.

Economic dependency on Russia put certain limitations on Ukraine's independent foreign policy. The countries were truly interconnected economically; let us only mention the fact that 50% of Russia's gas and 90% of its oil exports to Europe went through Ukraine (Balmaceda 1998, 259; Tsygankov 2015, 281). Although the greatest example of Ukraine's dependency on Russia related to its imports of energy resources (Balmaceda 1998, 257; Mroz and Pavliuk 1996, 58), its dependence in relation to the defence industry and military research was also substantial (Davis 2016, 174;

Dragneva-Lewers and Wolczuk 2015, 16; Rutland 2015, 131). Moreover, as mentioned earlier, many Ukrainian oligarchs were making money out of Russian gas (Dean 2000, 103; Dragneva and Wolczuk 2016, 681), which also hindered Ukraine's healthy economic development. Certain Ukrainian elites perceived the Russian economic system as friendly and preferred the country to move in the Eastern direction of integration to that of the Western, which would require the development of democracy and would reduce oligarchic influence (Dean 2000, 96; Kuzio 2005c). Thus, these economic and financial dependencies on foreign states left Ukraine's foreign policy with less room for manoeuvre.

In addition to economic instability, in the first years of its independence, Ukraine experienced some social fluctuations due to the hard economic situation and regional differences (Larrabee 1994; Pifer 2009, 388; Sasse 2001). Even the country's concept of national security in 1997 identified separatist tendencies in certain regions and among some political forces as one of the main threats (Verkhovna Rada of Ukraine 1997). Although some scholars noted regional, cultural and language differences in the political choices of Ukraine (Pogrebinskiy 2015), others argued that socio-economic divisions, but not those related to ethnicity and/or language, were more important in people's political affiliations (Sasse 2001, 73–74). However, different separatist tendencies even with local referendums (in Donbas and Crimea) on different kinds of regional autonomies existed in the 1990's (Sasse 2001). Moreover, social unrest and protests due to poverty, although not massive (Zon 2005, 18), were part of Ukrainian life in this period (Mroz and Pavliuk 1996). These domestic instabilities and economic problems took much of decision-makers' energy, which could otherwise have been used for building Ukraine's professional foreign policy. Moreover, economically weak Ukraine was less interesting to its foreign interlocutors and the country could not place itself as an equal partner on the world map.

My employment of a game theory-based framework for an analysis of Ukrainian elites' decision-making in 1991-2004 enabled me to determine that Leonid Kuchma and his team were quite good in their foreign policy analysis and strategic decisions. Although Leonid Kravchuk adopted more nationalistic policies, the economic fall during his presidency (1991-1994) resulted in Ukrainians' choice of Kuchma over Kravchuk in 1994 (Zon 2005, 13). Leonid Kuchma, the director of a huge "Yuzhmash" plant in Soviet times, had a substantial understanding of Ukraine's economic ties with Russia, and the mindset of the people ruling Russia. Proof of this contention is provided by his successful resolution of all sensitive situations which could have developed into an open Ukraine-Russia conflict (Mroz and Pavliuk 1996). Moreover, his ability to preserve all of the Ukrainian regions in one state is also remarkable (Sasse 2001; Zon 2005). Kuchma's awareness of Russia's preferences helped him to keep the required balance in Ukrainian-Russian interactions. Although aiming towards EU integration, Kuchma preserved good relations with Russia and thus avoided angering the country. However, the proclaimed foreign policy goals were not achieved and Ukraine was no closer to EU integration in 2004 (Kuzio 2005b, 61). One may say that policy-makers in the early years of Ukraine's independence were not able to correctly estimate the EU's preferences. On the other hand, it is probable that certain oligarchic circles were not interested in faster integration with the EU, and only acknowledged Ukraine's desire for EU membership from time to time in order to gain the support of Ukrainian voters (Dragneva and Wolczuk 2016; Dragneva-Lewers and Wolczuk 2015; Meister 2019). It seems as though Kuchma and his team were right in their estimation of trust in Russian actions most of the time (the Tuzla incident, pressure on Ukraine to join Russia's integration projects). They were also learning to distinguish between the EU's policy statements and its realistic strategies. Ukraine's payoffs overlapped with the payoffs of the most powerful oligarchs, who preferred to maintain the *status quo* and to continue their rent-seeking practices, including machinations over Russian gas. Thus, the application of my game theory analytical framework to Kuchma's decision-making in foreign relations proves that his policy was quite successful, but only until the beginning of the 2000s. Later, the previous equilibrium in foreign and domestic policy faltered, while at the same time it went against Russia's payoff (Ukraine's membership in its integration organisations), that of the EU (Ukraine as a democratic and stable trade partner), and that of the Ukrainian people (a decent standard of living). As long as Ukrainian oligarchs had the resources to prevent Russia and the EU from having too big influence on the country, and the Ukrainian population continued to be oppressed, the system maintained a fragile stability. The fraudulent 2004 elections, the EU's support for an opposition candidate, and the emergence of popular protests, ruined this balance and allowed a new elite to come to power. This change in the ruling elites also brought substantial change to EU-Ukraine-Russia relations.

2.2. The EU-Ukraine-Russia relations after the Orange Revolution

2.2.1. Post-revolution expectations and challenges

Scholars have argued that the election of Viktor Yushchenko following the Orange Revolution was a victory for democracy and the persistence of European values in Ukraine, which could be a strong justification for Ukraine's dream of membership in the EU (Dragneva-Lewers and Wolczuk 2015, 42; Kuzio 2005a). Therefore, with his big supply of trust from Ukrainians, Yushchenko and his team aimed to receive the EU's perspective for the country (Wiegand and Schulz 2015, 333). At the same time, changes within the EU — the 2004 enlargement, which made Ukraine its direct neighbour, and the introduction of the European Neighbourhood Policy — also increased the EU's interest in developing closer ties with Ukraine (Charap and Colton 2017, 96). The European Parliament resolution confirmed Ukraine's European aspirations and called on the Commission to consider "a revision of the European Neighbourhood Policy Action Plan … in the light of its [the new Ukrainian government] deep aspirations for European integration" (European Parliament 2005). Moreover, scholars have also argued that at that time there was no big Russia's objection to this, and that Ukraine's cooperation with Russia might even have helped to foster EU-Ukraine relations, while Russia achieved deeper economic cooperation with the EU (Charap and Colton 2017, 78–79). What Russia did mind was the change of power in Ukraine as the consequence of the revolution supported by the West.

The Orange Revolution could serve as a good example of the role of perceptions in international politics. On the one hand, the revolution was a matter of Ukrainian domestic politics, while on the other, it mirrored the country's choice between 'pro-Russian' Yanukovych and 'pro-European' Yushchenko. While neither candidate's foreign policy attitudes were that simple, Yanukovych did favour closer relations with Russia, was openly supported by Putin (Guy-Nizhnik 2017, 448; Kuzio 2005c) and was not as overly optimistic about EU integration as Yushchenko was perceived to be (Kuzio 2005b). Apparently, the EU and Ukraine did not take these Russia's perceptions into account. Scholars have confirmed that the Orange Revolution was seen in Russia as alarming Western interference in Russia's sphere of influence (Dragneva-Lewers and Wolczuk 2015a, 25–26; Malek 2009, 536–37; Pifer 2009, 394–95). For instance, Haukkala (2015, 31) has explained how 'the colour revolutions', combined with Russia's domestic terrorism resulting from the Chechen wars, made Russia less oriented towards cooperation with the EU and acceptance of its Western values. This might have decreased the trust of Russian political elite both domestically and in its foreign interlocutors. According to a senior EU official, who worked on EU-Ukraine-Russia trade relations for years, Russia was very concerned about 'the colour revolutions' and thereafter aimed to ensure that it remained a strategic partner for Ukraine (Int-37 2021). Others argued that Putin saw every revolution in Russia's vicinity as a spark that could trigger protests in Russia and consequently end Putin's rule (Int-13 2020; Wood et al. 2015). From yet another point of view, the international community recognised that the first election results giving victory to Viktor Yanukovych were fraudulent and only Russia accepted him as president (Gromadzki et al. 2004, 2). Therefore, the Orange Revolution was viewed differently by Russia, which to some extent further complicated the EU's and Ukraine's relations with the country.

Yet, there were diverse views on Ukraine's foreign policy also inside the country. For instance, only 10-20% of Ukrainians voted for Yushchenko in the East and South of Ukraine (DIF and KIIS 2005). While the majority of Ukrainians in the West and Centre were in favour of Ukraine's integration into the EU (68% and 55% respectively), the majority in the East and South preferred Ukraine to join the Single Economic Space (77% and 76%) (DIF and KIIS 2005). As noted both by the EU (European Parliament 2005) and some scholars (Gromadzki et al. 2004; Shmelova 2008, 31; Zon 2005, 20), the Orange revolution revealed divisions inside Ukraine, with the East (in particular the Donbas region) being more pro-Russian and cautious of EU integration. Thus, ties with Russia were especially crucial for a certain part of Ukraine, which, in addition to historical and cultural reasons, can be explained by the closer industrial connections of those regions to Russia (Mylovanov, Zhukov, and Gorodnichenko 2018). While Kuchma was able to maintain the unity of Ukrainians even in hard times (Mroz and Pavliuk 1996, 54–55), it was an important task for Yushchenko not to forget about people in Eastern Ukraine, who had voted for his opponent Yanukovych (Gromadzki et al. 2004, 5). Interestingly, but already in 2005, Yushchenko signed a presidential decree approving Ukraine's participation in the Russian-led Single Economic Space, but only if this participation did not prevent integration into the EU (President of Ukraine 2005). Thus, Yushchenko's victory revealed certain regional differences in Ukraine, which could influence the country's domestic and foreign politics.

Although the new authorities wanted rapid integration into the EU, the promised negotiations of the Association Agreement (AA) started only in 2007, after the EU had confirmed the democratic nature of the 2006 elections in Ukraine. The EU "welcomed Ukraine's European choice" and confirmed that the new Association Agreement was to be "aimed at gradual economic integration and deepening of political cooperation" (European Council 2007). However, scholars pointed out that like the previous Ukrainian government, the new one did not develop a strategy to integrate with the EU and did not involve itself enough in the AA negotiations until 2011 (when there was already a new president and he involved core oligarchs in this process) (Dragneva-Lewers and Wolczuk 2015, 43-44). This could be explained by the Ukrainian domestic political crisis[29] and the lack of internal coordination regarding negotiations with the EU (Dragneva-Lewers and Wolczuk 2015, 44). On the other hand, the EU's unwillingness to offer a membership perspective to Ukraine could be due to its concern that this could result in a deterioration in relations with Russia (Malek 2009, 524). Yet the EU-Ukraine negotiations had already captured Russia's attention, and the prospective cooperation in security matters from article 7 was viewed by Russia as a step towards NATO membership (Dragneva-Lewers and Wolczuk 2015, 47). Immediately after the start of the AA negotiations in 2007, Russia started to develop the Customs Union, which was to be based on an integration model of the EU and was to include Ukraine (Dragneva-Lewers and Wolczuk 2015, 26). Whilst a country can be a party of different free trade agreements (FTA), it cannot simultaneously join a customs union and a free trade union, which was confirmed by the EU (Baranovskaya and Stepovik 2011; Int-21 2020; Int-34 2021). Therefore, via this step, Russia wanted Ukraine to make a choice about integration and to abandon its East-West policy.

In 2008, the EU developed the Eastern Partnership (EaP), which was "a special dimension of the European Neighbourhood Policy" and involved "the EU, its Member States and six Eastern European Partners: Armenia, Azerbaijan, Belarus, Georgia, the Republic of Moldova and Ukraine" (European External Action Service 2016). Scholars have argued that its introduction, after the start of the negotiations over AA, did not bring substantial change to EU-Ukraine relations (Dragneva-Lewers and Wolczuk 2015, 45). However, it was viewed very differently in Moscow, which thought it represented a threat to Russia's own integration pro-

---

29 Firstly, I refer to President Yushchenko's 'power wars' with Prime Minister Tymoshenko and her government in 2005-2006. Secondly, the 2006 elections to the Verkhovna Rada of Ukraine saw the victory of the opposition party ("Party of Regions" led by Yanukovych), which made it more difficult for Yushchenko to push forward his pro-EU agenda. The return of Tymoshenko as Prime Minister in 2007 continued the confrontation between the president and the cabinet of ministers (Pifer 2009, 391).

jects, that it could result in a loss of influence over its 'near abroad'[30] (Haukkala 2015, 32), that it could extend the EU's sphere of influence (Charap and Colton 2017, 100) or even that it was a way to get its members into NATO (Moshes 2012, 23; Tsygankov 2015, 290). The vagueness of the EU's explanation of the EaP and its normative part (promotion of norms of democracy, market economy etc.) might have contributed to the development of such perceptions on the part of Russia[31] (Gretskiy, Treshchenkov, and Golubev 2014, 375-376). On the other hand, although President Medvedev was closer to Western values (Int-34 2021), Western hopes for improved relations with Russia under his rule were not realised, since no better EU-Russia agreement was reached and there were no substantial changes in Russian foreign policy (Moshes 2012). In 2008, Russia's anti-Western doctrine was also supported by the development and modernisation of its Army (Åtland 2016, 163). Scholars argued that the Eastern Partnership, together with 'the colour revolutions', were perceived by Russia as a threat to its goal of becoming a regional power by means of its influence over post-Soviet space (Dragneva-Lewers and Wolczuk 2015, 25; Moshes 2012, 26) and this subsequently made Russia's attitude to its 'near abroad' more defensive (Gretskiy, Treshchenkov, and Golubev 2014, 378). According to an EU official, the above, combined with the Russian-Georgian war of 2008, brought about a deterioration in EU-Russia relations (Int-2 2020). This was also a substantial challenge to Ukrainian decision-makers, which they did not manage to fully address. Therefore, my next section deals with the failures of President Yushchenko and his 'orange' team.

---

30 A Russian scholar argued that Russian leaders were most annoyed with the fact that these six post-Soviet countries joined the Eastern Partnership so rapidly and with no issues, whilst cooperation within the CIS was always complicated and slow (Int-26 2020)

31 Additionally, it was not helpful that Eastern Partnership's initiators, the foreign ministers of Poland and Sweden, were presenting the project as anti-Russian (Merry 2015, 36).

2.2.2. The failures of the Yushchenko presidency

After some time, it became clear both to Ukrainians and Ukraine's foreign partners that Viktor Yushchenko's big promises (the end of corruption, economic development, and integration with the EU) were not to be realised. The internal fight for power was not only preventing important reforms inside the country, but was also pushing Ukraine further from the EU (Guy-Nizhnik 2017, 448; Pifer 2009, 391). Additionally, it was mentioned, that despite Yushchenko's promise to end the oligarchy, he involved himself in some of its projects (Szeptycki 2008, 43). In 2008, the European Commission expressed concern over corruption in the country and dissatisfaction with what was clearly a falsely expressed desire of the new political elites to fight it (Gretskiy 2013, 11). In 2009, the EU postponed signing the AA, and the European Commission's President criticized the Ukrainian authorities for corruption and lack of structural economic reforms (Ivakhnenko 2009). In addition, the Ukrainian economy shrank by 14.8% in 2009 due to the 2008 financial crisis, and 78% of Ukrainians found themselves living below the poverty line (Poverty line in Ukraine and Europe 2010). Therefore, Ukrainians and the country's foreign partners were rather unsatisfied with Yushchenko's presidency.

While progress in relations with the EU was not visible, the deterioration of relations with Russia was evident from the start of Yushchenko's presidency (Shmelova 2008, 31; Szeptycki 2008, 52; Tenerowicz 2012, 158). His electoral rhetoric was already touching on issues which were of high concern to Russia, such as the status of the Black Sea Fleet, closer ties with both NATO and the EU and the use of the Russian language in Ukraine (Gretskiy 2013, 20). Unlike Kuchma, Yushchenko used language which was too tough (for Russia) in respect of the pro-EU course, which annoyed Russian policy-makers (Int-26 2020). In spite of attempts "to reset Russia-Ukraine relations", they were deteriorating, due, for example, to Ukraine's plans not to prolong the lease of Sevastopol bay to the Russian fleet (Gretskiy 2013, 20-21). The 2005 gas dispute with Russia or the 2008 interruption of gas supplies both to Ukraine and Europe showed once again the link between gas prices and Ukraine's integration choices (Guy-Nizhnik 2017; Tsygankov 2015, 283). Subsequent attempts by Ukraine to integrate with NATO and the Bucharest Declaration's[32] confirmation that Ukraine would join at some unspecified time were received by Russia as direct threats (Charap and Colton 2017, 88–89; Malek 2009, 534–35). It was during this NATO Summit that Putin told Bush that Ukraine was not a state and suggested that if Ukraine was to join NATO, it would do this without Crimea and the Eastern part of Ukraine (NATO is dissolved into packages of blocks 2008). Moreover, the Russian Parliament asked the president to break the Treaty on Friendship with Ukraine because of Ukraine's efforts to join NATO (Russia is ready to break the treaty with Ukraine 2008). In spite of Russia's dissatisfaction with Ukraine's pro-Western policy, some scholars pointed out that Tymoshenko's government[33] "pursued policies — especially in the energy sphere — that were almost entirely satisfactory to Moscow" (Merry 2015, 32). However, Russia's recall of its ambassador to Ukraine in 2009 and unwillingness to appoint a new one was a low point in the countries' relations (Gretskiy 2013, 23–24; Guy-Nizhnik 2017, 453). Therefore, one could say that, unlike Kuchma's, Yuschenko's strategy backfired: although he hardly achieved his goals with the EU or NATO, he managed to provoke Russia.

In spite of huge hopes for progress in foreign policy, Yushchenko's team did not show any substantial achievements, apart from joining the WTO. Receiving 5% of the votes in the 2010 presidential elections, and the victory of his opponent who had almost the opposite agenda, might be a sign of the people's verdict on Yushchenko's presidency (Central Electoral Committee of Ukraine 2010). It could be that over-optimism after the Orange Revolution and concentration on domestic political battles distracted Ukrainian politicians from assessing foreign policy information (Guy-Nizhnik 2017). Kyiv leaders trusted the EU's will to integrate with

---

32 The Bucharest Declaration, accepted at NATO Summit in Bucharest in April 2008, among others stated: „NATO welcomes Ukraine's and Georgia's Euro-Atlantic aspirations for membership in NATO. We agreed today that these countries will become members of NATO." (NATO 2008).
33 Yulia Tymoshenko was Ukraine's Prime Minister in 2005 and in 2007-2010.

Ukraine, even if the actual signals from Brussels were moderate or negative. It is hard to say whether the president and his team truly believed in the possibility of the EU opening accession negotiations with Ukraine in this period. In their public appeal, indeed, they seemed to be convinced of this. This unrealistic message, together with the poor progress in integration with the EU, was criticised even by some of Ukraine's powerful oligarchs (Szeptycki 2008, 55). The EU's preferred payoff for that time might have been closer relations with Ukraine (but only after the country's 'homework' would have been done), but there was no way of the EU's enlargement by Ukraine in the foreseeable future (Maass 2019, 6). Russia wanted Ukraine to join its own integration organisations and showed this clearly with political and economic (gas wars) signals. It is crucial to mention that oligarchic influence on the country's domestic and foreign policies (and the country's payoffs) was not brought to an end during the Yushchenko era (Szeptycki 2008). Looking at the country's resources of that time, it can be observed that Ukraine's international image did improve after the Orange Revolution and later after the country's entrance to the WTO in 2008, which added some credibility to Ukraine's desire to become a candidate for EU membership. However, a poor level of democratic standards (and most importantly, a high level of corruption), as well as weak economic development, ensured that the country did not turn into a powerful player in Europe. Energy dependency on Russia and Russia's use of this as a leverage confirmed Ukraine's inability to back its aims with means, and Russia's readiness to use this tool to pursue its foreign policy goals. Thus, looking through my game theory analytical framework, Yushchenko's team did not conduct a proper foreign policy analysis, which resulted in its defeat both domestically and on the international level. My next section deals with the presidency of Yanukovych, whose even worse decision-making resulted in a war in 2014.

2.3. The Yanukovych regime and its fall (2010-2014)

2.3.1. The bargaining between East and West

The presidency of Viktor Yanukovych is essential for understanding the 2014 conflict. It is that moment when previous antagonisms came out and Ukraine found itself inside some kind of 'geopolitical game', which did not reflect the interests of the country. In this section, I study the decision-making process of President Yanukovych and those around him during the formation of this dangerous conflict environment in Ukraine's foreign relations. Scholars name the Yanukovych presidency "a return to Ukraine's usual East-West bargaining foreign policy"[34] (Samokhvalov 2015) and call him an advocate of nonalignment foreign policy (Birchfield and Young 2018, 56). On the one hand, the EU strategic course was officially unchangeable, while on the other, involvement in cooperation with Russia was quite strong (Tenerowicz 2012, 159). As scholars have pointed out, during the Yanukovych presidency "the gap between domestic developments and pro-European declarations was the widest" (Dragneva-Lewers and Wolczuk 2015, 52). Relations with Russia looked idyllic compared to those of the Yushchenko era (Mukhametov 2011). For instance, Yanukovych gave up the NATO membership aspiration, signed a treaty to prolong the Black Sea Fleet's stationing in Crimea[35] (see Table 2), expanded the legitimate use of Russian as a language of the minority in some regions, and did not challenge the Soviet view of the history (Mukhametov 2011; Tsygankov 2015, 281). This gave Russia the hope of developing closer relations, possibly even in common integration projects (Charap and Colton 2017, 114; Tsygankov 2015, 281). A senior EU official specialising in EU-Ukraine-Russia relations also argued that Russia

---

34 I mean Ukraine's policy of getting benefits both from the EU and Russia, but integration with neither of them. This policy was most visible during the Kuchma era. Meister (2019, 306) argues that the vast majority of post-Soviet countries follow such multi-vector foreign policies.

35 The Kharkiv Accords, signed by Yanukovych in April 2010, prolonged the lease of the Sevastopol bay to the Russian fleet until 2042 in return for 30% discount in gas prices for Ukraine (Dragneva and Wolczuk 2016, 690).

wanted to use the opportunity of the pro-Russian Yanukovych presidency to take back control of Ukraine and prevent the country's integration with the EU (Int-37 2021). Thus, Russia saw Yanukovych's presidency as a chance to achieve its own goals in Ukraine.

However, together with the improvement in relations with Russia, Yanukovych's team did not change Ukraine's policy of closer partnership with the EU and actually pursued it further, at least initially, as was reflected in the ongoing negotiations of the Association Agreement (Dragneva-Lewers and Wolczuk 2015, 55; Tenerowicz 2012, 167). Article 11 of the Law 'On the Foundations of Internal and Foreign Policy', passed in July 2010, stated that one of the core tasks of Ukraine's foreign policy was "ensuring Ukraine's integration into the European political, economic, legal space to become a member of the European Union" (Verkhovna Rada of Ukraine 2010). On the one hand, Yanukovych might have considered closer relations with the EU only to gain the support of Ukrainians, in particular before the 2015 elections; on the other, his close oligarchs were eager to get access to the EU market (Dragneva-Lewers and Wolczuk 2015). Although Yushchenko started discussions about the new agreement with the EU in March 2007 (Burlyuk and Shapovalova 2017), it was Yanukovych who brought the talks to their final phase. This resulted in the initialling of the EU-Ukraine Association Agreement on 30 March 2012 and the Deep and Comprehensive Free Trade Agreement (DCFTA) on 19 July 2012 (see Table 1). Ukraine did not have to wait for Russia's retaliation in relation to these steps.

At the same time, Russia was pursuing the goal of getting Ukraine into its sphere of influence via the development of its integration projects in defiance of the EU (Charap and Colton 2017, 101; Gretskiy, Treshchenkov, and Golubev 2014, 380; Haukkala 2015, 32). The previously mentioned Customs Union of Russia, Belarus and Kazakhstan was finally established in 2009 and launched in 2010 (Eurasian Economic Commission 2009).

Preparing his return to the presidency[36], Vladimir Putin was promoting the Customs Union as an integration alternative to the EU for post-Soviet countries, and especially for Ukraine, which was seen as an inevitable member of the Union (Birchfield and Young 2018, 60; Putin 2010). However, in April 2011, Ukraine announced its decision not to join the Customs Union (Baranovskaya and Stepovik 2011; Moshes 2012, 26–27). Consequently, in summer 2011 the Commission of the Customs Union introduced trade duties on some Ukrainian foodstuffs and metal products (Yanitsky 2011). In autumn of the same year, Putin was promoting yet another project – the Eurasian Union, pointing to the flexible nature of its membership and economic advantages, e.g., an increase of trade, modernization and improvement of living standards (Tsygankov 2015, 284). Russia's foreign policy became even more assertive when Putin won the presidential election once again.

Scholars and policy-makers are in agreement that Putin's return to power in 2012 brought a substantial deterioration in Russia-EU relations (Int-2 2020; Int-34 2021; B. Smith 2016; Trudolyubov 2015). It was argued that Putin not only blamed the West for 'the colour revolutions', but also pursued a policy of hostility, unprecedented since Soviet times, towards the global system, and a struggle for Russia's 'deserved' place in it (Trudolyubov 2015, 80). Others have pointed out that Putin viewed the EU-Ukraine Association Agreement as a threat to his geopolitical goal to create an integration union with global influence formed of post-Soviet countries (Walker 2015). However, not even Ukraine's important economic relations with Russia could convince Ukrainians to undertake closer integration, because entering any union with Russia would mean 'a big brother' relationship instead of an equal partnership (Dragneva-Lewers and Wolczuk 2015, 73). Therefore, the Ukrainian government offered a 3+1 formula—a

---

36 Vladimir Putin was Russia's president for two terms from 2000 until 2008. From 2008 to 2012 he was replaced by Dmitriy Medvedev due to the legal restriction that no more than two consecutive presidential terms could be served in Russia. During that time, Vladimir Putin was Prime Minister and kept most of his power. The more assertive Russian foreign policy could be explained by Putin's preparations and return to the presidency in 2012 (Moshes 2012, 30).

special limited integration for Ukraine—which, however, was rejected by Russia (Azarov: Ukraine is very cautious about relations with the Customs Union 2012). Pursuing his 'sitting on two chairs' foreign policy, Yanukovych signed the FTA, which was unpopular in Ukraine, with the CIS in autumn 2011, even after Russia had added an article on the unilateral withdrawal of preferences, making this FTA incompatible with EU-Ukraine DCFTA (Dragneva-Lewers and Wolczuk 2015, 76-77). Later, in May 2013, Yanukovych agreed to Ukraine's observer status in the Customs Union (Ukraine and the Customs Union 2013). Thus, Russia's pressure and Ukraine's unstable foreign policy path resulted in Ukraine making a turn towards the East (although the West was still its priority). In spite of political attitudes, the economic reality might have been that economic ties with Russia and the EU were both relevant for Ukraine.

Whilst Ukraine's industry was very connected to that of Russia as a result of historical cooperation in the Soviet Union (Dragneva-Lewers and Wolczuk 2015, 13; Odushkin 2001, 373), a rapid breach of all ties with Russia would have been harmful to the Ukrainian economy in the short term. In 2012, the Customs Union's countries accounted for 36.3% of Ukraine's foreign trade turnover, while the EU only accounted for 29.2%[37] (Ukraine and the Customs Union 2013). However, in the longer perspective, closer integration with the European Union was seen as more beneficial (The EU-Ukraine Association Agreement 2014; Tenerowicz 2012; Yelisieiev 2013). An EU official involved in AA negotiations confirmed that the Ukrainian government had a clear desire to have this agreement and that they were under no EU pressure (Int-35 2021). On the other hand, scholars acknowledged the West's lack of understanding of Russia's perceptions, aims and values (Meister 2019; Tsygankov 2015). Russia's trade wars against Ukraine made clear the price of the country's integration with the EU (Gretskiy, Treshchenkov, and Golubev 2014, 381; Int-

---

[37] In 2012, 36.7% of Ukraine's export and 40.7% of import was with CIS countries (25.6% and 32.4% respectively was with Russia) (State Statistics Service of Ukraine 2020).

35 2021). In the summer of 2013, Russia halted a substantial part of Ukraine's export (Olearchyk 2013; Trading insults 2013). A senior EU official explained that "Russia put Ukraine under extremely strong economic and political pressure, also using methods like blocking Ukrainian export, cutting off oil supplies in order to ensure that Ukraine or personally president Yanukovych would not sign this agreement" (Int-37 2021). Scholars also noted that long before Euromaidan, Russian hard power towards Ukraine was outmanoeuvring the EU's soft power (Burlyuk and Shapovalova 2017; Lightfoot, Szent-Iványi, and Wolczuk 2016; Pastore 2014). For instance, whilst the EU condemned Russia's trade wars against Ukraine in 2013 (European Parliament 2013), it was not eager to do more to help the struggling Ukrainian economy to deal with its consequences (Pastore 2014). The President of the European Council explained that Russia had never given a signal to the EU that "the AA [with Ukraine] was a red line" for Russia, but "their tactic was — to put enough pressure on Yanukovych to abandon the project" (Int-34 2021). Thus, it was understood that economic dependence on Russia would make EU integration a bitter choice for Ukraine because of Russian retaliation. The situation in the country was even more complicated by the fact that its political elites followed their own interests instead of those of the country and its people.

It is important to examine how Ukraine's foreign policy during Yanukovych's presidency reflected his personal interests. Scholars acknowledge that Russia was able to anticipate and use Ukraine's domestic power dynamics in its foreign policy goals (Dragneva-Lewers and Wolczuk 2015, 28). In a situation in which the EU was imposing conditions of democratic change in Ukraine (e.g., the end of the political persecution of Tymoshenko[38]) for signing the AA, Russia was more than happy to welcome authoritarian Yanukovych, who had been rejected by the EU (Charap and Colton 2017, 116–17; Dragneva-Lewers and Wolczuk 2015, 52;

---

38 The former president of the European Council explained how the European Parliament slowed down the signature of the AA due to its condition that Tymoshenko be released (Int-34 2021).

Tenerowicz 2012). In the meantime, Yanukovych was gambling on Ukraine's foreign policy. Meister (2019, 311) has explained how Yanukovych was using the gas transit system and negotiations with the EU to get better deals with Russia, although he did not want Ukraine to move too close either to the EU or to Russia. Moreover, Ukraine's difficult economic situation was the opposite of Yanukovych's electoral promises of economic growth and a decent standard of living, his support was low and he needed financial help to get re-elected (Charap and Colton 2017, 117; Dragneva-Lewers and Wolczuk 2015, 85). Wilson (2015, 104) characterised Ukraine at that time as "a pathologically predatory state, with an alleged 50% cut from all significant business and a tax-and-destroy policy against SMEs, driving the economy into the ground". Although Yanukovych initially rejected Ukraine's membership in the Customs Union and was implementing the EU course, after Russia's offer of a discount in gas prices and a $15 billion loan for the country, the president changed his mind and did not sign the EU-Ukraine AA in November 2013 (Charap and Colton 2017, 120–21; Tsygankov 2015, 284). According to a former EU Commissioner on Enlargement (who was in regular contact with Yanukovych), although Yanukovych did want to bring Ukraine into the EU, he did not understand all of the consequences (to both the judiciary and his own rule), and his desire to get re-elected was also greater (Int-21 2020). This, as well as Russia's pressure on Ukraine and Yanukovych, was confirmed by the president of the European Council and an EU official involved in AA negotiations (Int-34 2021; Int-35 2021). It looks like Yanukovych trusted Russia's threats this time. Thus, Yanukovych's fear of Russia's threats and the possibility of using Russian money for his re-election in 2015, outweighed the preferences of the vast part of Ukrainians[39]. However, a certain section of Ukrainian society did

---

39 Different polls showed that around half of Ukrainians were in favour of EU-Ukraine integration in 2013. The May 2013 poll from Democratic Initiatives Fund found 41.7% support for Ukraine's integration into the EU (Democratic Initiatives Foundation 2014), the June 2013 Deutsche Welle poll - 59% support (Ukraine 2013), and November 2013 GfK Ukraine poll - 45% support for signing the AA (Study by GfK Ukraine 2013).

not accept this foreign policy U-turn and came out on the streets of Kyiv to protect 'the European choice' of the country.

2.3.2. Euromaidan

When on 21 November 2013 Viktor Yanukovych halted preparations for signing the Association Agreement with the EU, which was planned to take place during the Eastern Partnership Vilnius Summit on 28-29 November 2013, Euromaidan protests erupted in Kyiv (Onuch 2014b, 44). This decision on the part of Yanukovych added the last brick to the overall dissatisfaction with his presidency in Ukraine. An EU official has told me that "it was already clear at the Vilnius Summit in 2013 that what we are witnessing is historic and that while the Vilnius Summit ended the way it ended that this was not the end" (Int-12 2020). Scholars have argued that Yanukovych did not expect such a level of protests against his refusal to sign the AA (Meister 2019, 311). However, it was also noted that this decision was just a catalyst, and not the main reason for Euromaidan. The real causes were his authoritarian rule, wide-spread corruption, Russian influence and the aggressive police response to the initial pro-EU demonstrations (Meister 2019, 311; Wilson 2015, 106). Only after the use of violence against protesters, the demand to remove Yanukovych from power became the core issue for Euromaidan (Charap and Colton 2017, 122; Wood 2015b, 12). Scholars have argued that "for the second time people's discontent with the political regime, coupled with a destabilizing confrontation between Russia and the EU, had led to a revolution" (Gretskiy, Treshchenkov, and Golubev 2014, 381). Thus, we can see that flaws in Yanukovych's foreign policy calculations backfired via the revolution.

Analysing the Euromaidan protests, it is relevant to note the regional differences in support for these protests. Scholars have determined that Eastern Ukraine, where many people were employed in heavy industry which had the biggest connections to Russia, was less enthusiastic about EU integration (Mylovanov, Zhukov, and Gorodnichenko 2018). The studies of revolts in Donbas in spring 2014 also showed that workers in industries with the closest connections to Russia were far more likely to protest against the pro-EU course taken by post-Euromaidan elites (with the language of communication and ethnicity being less relevant factors) (Mylovanov, Zhukov, and Gorodnichenko 2018, 37). On the other hand, scholars confirm some alienation on the part of Donbas from the rest of Ukraine, e.g., its greater nostalgia for the Soviet Union[40] (Wilson 2016, 638). Some scholars go so far as to suggest that after Yanukovych's removal from power "the delicate balance of interests forged between Galicia and Donbas" was destroyed, which could be seen as a threat to pro-Russian Ukrainians (Petro 2015, 31). Thus, some regional specificities could be identified already during the Euromaidan, and these could easily be used by foreign countries, in particular Russia.

Whilst Russia blamed the EU for its support and financing of Euromaidan[41], the EU's support, and its condemnation of the use of force against protesters (European Parliament resolution on the situation in Ukraine 2014), was largely symbolic. However, Russia's involvement in Ukraine during Euromaidan, both through regular contacts with Ukrainian decision-makers and its organisation of separatism in Crimea in January-February 2014, is documented by scholars (Wood et al. 2015, xii) and policy-makers (Tikhonova 2015). For instance, there are confirmations of Russia's actions in Crimea from the start of Euromaidan, such as anti-Euromaidan news in the media, the activation of pro-Russian politicians in the Crimean parliament and their promotion of Crimean secession from Ukraine (Wood 2015b, 13). Moreover, some see Russia's hand in Yanukovych's hard stance towards the protesters, the brutality of policy and the acceptance of January's anti-protest laws (Charap and Colton 2017, 123). After the mass shootings of 20-21 February 2014, protesters, opposition leaders, Ukrainian authorities and the EU were all anxious to find a peace-

---

40 The majority of people in Donbas - 57% - regretted the collapse of the Soviet Union in 2013 (as compared with 41% for the whole of Ukraine) (A few points about Ukrainians' value orientations 2013).
41 In a conversation with the EU leaders, Putin compared the EU's support for Euromaidan to the idea of him sending a Russian Minister of Foreign Affairs to take part in anti-EU demonstrations in Greece (Merry 2015, 40).

ful solution (Charap and Colton 2017, 123–24). On 21 February, a consensus was reached (Agreement on the Settlement of Crisis in Ukraine 2014), which, however, did not stop Viktor Yanukovych from fleeing the country. The events that followed will be studied in detail in the next chapters.

Yanukovych's presidency can be seen as a decisive period for Ukraine's relations with both Russia and the EU. The fact that he was overthrown by a revolution could be a sign that his domestic and foreign policies did not work the way he imagined. Through my game theory analytical lens, it can be observed that Yanukovych and his trusted circle were not successful in the assessment of information received from both Russia and the EU. It looks as though they trusted Russia's threats, which resulted in Yanukovych making a U-turn from signing the EU-Ukraine Association Agreement. While Russia dared to annex Crimea after the opposite post-Euromaidan U-turn, Yanukovych apparently was right in his assessment of Russia's preferences. It seems that before autumn 2013, Russia's and the EU's payoffs regarding Ukraine were not estimated correctly, as the EU was not ready to sign the agreement with undemocratic Ukraine and Russia was not willing to accept Ukraine having 'friendlier' relations with the EU than with Russia. Yanukovych's estimation of the actors' resources looks the worst in the context of his strategic decision-making. He was overusing Ukraine's resources for his and his 'family's'[42] enrichment during his presidency. Then, by the end of 2013, it appeared that he had no resources left to sustain his re-election and he needed to get funds from abroad. However, he could not accurately assess the EU's ability and readiness to provide him with the necessary financial help. He was also unable to predict Russia's readiness to use trade wars as a mechanism of foreign policy. Whether Yanukovych's team lacked professionals who could provide careful analysis of the foreign policy environment, or the ruling elites were preoccupied with their personal prefer-

---

42 Yanukovych's close circle of oligarchs and family members, who had a big influence on Ukraine's policymaking and were robbing the country's resources during his presidency, is popularly referred to as 'the family'.

ences (e.g., rent-seeking and re-election), is hard to estimate. What we need to keep in mind is that Yanukovych's presidency was considered by many to be a big failure in Ukraine's foreign policy and the war in Ukraine is its direct consequence.

Conclusion

This chapter presented the overview of the EU-Ukraine-Russia relations since Ukraine's independence in 1991 until the end of Euromaidan in February 2014. As a newly independent country, Ukraine had many state-building challenges, one of which was the positioning of the country on the geopolitical and geo-economic maps of the world. This difficulty was exacerbated by the fact that Ukraine is situated in a rather important place in the world and has a concentration of a variety of potentials, which provoke the interest of major powers. For the most part, three global actors were shaping the background of the international environment for Ukraine — Russia, the EU, and the USA. In my research, I focus solely on actors in Europe, and I analyse the history of Ukraine's decision-making in its relations with the EU and Russia. In conclusion, I would like to accentuate several important findings, which came out of the analysis in this chapter.

First of all, the existence of a certain indecisiveness in Ukraine's foreign policy integration direction caused difficulties both inside (polarisation of the population) and outside (competition between the EU and Russia over Ukraine). The country is situated at the crossroads of different civilisations, and during the course of history it was part of various neighbouring empires. Moreover, 70 years of coexistence in the Soviet Union not only connected the economies of the countries, but also left the footprints of the Soviet planned economy, organisation of political life etc., which made it harder for Ukraine to integrate with the countries of Western Europe. Scholars have pointed out that all Ukrainian presidents were trying to play 'an integration game' with Russia and the EU (Dragneva and Wolczuk 2016). Due to substantial economic ties with both Russia and the EU, and a certain difference of opinion among Ukrainian elites and the public on this matter, in 1991-2014 Ukraine was not able to choose one integration option over the other. This was, unfortunately, used both by oligarchic circles inside the country and the country's foreign partners, e.g., Russia, to further their own goals, which were often not to the benefit of the broader Ukrainian population.

Secondly, due to a number of factors, Ukraine holds substantial importance for major world powers, for instance Russia and the EU (as well as the USA). Ukraine is a large country endowed with large deposits of natural resources, black soil and a geopolitically relevant position (Odushkin 2001, 371). As a consequence of the latter, important energy transportation routes from Russia to the EU go through Ukraine, which raises the country's importance for its neighbours (Odushkin 2001, 371). Because of its history and its geopolitical position, the country has also become crucial in European security (Pifer 2009). During Soviet times it bordered Warsaw Pact countries, and after the 2004 EU enlargement, it became the EU's eastern neighbour. Although in 1994 Ukraine relinquished its nuclear weapon arsenal, the third largest in the world, it kept some Army potential and 30% of the former Soviet military industry. Since its independence, Ukraine has had close cooperation with NATO and has been a regular contributor to its peacekeeping missions (Odushkin 2001, 374). Russia objected to Ukraine-NATO ties due to its security interests in Ukraine, for instance in Crimea, where its Black Sea Fleet was stationed (Odushkin 2001, 375). The EU was interested in having a stable economic partner in Ukraine; partnership agreements, the introduction of the Eastern Partnership and the offer of signing the Association Agreement all confirm this. For its part, Russia was not ready to let Ukraine leave its sphere of influence and was developing its own integration projects, which could not be fulfilled and could not make Russia a global (or at least a regional) power, without Ukraine's membership in them. Some scholars agree that Ukraine is more important to Russia than it is to the EU (Dragneva-Lewers and Wolczuk 2015; Odushkin 2001).

Thirdly, I was able to identify certain issues in Ukraine's foreign policy-making, which diminished the country's capacity to forge relations with foreign interlocutors during all of the years of its independence. Most important of them are the wide-spread corruption, the polarisation in the views of its population, the weakness of its institutions and the lack of transmission of both information and experience between the changing political elites. Corruption prevented many Ukrainian leaders from working for the country's wellbeing, whilst they used the chance to create a perfect rent-seeking environment for themselves and their colleagues. Ukraine's turbulent history, its size, its poor economic development, and ineffective national policies, all encouraged the persistence of some kind of political polarisation in Ukraine. Instead of eradicating this by addressing the core problems common to the whole country, politicians often played on people's emotions to try to get support either from eastern or western Ukraine. The second Ukrainian President, Leonid Kuchma, was able to keep the balance in the country. However, Viktor Yushchenko was primarily pleasing his supporters in the West, to which the East often objected, while Viktor Yanukovych was doing the opposite. Euromaidan and the ousting of Yanukovych brought the pendulum arrow to the other side once again and encouraged the alienation of parts of the population. This was used by Russia as a legal justification (the protection of Russian-speakers) for its actions in Crimea and Donbas (Dubinsky and Rutland 2019). On the other hand, for the first 23 years of its independence, Ukraine was not able to develop strong institutions, democracy, and good governance. Rapidly changing governments and ministers, political crises (including president-parliament fights for power) and constitutional changes were not good for the country. The perception of a politically and economically unstable country was scaring Ukraine's foreign partners and making the perspective to join the EU even less workable. A chief of the State Border Guard Service of Ukraine in 2001-2013 (who worked with four presidents) pointed at the difficulties in the country's policy formation caused by the clear out of professionals after each revolution (Int-10 2020; Lytvyn 2019). It could be that Ukrainian decision-makers preferred allegiance over qualification in their employment strategies. Thus, all of the above led to a deterioration in the creation of Ukraine's professional foreign policy.

A Backward Look

In the studied period (1991 – 2014), Ukraine's foreign policy in the country's interactions with the EU and Russia had certain issues and thus it could not fully serve the interests of the country. My application of the previously proposed game theory-based analytical framework makes it clear that strategic decision-making in the country's foreign policy was most successful under 'the reign' of President Kuchma, since he kept the country united and did not provoke either Russia or the EU. All in all, in 1991-2014, information about foreign interlocutors' preferences was often either not available or missed by Ukrainian political elites. Their trust in foreign partners was sometimes more adequate (trust in Russia's threats), sometimes less (trust in the EU's readiness to integrate with Ukraine under Yushchenko). It appears that Ukrainian politicians were too concerned with each election and failed to invest enough efforts in the analysis of Ukraine's, Russia's, and the EU's payoffs. They were not always able to properly assess Ukraine's own and other actors' resources, and their readiness to use them in reaching their payoffs. Corruption could be a reason for the disappearance of a vast part of Ukraine's resources. This unhealthy policy hit Yanukovych the hardest. He was playing on Ukraine's foreign policy choices to get benefits for his 'family' and to try to fool both Ukrainians and his foreign partners. When Russia pushed hard on him and he refused to sign the Association Agreement with the EU, he did not expect the Ukrainian population to be tired of his policies and to protest on the country's main square. The annexation of Crimea and the war in Donbas is the price which Ukraine had to pay both for the importance it holds for its neighbours, and the mistakes of its ruling elites.

Table 1: Key moments in EU-Ukraine relations in 1991-2013

Date	Event
2 December 1991	Recognition by the European Community of Ukraine's referendum on its independence of 1 December 1991
14 June 1994	The signature of the Agreement on Partnership and Cooperation between the EU and Ukraine
5 September 1997	The first Ukraine-EU summit approved Ukraine's European choice
1 March 1998	Agreement on Partnership and Cooperation Between Ukraine and the EU comes into force
8-9 June 1998	Ukraine officially announces its intention to become an EU associate member at the first meeting of the Council on Co-operation between Ukraine and the EU
11 June 1998	The Decree of the President of Ukraine approved the Strategy of Ukraine's integration into the EU
11 September 2001	At the 4th EU-Ukraine Summit in Yalta, EU leaders and the President of Ukraine, Leonid Kuchma, reaffirmed their commitment to reinforce the strategic partnership between Ukraine and the EU
12 May 2004	Adoption of a Strategy Paper on the European Neighbourhood Policy
9 December 2004	European Commission approves Action Plan for Ukraine
18 February 2008	The launch of free trade agreement negotiations
7 May 2009	The launch of Eastern Partnership initiative
19 October 2011	Ukraine and the European Union finalised negotiations of the Deep and Comprehensive Free Trade Agreement
19 July 2012	Initialling of the Deep and Comprehensive Free Trade Agreement between the EU and Ukraine
28-29 November 2013	Third Eastern Partnership Summit in Vilnius

Source: (Delegation of the European Union to Ukraine 2016)

Table 2: Key moments in Ukraine-Russia relations in 1991-2013

Date	Event
24 August 1991	Act of Declaration of Independence of Ukraine
23 June 1992	The agreement "On the further development of interstate relations"
15 April 1994	The agreement between the Russian Federation and Ukraine on a Phased Settlement of the Black Sea Fleet problem
4 December 1994	Budapest Memorandum on Security Assurances in connection with Ukraine's accession to the Treaty on the Non-Proliferation of Nuclear Weapons
31 May 1997	Signing of the Treaty on Friendship, Cooperation and Partnership
September – October 2003	The conflict over Tuzla Island
April 2004	Kuchma's signing and the Verkhovna Rada's ratification of the agreement for Ukraine to join the Common Economic Space with Russia, Belarus and Kazakhstan
December 2005	The first 'gas war' between Russia and Ukraine
10 February 2007	The Munich speech of Vladimir Putin with his critique of NATO enlargement
August 2008	The Russo-Georgian war, Ukraine's support for Georgia, Russia's use of the Black Sea Fleet against Georgia and Ukraine's protest against this
Winter 2008-2009	The second 'gas war' between Russia and Ukraine
April 2010	The agreement between Ukraine and Russia on the Black Sea Fleet in Ukraine (the Kharkiv Accords) prolongs the stationing of the Russian Black Sea Fleet in Crimea until 2042
18 October 2011	Ukraine's signing of the FTA with the CIS
Summer 2013	Russia's trade war against Ukraine (chocolate, dairy products)
21 November 2013	The Verkhovna Rada of Ukraine suspends preparations for signing EU-Ukraine Association Agreement and announces the development of closer relations with Russia

Source: (Olearchyk 2013; Tsitsuashvili 2009; Vynogradova and Chervonenko 2017)

3 Crimean *Blitzkrieg* (21st February – 26th March 2014)

Introduction

We have seen how Ukraine's foreign policy choices caused confrontations both inside and outside the country. Russia exploited this instability after Euromaidan to pursue its own goals. This chapter studies the Crimean annexation, which took place between 21st February and 26th March 2014[43]. Antagonisms between the parties were growing in this first period of the war, and could be noticed more easily, thus making this month crucial for the understanding of EU-Ukraine-Russia interactions and their further developments. This short period will be examined in detail by means of the game theory analytical framework which I introduced above: information, trust, payoffs, and resources. I look at Ukrainian leaders' actions both on the country's territory (e.g., Ukraine's domestic response to Russia's actions in Crimea, which was based on previous consultations with the EU) and in their foreign interactions with the EU and Russia. My main empirical findings suggest that post-Euromaidan instability did not allow new Ukrainian decision-makers to react quickly to Russia's rapid actions in Crimea, and in particular leaders in Kyiv were too trusting of Russia's respect for international laws and the EU's ability to stop Russian aggression (see Table 4 at the end of the chapter).

Firstly, it is important to remember that historically Crimea had been the cause of discord for many nations: it was occupied by the Greeks in the seventh century BC, later by the Golden Horde, then the Ottoman Empire for 300 years, and afterwards it became a part of the Russian Empire in the eighteenth century (D'Anieri 2019, 38; Magocsi 2014; Wood et al. 2015, 3). The indigenous people of Crimea, the Crimean Tatars, who had formed the majority of the population in Crimea for centuries, were deported

---

[43] For justification of my periods of the conflict, please see the introduction.

from the peninsula by Stalin in 1944[44], since he perceived them as traitors to the Soviet Union (D'Anieri 2019, 38; Int-6 2020; Katchanovski 2015, 81–82). In Soviet times, the Crimean peninsula was part of the Russian SSR until its transfer to the Ukrainian SSR in 1954 (Magocsi 2014). After the deportation of Crimean Tatars, the Soviets repopulated Crimea with Russians and succeeded in making them the majority (Int-6 2020). The Russian majority, the presence of the Russian Black Sea Fleet, Russian propaganda, and its political and cultural activities in Crimea during the period of Ukraine's independence, — all facilitated the annexation (Int-5 2020; Int-10 2020; Wood et al. 2015). I will also touch on the impact of these factors on Ukrainian leaders' decision-making during the crisis in Crimea in February-March 2014.

Secondly, there are several different scholarly perspectives on the Crimean annexation. Although many consider that Russia broke international law by its annexation of the peninsula, others have argued that Russia was "exploiting areas of uncertainty in international law" to justify its actions in Ukraine (R. Allison 2014), or they studied Russia's self-justification concerning the 'legality' of this annexation[45] (Dubinsky and Rutland 2019). There is also no scholarly agreement on whether the takeover of Crimea was well planned by Moscow or was a spontaneous decision triggered by the fleeing of Yanukovych and the fragility of the new government in Kyiv (Dubinsky and Rutland 2019, 50; Wood 2015a, 98). Hence one approach suggests that the motivation for the annexation was Putin's concern about the Russian Black Sea Fleet in Crimea; he feared the possibility of NATO getting control of the peninsula because of Ukraine's vulnerability (Wood 2015a, 98). Some studies show that the planning of 'the return of Crimea' was developing "for some time" (Freedman 2014, 15), perhaps immediately after Ukraine's independence, and that the events in

---

44   Only after the collapse of the Soviet Union could Crimean Tatars return to Crimea, but then they were a minority in their historical motherland.
45   According to a relevant person in the Crimean annexation – the Chief Prosecutor of Crimea, Natalia Poklonskaya — the change of power in Kyiv was illegal and, thus, the Crimean referendum should be viewed not in accordance with the Ukrainian Constitution, but with international law, e.g., the right to self-determination (D. Gordon 2020).

Ukraine resulted in the plan's amendment and application (McDermott 2015, 10). Moreover, the post-Euromaidan government's decision to overturn the language law could have given Russia a pretext to protect Russian speakers in Crimea (McDermott 2015, 10). Others argued that the Crimean decision was completely spontaneous, and President Putin confirmed that he took this decision himself after consultations with a few senior officials[46] on the night of 22nd-23rd February 2014 (Kondrashov 2015). A number of scholars also suggest that Putin's comparatively low approval rating in Russia and public protests of 2011-2012 could have inclined him towards the invasion of Ukraine with the aim of strengthening his domestic power (Charap and Colton 2017, 25–26; Stoner and Mcfaul 2015; Wood 2015a). In my subsequent discussion, we will see which of these perspectives are confirmed by my original data and we will discover the specificities of Ukraine's decision-making in its relations with the EU and Russia during the events in Crimea between 21st February and 26th March 2014.

3.1. Information: The problem of a knowledge vacuum

As mentioned earlier, scholars have argued that in order to make decisions about relations with other states, officials need to have information about the preferences of all actors involved in a given international interaction (Bennett 1995; Khumalo and Baloyi 2018; Michel 2013; Milner 1997; L. Thompson 1995). This section will examine the role of information about opponents' preferences in Ukrainian leaders' decision-making during the Crimean annexation. My key findings uncover flawed information collection and analysis by the new Ukrainian decision-makers due to a post-revolutionary environment and their consequent limited understanding of both the EU's and Russia's preferences regarding Ukraine. I start with a brief explanation of the situation after the

---

46 A Russian politician, Ponomarev, claimed that there were four people at that meeting, but he did not give their names.

Euromaidan. I then elaborate on Russia's and the EU's preferences regarding Ukraine at that time and how they were perceived by Ukrainian decision-makers. Finally, I describe the specifics of Ukraine's dealing with information during the annexation of Crimea and show how Ukraine's own preferences were situated within the broader geopolitical environment.

To begin with, the situation in Ukraine was unstable after the Euromaidan, which consequently resulted in misunderstandings in the EU-Ukraine-Russia triangle. After the mass-killings on the Maidan Square on 18-19 February 2014[47], on 21st February the agreement between Ukrainian authorities and opposition leaders, under the supervision of the EU's and Russia's representatives, was signed (The agreement on the Settlement of the crisis in Ukraine 2014). However, the protesters on Kyiv's streets refused to accept the conditions of the agreement (in particular, to have Yanukovych remain as president for a year) and threatened to retaliate if Yanukovych did not give up the presidency (Maidan online. The truce 2014). The following night, Viktor Yanukovych fled Kyiv, and, later, Ukraine[48] (see Table 3). Power was seized by the opposition leaders, which one Ukrainian social activist I interviewed perceived as unconstitutional (Int-3 2020) and Russian journalists as a *coup d'état* (Int-19 2020; Int-28 2021). The latter view was also stressed by Vladimir Putin at his press-conference on 4th March (Putin 2014) and later in November 2014 (Seipel 2014). Putin confirmed that it was on the night of 22nd-23rd February that he discussed the situation in Ukraine with Russia's security forces and in the morning decided to start the operation of the annexation of Crimea (or its 'return to Russia', according to Russia's viewpoint)[49] (Kondrashov 2015). The message about the *'coup*

---

47 According to different estimates, on 18-19 February, during the Euromaidan protests, more than 100 people were killed and many more injured, the vast majority of whom were protesters.
48 Vladimir Putin claimed that there was a threat to Viktor Yanukovych's life and that it was he – Putin – who saved Yanukovych with the help of the Russian Federal Security Services (Kondrashov 2015).
49 As I mentioned earlier, there is no scholarly agreement on whether the annexation of Crimea was planned for some time or was a spontaneous decision. We certainly cannot trust in the credibility of Putin's words. Scholars experi-

d'état' was transmitted in the Crimean Russia-controlled media, which added to the confusion about the legality of the new power in Kyiv and possibly influenced numerous defections of Ukrainian military and authorities to Russia (which will be studied in detail in the section about resources). Therefore, the change of power in Ukraine in February 2014 was an event that was viewed differentially in Ukraine and Russia.

In regard to Russia's preference regarding Ukraine, my research shows that its core aim was keeping control over Ukraine[50], which was not understood in full either by the EU or Ukraine. Earlier, I mentioned the arguments of a group of scholars that the West's lack of understanding of Russia's preferences (its influence over the post-Soviet space, slowdown of NATO/EU enlargements) led to the conflict in Ukraine (Kissinger 2014; Mearsheimer 2014; Sakwa 2015b). My interviewees (Ukrainian and EU policy-makers) also reported that Russia's long-term preference was to prevent Ukraine from integration into NATO and the EU (Int-3 2020; Int-5 2020; Int-7 2020; Int-31 2021) or even to take full control of Ukraine (Int-9 2020). In another interview, a former president of the European Council explained: "they [Russia] try to keep all those countries in the Western neighbourhood [Georgia, Moldova, Ukraine] weak, in some way dependent on Russia (Int-34 2021). On the other hand, an EU official told me that Russia saw DCFTA as "a geostrategic move", but at the same time that "Russia's position was clearly understood and seen" (Int-12 2020). Scholars have explained how wars can start due to a mistaken understanding of the opponent's commitment to fight (Bennett 1995, 32; Fearon 1995, 393–94; Snyder 1971, 100). An EU Commissioner on En-

---

ence hardship in getting reliable information about Russia. Nevertheless, I aim to provide the reader with different sources and my analysis of them.

50 As we will see, this Russia's preference – to have control over Ukraine – persisted during the whole first year of the war and Russia's invasion in 2022 confirmed this preference once again. Based on the previous chapter, we can assume that the situation before 2014 was acceptable for Russia – formal (economic partnership with Russia, in the best case scenario – Ukraine's joining Russian-led integration projects) and informal (statements of Ukrainian politicians about friendship with Russia) cooperation with Russia and limited cooperation with the West (no attempts to join NATO, no closer economic cooperation with the EU than with Russia).

largement, a green MEP and an EU official certainly assumed that although Russia's preferences were very clearly understood by the EU, they were not able to predict how far Russia was ready to go to achieve its goals (Int-21 2020; Int-31 2021; Int-35 2021). Therefore, while I can observe some kind of understanding of Russia's long-term preferences from both Ukraine's and the EU's positions, there was clearly no deep awareness of the importance of these preferences for Russia and thus its readiness to fight for them. A look at information analysis in Ukraine will help us to study this misperception further.

My evidence suggests that Ukrainian decision-makers had access to different sources of information but could not properly analyse and use them. My respondents provided a number of examples. One of them, who had access to senior Ukrainian decision-making echelons at that time, told me that state organs were often providing inaccurate information either on purpose or unintentionally, and that decision-makers "had to rely heavily on people on the ground" (Int-7 2020). Ukraine's foreign minister at that time acknowledged that he might have been receiving outdated information when the situation was too dynamic (Int-36 2021). An independent foreign journalist in Ukraine explained that information was available, but that the new politicians were in disarray and could not sit down and analyse the information they needed for key decision-making (Int-15 2020). Moreover, certain state organs, like the Security Service of Ukraine and the Intelligence Office, were incapable of performing their tasks properly, because many of their previous workers had either left or were in a state of disorientation (Int-8 2020; Int-11 2020). Lastly, the acting foreign minister of Ukraine mentioned that there was no official communication with Russia before April 2014 (Int-36 2021). Thus, Ukrainian decision-makers not only lacked information, but were not in a position to be able to properly analyse and process available information. This, according to game theory assumptions, could be an obstacle to decision-making.

Turning to Russia, one may say that in terms of access to information, it was well-equipped to carry out its operation in Crimea. My informants argued that Russian intelligence had been very successful in penetrating various Ukrainian services, which gave it accurate information about the thinking of Ukrainian policy makers (Int-1 2020; Int-6 2020; Int-7 2020; Int-8 2020; Int-9 2020). This is confirmed by other scholars' research (e.g., McDermott 2015) and was mentioned by senior Ukrainian officials during the meeting of the National Security and Defence Council on 28th February 2014 (National Security and Defense Council of Ukraine 2014). An independent foreign journalist in Ukraine also said that "Russia was always three or four steps ahead of them [the Ukrainian authorities]" (Int-15 2020). Therefore, I would conclude that Russia had a certain information supremacy during the crisis in Crimea, which certainly contributed to its success with the annexation.

Looking at Ukraine's own preferences, post-Euromaidan decision-makers in Ukraine chose the pro-EU course of the country but misunderstood to a certain extent the views of the EU and Russia in this respect. The post-Euromaidan leaders settled Ukraine's final goal—integration with the EU and the end of dependence on Russia (Int-7 2020; Int-15 2020; Int-22 2020; Int-35 2021; Int-38 2021). However, it emerged from my interviews with EU officials and the EU's official communication that the Union wanted to cooperate with Ukraine and to preserve some kind of stability in the country (Council of the European Union 2014; Int-2 2020; Int-12 2020; Int-21 2020), but that this preference appeared to be far less important for the EU (this is discussed in more detail below) than was perceived in Ukraine (Int-15 2020). An EU analyst and EU officials confirmed that the EU wanted to sign the Association Agreement with Ukraine in order to have a stable partnership with the country (Int-2 2020; Int-12 2020; Int-13 2020; Int-38 2021), but according to a leading EU journalist, the EU could not offer anything more (Int-20 2020). In this way, avoiding the outbreak of war (or any other instability), and achieving economic cooperation with Ukraine, could be seen as the EU's preferences. However, it will become clearer in further discussion that the EU's readiness to reach these preferences may also differ from Ukraine's perception.

My main findings regarding Ukrainian leaders' operation with information about others' preferences is that they did not make full use of the available information and had incomplete awareness of the EU's and Russia's preferences. Concentration on Ukraine's preference—integration with the EU and independence from Russia—might have resulted in Ukrainian decision-makers missing some of the EU's and Russia's preferences. Their inattention to the interests of their foreign partners was said by an independent foreign journalist to be a key failure of Ukraine's foreign policy (Int-15 2020). First of all, I have explained that Russia's core preference of preserving control over Ukraine, although this was understood in Kyiv and Brussels, was still not taken seriously enough either by Ukrainian or EU decision-makers. Secondly, the EU's preference was to avoid a war near its borders and to have economic cooperation with its neighbours, which also differed from Ukrainian leaders' perceptions about rapid EU-Ukrainian integration. Some of Ukraine's state organs were not operating properly, the circulation of information was poor and there were many Russian agents in Ukraine, which further complicated decision-making. As an advisor to a senior Ukrainian official pointed out when reflecting on that period, "in order not to take the wrong decisions, often the decision was not to take any decisions at all" (Int-7 2020). It can be argued, then, that the post-Euromaidan authorities were not fully prepared for such a difficult international chess game. Thus, in order to see the whole picture, an analysis of other dimensions of the game theory analytical framework is required.

3.2. Trust in international law

Apart from decision-makers having information about others' preferences, game theory rests on the assumption that they assess whether other actors' signals and strategies can be trusted. This is particularly the case when information is limited. Scholars have argued that lack of trust in the intentions of interlocutors may lead to conflict even among players with similar preferences (Devetak, George, and Percy 2017; Fearon 1995; Kydd 2000; Lieberman 1964;

A. Thompson 2002). This section examines the role of trust in Ukrainian decision-makers' interactions with the EU and Russia. My evidence led me to an important discovery—Ukrainian leaders did not trust Russia's threats but trusted the EU's willingness to 'save' Ukraine during Crimea's annexation. I start with a discussion of Ukraine's trust in a brotherhood with Russia and the consequences of such trust. Later, I look at Ukraine's trust in the Budapest Memorandum and support from the EU. I sum up with an analysis of how trust directed Ukrainian leaders' strategic decision-making and how this trust became the biggest miscalculation during the annexation of Crimea.

First of all, my Ukrainian respondents (both analysts and decision-makers) stated that Ukrainian decision-makers had information about Russia's unusual and aggressive actions in Crimea at the end of 2013 and the beginning of 2014, but they could not believe that Russia would dare to annex Crimea (Int-3 2020; Int-5 2020; Int-7 2020; Int-8 2020). One example of this position was provided by a commander of a volunteer battalion, who said that "Ukrainian soldiers in Crimea could not shoot at Russians, whom they considered brothers, not believing that they had launched aggression against their brotherhood nation" (Int-11 2020). Another comes from a deputy commander of a battalion in Crimea, who told journalists that he was "101 % confident" that Russians would not shoot, because they had previously even trained together (5 Channel 2014). On the other hand, informants mentioned Ukraine's substantial trust in the declared readiness of signatories of the Budapest Memorandum—the UK, the US and Russia—to guarantee the territorial integrity of Ukraine[51] (Int-1 2020; Int-4 2020; Int-7 2020; Int-8 2020; Int-10 2020). Interestingly, an EU Ambassador to Russia also pointed out that despite having warnings about possible aggressive actions on the part of Russia in Crimea from intelligence, researchers and through interactions with Russians, the EU leaders' common sense understanding was

---

51 Here, I refer to Ukraine's trust that Russia would not break the Budapest memorandum and if so, that there would be an immediate and strong response from the UK and the USA.

that "No, that is impossible" (Int-23 2020). Thus, Ukrainian policy-makers' trust in Russia's respect for Ukraine's territorial integrity could be explained both by a historical brotherhood myth and by guarantees made by Russia (and other countries') under international agreements. Consequently, the existence of such beliefs might have influenced rational foreign policy analysis.

While we know that Ukrainian policy-makers had too much trust in Russia, it is worth considering the nature of trust in EU-Ukraine relations. In this respect, my analysis shows that Ukrainian decision-makers had substantial trust in the EU's desire to involve itself in this war on Ukraine's side and this apparently influenced their decision not to confront Russia in Crimea. My data clearly shows that Ukrainians had high hopes for EU actions against Russian aggression (Int-3 2020; Int-5 2020; Int-6 2020; Int-27 2020), which could partially be explained by their misunderstanding of the EU's foreign policy procedures (Int-5 2020; Int-12 2020; Int-20 2020). However, both a Ukrainian and a Polish politician assumed that Ukrainian politicians could also use EU statements of support as justification of their inaction, misleading the population in this way (Int-22 2020; Int-25 2020). Looking at the EU's trust towards Ukraine, EU officials acknowledged a certain trust in the words of their Ukrainian counterparts, although they had doubts about their ability to deal with all the problems the country had (Int-2 2020; Int-12 2020; Int-25 2020). In spite of this, the EU did not break all ties with Russia, but searched for "a way to deal with Russia in these circumstances" (Int-12 2020) and had "a policy based on necessity" and not on trust (Int-20 2020). Apparently, then, the EU and Ukraine had different perceptions of their mutual trust: Ukrainians imagined the EU had an 'obligation' to support Ukraine, while the EU condemned Russian actions, but did not openly confront them.

Turning now to Russia, my research demonstrates that Putin rejected the possibility of dealing with new Ukrainian decision-makers and also distrusted the EU. Russian respondents pointed out that Russia could not trust the new leaders in Kyiv precisely because they broke the 21st February agreement with Yanukovych (Int-16 2020; Int-17 2020; Int-19 2020). Moreover, this also diminished Russian leaders' trust in the EU, whose representatives were present during the signing of the agreement[52] (Int-19 2020; Seipel 2014). The acting foreign minister of Ukraine also mentioned that Russia did not recognise the new government and refused to deal with it (although remaining in contact with some of Yanukovych's people) (Int-36 2021). Several Russian respondents highlighted the fact that in Putin's view both Ukraine and the EU were highly dependent on the US in their policy-making (Int-16 2020; Int-17 2020; Int-18 2020; Int-19 2020). Moreover, with no trust in multinational organisations, and in particular in the EU (Int-2 2020; Int-20 2020; Int-28 2021), Putin apparently preferred to discuss the situation in Ukraine with individual EU member-states or with the US (the perceived main decision-maker)[53] (Int-16 2020; Int-18 2020). Thus, the discrepancy between Russia's own perception of the situation and the views of other actors diminished the country's trust in the EU and Ukraine. This also created opportunities for purposeful misleading on the part of Russia of its EU and Ukrainian interlocutors.

My analysis of the annexation of Crimea confirms scholarly arguments that in an uncertain environment actors may use bluffing and threats (Bennett 1995, 20–21) to change opponents' perceptions and hence their actions (Fearon 1995). Ukrainian and EU policy-makers highlighted the fact that during the Crimean annexation, Russia used bluffing strategies effectively (Int-2 2020; Int-6 2020; Int-11 2020; Int-13 2020), e.g., in denying its military presence in Crimea (Int-4 2020; Int-9 2020; Int-23 2020). A former Ukrainian Foreign Minister explained: "Of course, it [Russia] was deceiving everyone. From the beginning, we heard about the "green men"[54], right? And only after a certain period of time did

---

52 In his interview in November 2014, Putin was harshly critical of the fact that Polish, German and French foreign ministers put their signatures on the agreement of 21st February and later supported the *'coup d'état'* in Ukraine (Seipel 2014).
53 Thus, Putin's own perceptions (distrust in the EU's and Ukraine's subjectivity) formed his strategy to deal with individual EU member-states and the US.
54 Here, the interviewee refers to Russia's original claim that there was no Russian military in Crimea, but the armed men (so called „green men") were local people dressed in uniforms bought in regular shops.

Putin have to admit that these were Russian troops." (Int-4 2020). On the other hand, a leading analyst in Brussels explained how this influenced trust in Russia's words: "Russia had initially been denying that these were its troops and Putin later said: "Well, you know, we had to lie." This was a very strong reduction of trust." (Int-13 2020). Already on 17th April 2014, Putin confessed that the Russian military "helped to conduct the referendum" (President of Russia 2014c), which he later confirmed in a 2015 Russian 'documentary' about Crimea (Kondrashov 2015). EU and Ukrainian officials recognised that these kinds of inconsistent and contradictory actions on the part of Russia made it harder for the EU and Ukraine to react (Int-12 2020; Int-36 2021). Therefore, Russia managed to deceive Ukraine and the EU regarding its actions in Crimea, which complicated their reactions, but also diminished the EU's and Ukraine's trust in Russia.

On the other hand, Ukrainian policy-makers assumed that Russia would possibly threaten physical violence towards Ukrainian politicians (Int-4 2020; Int-8 2020). As a former Ukrainian Foreign Minister put it: "Blackmail is one of the elements of Russian foreign policy … and fear of this blackmail, unfortunately, did not allow our Ukrainian leadership in 2014 to make very tough decisions to resist the aggression." (Int-4 2020). Even more interesting is the claim made by the former ambassador of one of the Baltic states to Ukraine, that acting President Turchynov was ready to fly to Crimea when the dangerous situation was developing, but in a threatening phone call from Russia he was told that if he did so, his plane would be shot down, and that this resulted in him abandoning the trip (Int-14 2020). Russia's telephone threat that it would start a full-scale war against Ukraine was also confirmed by Turchynov on 28th February 2014 (National Security and Defense Council of Ukraine 2014). These statements acknowledge the possible use of threats by Russian top officials in dealing with Ukrainian decision-makers, and also their partial trust in these threats.

Another important point is that trust may take different forms in a prisoner's dilemma and a game of chicken: for a better outcome, actors in a prisoner's dilemma need to trust the cooperative intentions of their interlocutors, while in a game of chicken, an actor cooperates if it trusts its opponents to defect (Bennett 1995, 24; G. H. Snyder 1971, 82–87). On the one hand, Ukrainian decision-makers might have engaged in a prisoner's dilemma and thus trusted Russia not to annex Crimea. On the other, the case of Crimea could be a chicken game, where certain Ukrainian policy-makers trusted in Russia's readiness to start a war and thus Ukraine did not react militarily for fear of an all-out conflict. The same might have been true for the EU – its policy-makers were afraid to provoke Russia and urged Ukrainian colleagues to do the same (as discussed below). Another possibility is that, like in Snyder's example (1971, 91-92) of World War I, the parties adhered to different games. If Ukraine and the EU thought that everybody was in a prisoner's dilemma and sought cooperation, Russia might have been in a chicken game and, noticing Ukraine's and the EU's weakness, it decided to annex Crimea in order to get a better payoff, following the rules of a chicken game. Thus, we have seen that Ukrainian decision-makers' trust in their interlocutors' intentions was not always based on realistic estimations: originally, they trusted in friendship agreements with Russia and the EU's intentions to help Ukraine. This misperception regarding the appropriateness of trust in foreign interlocutors is seen as the biggest issue in Ukraine's decision-making in this period. The further analysis of payoffs and resources will add more clarity to Ukraine's decision-making process.

3.3. Miscalculation of payoffs

We will now consider how Ukrainian leaders perceived the payoff structure for Ukraine, the EU, and Russia in February-March 2014. Scholars have argued that payoffs—possible values which opponents can receive from a given interaction—have to be estimated correctly if one wants to get the most desired outcome (Bennett 1995; Snidal 1985). My evidence suggests that Ukrainian decision-makers' concentration on the country's preferred payoffs—closer ties with the EU and the preservation of Crimea as part of Ukraine—obstructed their analysis of the core payoffs for Russia (all parties respecting the 21st February agreement, stopping Ukraine's integration with the EU, and, in the case of Putin, winning domestic popularity) and of the EU (to avoid a war over Crimea and to have the AA signed).

In February-March 2014, Ukrainian decision-makers saw two payoffs for the country — integration with the EU and the preservation of territorial integrity. After Euromaidan, new Ukrainian decision-makers were advocating for faster integration with the EU (Int-5 2020; Int-7 2020; Int-24 2020), which was confirmed by EU policy-makers (Int-21 2020; Int-38 2021). A foreign journalist in Ukraine expressed his shock that many politicians were really confident that Ukraine could join the EU within the next five years (Int-15 2020). On the other hand, Russian correspondents and a Ukrainian official observed a certain division amongst Ukrainians after Euromaidan (Int-10 2020; Int-19 2020; Int-28 2021). For instance, support for EU integration on the part of Ukraine's South and South-East was low. In Ukraine as a whole, 45.3% favoured EU integration in March 2014 and 50.5% in May 2014, but only 28% did so in the South, 30.5% in the East and 13.1% in Donbas (Democratic Initiatives Foundation 2014). When the occupation of Crimea became a reality, Ukrainian decision-makers concentrated on saving the country's territorial integrity (Int-1 2020; Int-2 2020; Int-4 2020; Int-5 2020; Int-8 2020; Int-21 2020). The situation with Ukrainian elites was quite similar: although the new decision-makers were pro-EU, some powerful regional elites in the South and East of Ukraine were pro-Russian (we will see this in the discussion below). This is another confirmation of the importance of domestic politics for foreign policy relations. Therefore, we can see that although many Ukrainians had a clear desire for Ukraine's integration with the EU, this did not have unanimous support and was also never offered by the EU. Later, the focus of Ukrainian policy-makers switched to preserving Crimea as part of Ukraine. Below, we will study other actors' payoffs and how they were assessed in Ukraine, which will show that Ukrainian decision-makers' perceptions did not always have realistic grounds.

We already know that Russia's foreign policy preferences were to keep control over Ukraine and to avoid close EU-Ukraine ties. Now we will see how Russia tried to achieve these goals. Whilst Euromaidan moved the Ukrainian foreign policy pendulum to the West, the last option for Russia to keep its influence was the 21st February agreement (if Yanukovych had remained in the presidency for a year), which was rejected both by the EU and Ukraine. Scholars have argued that after Yanukovych fled Ukraine, the West celebrated its victory without paying attention to Russia, whose preferred option was that all parties respected the 21st February agreement (Charap and Colton 2017, 126). This is confirmed by the 22nd February request of the Foreign Minister of Russia to France, Germany and Poland to put pressure on Ukraine to endorse the agreement (Lavrov urged them to implement the agreement of 21st February 2014) as well as the 7th March reiteration of commitment to the agreement, as expressed by the Russian Ministry of Foreign Affairs (Ministry of Foreign Affairs of the Russian Federation 2014). However, the 21st February agreement was followed neither by Ukraine, nor the EU. It seems that both the protesters and the new decision-makers failed to analyse Russia's possible actions (payoffs), although they all were aware of Russia's preference to keep control over Ukraine. Rutland (2015, 137) has argued that Russia saw the breaking of this agreement as "the point of no return". A former Deputy of the Russian State Duma stated that Putin perceived this as "a rude scam on the part of the West" (Int-17 2020). Thus, inattention to Russia's commitment to the 21st February agreement[55] led to further changes in the payoffs structure.

When the new leaders came to power in Ukraine and the 21st February agreement was forgotten, Russia moved to a different form of action — the annexation of Crimea. A number of Ukrainian respondents argued that Russia hoped to achieve its preference of stopping Ukraine from integrating into the EU/NATO by means of its actions in Crimea (Int-3 2020; Int-7 2020). A German

---

55 According to a foreign journalist, who was in Ukraine and followed Euromaidan events, the protesters did not have a plan of what to do after the revolution, since they did not believe that they could actually win (Int-15 2020). This post-revolutionary moment of re-adjusting could partly explain the new leaders' failure to analyse the foreign environment better.

115

MP also considered that Russia wanted "to cut any further development of Ukraine going in the EU direction" (Int-38 2021). Some scholars observed that, by the end of Euromaidan, Putin had exhausted all possibilities from his toolbox for achieving Russia's aims in Ukraine: a trade war in summer 2013, $15 billion support for Yanukovych and the negotiations with the West on 21st February (Charap and Colton 2017, 127). A former ambassador of one of the Baltic states to Ukraine also stated that "at the end of February, it was clear that Russians do not accept what happened" (Int-14 2020). Thus, it could be that after the change of power in Ukraine and the new decision-makers' inattention to the 21st February agreement, Russia's preferred payoff changed to the annexation of Crimea[56].

How did Ukrainian politicians estimate Russia's payoffs at that time? One of the leaders of the Crimean Tatars stated that Russia wanted to settle the score with the EU and the US via the annexation of Crimea (Int-6 2020). In the same way, Russian analysts argued about Russia's resentment (that of both Putin and Russian society) towards the West (Medvedev 2015). The acting Foreign Minister of Ukraine even thought that Russia wanted to capture the whole of Ukraine (Int-36 2021). The chairman of the Mejlis of the Crimean Tatar People, and an MP, originally considered that Russia's actions in Crimea were aimed at giving Kyiv an ultimatum regarding integration into the EU, but later he understood that the actual goal was the annexation of Crimea (Int-5 2020). During the meeting on 28th February 2014 of the National Security and Defence Council of Ukraine, the acting President of Ukraine stated that it appeared from various sources that Russia

---

56 Apart from its preference to preserve control over Ukraine, we remember from the previous chapter that Russia had a strategic interest in Crimea (i.e. due to its Black Sea Fleet stationing in Sevastopol, Russian majority there and Russians' perception of Crimea to be Russian), it had already tried to destabilise the situation in Crimea in the 1990's and preserved a certain influence over the peninsula via pro-Russian politicians, media and organisations. Thus, a few coincidences might have inclined Russia for the annexation of Crimea – losing control over Ukraine due to the new pro-EU leaders, persistent interest in Crimea, post-revolutionary unstable situation in Ukraine and an opportunity to rise Putin's popularity at home.

was really considering the possibility of annexing Crimea (National Security and Defense Council of Ukraine 2014). However, the Head of the Security Service of Ukraine suggested that Russia was waiting for Ukraine's response in order to use this as a pretext for starting a full-scale war against Ukraine (National Security and Defense Council of Ukraine 2014). The acting Foreign Minister of Ukraine called Russia's decision to annex Crimea "very emotional", and said that it happened because of Putin's desire "to take anything and rapidly", when everything else in relation to Ukraine was lost ("none of his forces, none of his politicians in Ukraine") (Int-36 2021). I can observe, then, that different political actors in Ukraine had diverse views on what was Russia's preferred payoff, which prevented them from forming a workable and consistent foreign policy in this respect[57].

There could be also another reason for Russia's annexation of Crimea — the domestic goals of President Putin. Russian and EU analysts and politicians have suggested that Putin's decision to annex Crimea could be explained by his aim of increasing his popularity at home, which was decreasing following the protests in 2011-2012 (Int-9 2020; Int-13 2020; Int-17 2020; Int-26 2020; Int-31 2021). For this reason, a former Baltic Ambassador in Ukraine assumed that Russia would annex Crimea even if President Yanukovych remained in office (Int-14 2020). The huge support on the part of Russians for the annexation—according to a Russian journalist, it was "bigger than their love for their mother" (Int-28 2021)—could justify Putin's decision. A former President of the European Council also explained that for Putin "the annexation of Crimea was a major nationalistic achievement" (Int-34 2021). In my first chapter, I explained that countries' leaders may use wars to stay in power; thus an analysis of their interests is important in strategic decision-making (De Mesquita 2006, 638; Kydd 2000, 352; Nye 2005). A former deputy of the Russian State Duma and a

---

57 During the meeting of the National Security and Defense Council of Ukraine, the acting President Turchynov proposed the introduction of martial law in order to protect Crimea, whilst other participants did not support this, fearing an all-out war with Russia, in which Ukraine would, they believed, be defeated (National Security and Defense Council of Ukraine 2014).

leading EU analyst both stressed that Russia's payoffs were concentrated on the payoffs of the country's president[58] (Int-13 2020; Int-17 2020). Therefore, it can be argued that successful decision-making in relation to Russia required analysis of the personal preferences of President Putin. However, my Ukrainian informants did not mention this kind of analysis.

Turning to the EU's payoffs, I also found certain misperceptions on the part of Ukrainian decision-makers. Although during the start of events in Crimea Ukrainian policy-makers viewed the EU's core interest as the preservation of the international rule of law (Int-4 2020; Int-5 2020), after the annexation they understood that the main aim for the EU was to not have a war break out in Europe (Int-3 2020; Int-4 2020; Int-5 2020; Int-11 2020). A number of Ukrainian policy-makers, who were in regular contact with their EU counterparts, confirmed that the EU was opposed to open warfare more than anything else, and so asked Ukraine "not to provoke Russia in Crimea" (Int-4 2020; Int-5 2020; Int-7 2020; Int-36 2021). Accordingly, an advisor to a senior Ukrainian official highlighted the fact that the EU promised Ukraine that it would resolve the situation with Russia over Crimea and urged Ukrainians not to take any further action (Int-7 2020). In this regard, it is worth seeing how EU policy-makers described the EU's payoffs in Ukraine. An EU official confirmed that the EU understood Ukraine's preference for a stronger global reaction, which could possibly change Russia's behaviour (Int-12 2020). However, according to EU officials, the EU did not see itself as a party to the conflict, but rather a partner in its mediation and a supporter of Ukraine (Int-2 2020; Int-12 2020), or "an involved observer" (Int-21 2020). On the other hand, an EU analyst and Ukraine's acting Minister of Foreign Affairs suggested that at that time the EU was most concerned about the signing of the Association Agreement (Int-13 2020; Int-36 2021). A German MP also confirmed that the EU wanted the AA to be signed, but said there was no option for

---

58 An EU analyst pointed out that "Russia today is more centralised on one person than ever since Joseph Stalin" and "when I say Russian interest, what I really mean, of course, unfortunately, is Vladimir Vladimirovich Putin's interest" (Int-13 2020).

Ukraine to integrate with the EU in 2014 (Int-38 2021). This shows that there were certain misperceptions on the part of Ukrainian policy-makers, who originally expected the EU to 'save' Crimea from Russia and imagined fast integration with the EU.

It can be seen, then, that Ukrainian decision-makers concentrated on Ukraine's desire to integrate with the EU and to preserve the territorial integrity of the country and did not analyse either Russia's payoffs (all parties' respect for 21st February agreement, stopping Ukraine from integrating with the EU, and boosting Putin's domestic popularity), or those of the EU (avoiding war and having economic cooperation with Ukraine). Firstly, both Ukrainian and EU politicians did not fully realise the importance of the 21st February agreement for Russia. Secondly, only some Ukrainian policy-makers could sense that Russia was annexing Crimea with the aim of blocking EU-Ukraine integration. Thirdly, none of my Ukrainian respondents mentioned the analysis of Putin's payoff of boosting his national support via Crimea, although this possibility was acknowledged by scholars, and by both Russian and EU policy-makers. In regard to the EU, Ukrainian decision-makers thought the EU's payoff was to preserve the rule of law in Ukraine. Although there are several confirmations of the EU's request to Ukrainian authorities not to constrain Russia in Crimea and to let the EU to take care of this, EU officials stated that the EU was not an actor in this conflict, only a mediator and a supporter of Ukraine. On the other hand, post-Euromaidan leaders aimed at EU-Ukraine integration, although there was not majority support for this in Ukraine (in particular, the vast majority in the East and South opposed this). In this respect, the EU's true payoff was to have the AA with Ukraine signed, but there was no perspective of full integration. With Russia's actions in Crimea, the key Ukraine's payoff became the preservation of the country's territorial integrity. It will also become clear that these payoffs were confirmed by the readiness of different actors to employ resources for their achievement.

3.4. Low awareness of resources

In this last section, I discuss Ukraine's awareness of self and other actors' resources and their readiness to apply them in order to achieve their payoffs during the Crimean annexation. Scholars have pointed out that not only the opponents' resources, but also their willingness to invest these resources in a particular interaction, strongly determines its outcome (Clausewitz, Howard, and Paret 1976; Moravcsik 2010; G. H. Snyder 1971). While my empirical findings confirmed these game theory assumptions concerning the importance of resources in decision-making, I also discovered a lack of full awareness on the part of Ukrainian leaders of everyone's resources during the annexation of Crimea. I start with a discussion of the nuclear weapons resource; I then compare Russia's and Ukraine's military, both in general terms, and in relation specifically to the Crimean Peninsula. After this, I look at the EU's resources and its readiness to apply them in Ukraine. Finally, I sum up the ability of Ukrainian decision-makers to estimate Ukraine's, the EU's and Russia's resources and their willingness to use them in Ukraine.

Scholars have emphasised that a nuclear resource is a unique tool to increase a country's capabilities in its relations with others (Horowitz 2009; M. Simon 2004). Accordingly, Russia's nuclear status, *vis-à-vis* Ukraine's non-nuclear status, might have facilitated Russia's annexation of Crimea. Mearsheimer's prediction (1993) was realised and Russia did attack non-nuclear Ukraine. Although Ukrainians believed in the strength of the Budapest Memorandum, under which the country gave away its nuclear arsenal in exchange for a guaranty of its territorial integrity, it could be argued that if Ukraine had still possessed nuclear weapons, this could have been a more effective deterrent to Russia during the Crimean crisis (Int-4 2020; Int-8 2020; Int-27 2020). It is interesting to note that a former EU ambassador to Russia explained that there was no mechanism or organisational structure for the Budapest Memorandum to work (Int-23 2020). EU policymakers also mentioned that Russia's possession of nuclear weapon was a key element in its status as a military power (Int-2 2020;

Int-31 2021; Int-34 2021). It is highly likely that this contributed to Russia's strong position and the EU's caution in dealing with Russia.

Ukraine's resources

In respect to Ukraine's resources, the crucial ones were the political ability of the new leaders and the country's military might. On 28th February 2014, the Minister of Defence of Ukraine explained that in Crimea there was at most 1.5-2 thousand Ukrainian soldiers and, in contrast, 20 thousand Russians, with the latter on the increase (National Security and Defense Council of Ukraine 2014). Hence, Ukraine would not be able to protect itself against Russia in a full-scale war (National Security and Defense Council of Ukraine 2014). In accordance with the previous agreement, the whole of the Russian Black Sea Fleet was stationed in Crimea (Ukraine, Russian Federation 1997), which was seen as a threat by the Chief of the Ukrainian Border Guard Service (Int-10 2020). While many interviewees pointed out that having a strong army would have been very beneficial in this war (Int-4 2020; Int-6 2020), Ukrainian policy-makers confessed that during the events under discussion, the Ukrainian Army was disbanded (Int-8 2020; Int-36 2021). Moreover, acts of betrayal and the transfer of the Ukrainian Army, Security Services and politicians to the Russian state in Crimea, were widely reported (Int-5 2020; Int-8 2020; National Security and Defense Council of Ukraine 2014). To some extent this could be explained by a lack of clear orders from Kyiv (Int-10 2020; Int-19 2020). The Ukrainian state treasury was also drained after the fleeing of Yanukovych (Int-11 2020; Int-36 2021). Furthermore, the acting Foreign Minister of Ukraine mentioned that when Russia started its actions in Crimea, a new government in Ukraine had yet to be formed (Int-36 2021). Though we can see how scarce Ukraine's resources were, was there anything Ukrainian leaders could have done to protect Crimea?

According to one of the ambassadors of the EU countries in Ukraine, in February Ukrainian decision-makers understood that Ukrainians were not ready to fight for Crimea (Int-14 2020). Given the poor state of the Army, Ukraine would have had to rely on volunteers, who later did support the Ukrainian Army in Donbas (Int-5 2020; Int-7 2020; Int-13 2020). My informants pointed to the power of Ukrainian civil society after Euromaidan (Int-4 2020; Int-5 2020; Int-13 2020) and some even suggested that volunteers could have prevented the annexation of Crimea (Int-9 2020). However, during the events in Crimea, the leaders in Kyiv did not think of the possibility of involving volunteers. Additionally, some policy-makers mentioned that Ukrainian decision-makers did not have enough "political will" to resist Russia, which was seen by some Ukrainian policy-makers as a core factor in facilitating the annexation (Int-4 2020; Int-5 2020; Int-22 2020). Therefore, weak military resources and lack of political will on the part of high-up officials might have contributed to the annexation of Crimea. Let us move now to a discussion of the resources of Russia and the EU.

Russia's resources

Considering Russia's resources, I have found little agreement among my respondents as to whether Russia possessed all the resources it needed to achieve its aims in Ukraine, and whether Ukrainian decision-makers had full or limited understanding of Russia's capabilities. Some scholars (McDermott 2015) and respondents (Int-1 2020; Int-7 2020; Int-8 2020; Int-9 2020; Int-16 2020) apparently had evidence that Russian intelligence had penetrated Ukrainian services substantially and had gained information about Ukraine's military capabilities which facilitated the Crimean annexation. Moreover, the Chief of Ukraine's Border Guard Service confirmed that in February-March 2014 the Russian Federation was monitoring the situation at Ukraine's border and was increasing its forces along the entire perimeter of the border (Int-10 2020). The former Ukrainian Chief of the General Staff, Volodymyr Zamana, explained that he was in possession of information regarding Russia's movements in Crimea in January 2014, which he reported to Yanukovych in January-February 2014 and to the post-Euromaidan decision-makers at the beginning of

March (Tikhonova 2015). Moreover, the Chief of the State Border Guard Service of Ukraine and the commanders of military units in Crimea were conveying regular updates on the situation in Crimea to the Ukrainian authorities (Int-10 2020; Int-11 2020). Thus, although Russia gained access to information about Ukraine, decision-makers in Kyiv also received information about Russia's actions in Crimea.

Analysing Russia's capabilities, both scholars and decision-makers confirm that if Russia did "hold all the cards ... Ukraine would have collapsed by summer 2014" (Sherr 2017, 31) or even "by March 2014" (Int-7 2020). However, Russia easily achieved its goal regarding Crimea. As I was told by an EU official: "If the Ukrainian military was strong, would that have prevented the annexation of Crimea? No! The military means of Russia are so much stronger. Russia is stronger than Ukraine and many EU countries." (Int-2 2020). Later in 2014, Putin confirmed that the Russian military was holding back the Ukrainian military in Crimea but claimed that it did so only to allow people to vote in the referendum without bloodshed (Seipel 2014). However, according to yet another political expert, Russia had greater political will to combine its resources for achieving its aims in Ukraine, whilst "Ukraine did not have such will, desire and ability" to unite against Russia (Int-9 2020). Some respondents mentioned that Ukrainian policy-makers understood the extent to which Russia was ready to apply its resources in Ukraine (Int-2 2020; Int-8 2020), or that they quickly acquired this understanding in March 2014 (Int-7 2020). Others, however, doubt that this full understanding existed (Int-3 2020; Int-9 2020; Int-14 2020; Int-22 2020; Int-30 2021). Thus, we can see that Russia had substantial resources, both in terms of military and political decisiveness, to annex Crimea, and Ukrainian decision-makers, although getting information from Crimea, lacked a full understanding of Russia's resources.

Another resource—the will of the Crimean population—also helped Russia. Scholars (Wood et al. 2015) and policy-makers (Int-6 2020; Int-10 2020) emphasised the strong presence of Russia in Crimea before the annexation, in the form of its information policy and its cultural, youth, and also political organisations. Crimean

Tatar politicians and a foreign journalist in Ukraine pointed out that the Ukrainian authorities did not pay enough attention either to separatist issues in Crimea or the rights of Crimean Tatars during all of the 23 years of the country's independence (Int-5 2020; Int-6 2020; Int-15 2020). The victory of Euromaidan and the ousting of President Yanukovych were portrayed in Crimean media as a *coup d'etat*, organised by far-right Ukrainians with active support from the West (Kondrashov 2015). In February-March 2014, Ukrainian decision-makers were aware that the Crimean population was pro-Russian[59] (Int-10 2020; National Security and Defense Council of Ukraine 2014). However, the new authorities did not make a substantial effort to unite Ukrainians and were advocating for the cancellation of the language law, which allowed the usage of Russian as a regional language in Crimea. This was seen by many as a fatal mistake, which played into Russia's hands (Int-3 2020; Int-26 2020; Int-27 2020). The Russian 'documentary' "Crimea. The way home" argued that Crimeans were scared that they would be forbidden to use the Russian language (Kondrashov 2015). It also confirmed that the militia in Sevastopol started to form already in October 2013, and on 22nd February 2014 Crimeans gathered on Lenin square and declared their will to fight against the new power in Kyiv (Kondrashov 2015). On 18th March (after the referendum on 16th March), the Prime Minister of Ukraine recorded an appeal to Ukrainians, in which he promised not to cancel the language law, to begin decentralisation and to preserve good relations with Russia (Yatseniuk 2014). This came too late. In any case, an independent foreign journalist following these events stressed that if there had been a legitimate referendum in Crimea, it was very probable that the majority would have voted to join Russia anyway (Int-15 2020). Therefore, the alienation of the Crimean population from the rest of Ukraine was strengthened by certain steps on the part of the new authorities in Kyiv, and by Russia's actions in Crimea during and after the Euromaidan.

---

59 For instance, in February 2014, 41% of Crimeans wanted Ukraine to unite with Russia, with the average for Ukraine being 12% (KIIS 2014a).

The EU's resources

Understanding the scarcity of Ukraine's resources, Ukrainian politicians viewed the European Union as the last hope in their stand against Russia, but the EU was not ready to fulfil Ukraine's expectations. In the beginning of Russia's military actions in Crimea, senior Ukrainian officials decided to seek help from the EU (National Security and Defense Council of Ukraine 2014). However, a number of policy-makers emphasised that Ukraine could have used its diplomatic resource better, e.g., by using the Budapest Memorandum as a platform for an international solution to the conflict, when the first 'green men' appeared in Crimea[60] (Int-1 2020; Int-4 2020; Int-7 2020). While Ukraine attempted to convince the EU to give the country more help, the EU was not ready to do so (Int-5 2020; Int-7 2020). The acting Foreign Minister of Ukraine mentioned that until mid-March the EU was "stunned and confused" (Int-36 2021). An EU official working on EU-Ukraine and EU-Russia relations wondered: "How can we interrupt intervention in Crimea? We cannot interrupt this. It's the difference between those who take power by traditional means and those who project power with modern means." (Int-35 2021). Another EU official explained that in the beginning the EU tried to apply its "usual toolbox" and only some time later developed new mechanisms, and clarified:

> The European Union only got its, shall we say, new identity with the Lisbon Treaty in 2010 and a number of tools that the treaty had given to the EU were only effectively in use in exactly that way for the first time with the conflict [in Ukraine]. (Int-12 2020).

It was confirmed by both EU (Int-12 2020; Int-14 2020) and Ukrainian decision-makers (Int-7 2020; Int-36 2021) that in the beginning Ukrainian policy-makers lacked a full awareness of the limited extent of the EU's readiness to use its resources in Ukraine. Thus,

---

[60] The meeting of signatories of the Budapest Memorandum took place on 4-5 March 2014 in Paris (MFA Briefing 2014). However, consultations with the UK and the US did not result in anything but declarations about Ukraine's territorial integrity (MFA Briefing 2014). Ukrainian representatives also did not have a chance to meet with those from Russia (Int-36 2021).

Ukrainian misperceptions about the EU's help is an additional issue in the country's decision-making during the events in Crimea.

Lastly, time is also a resource, which plays an important role in international relations, and it was crucial during the annexation of Crimea. In Ukraine, the new post-Euromaidan decision-makers required time to establish control, which influenced their ability to manage the country's resources and to quickly react to the threats (Int-8 2020; Int-10 2020; Int-36 2021). The Chief of Ukraine's Border Guard Services confirmed that "with the time lag and such a rapid change of circumstances, it was very difficult to make comprehensive and correct decisions" (Int-10 2020). The EU's slow decision-making was mentioned by both a Ukrainian politician ("prolonged in time and sometimes not timely EU decisions") (Int-11 2020) and an EU official ("it took us a while before we actually fully understood and started to react") (Int-12 2020). On the other hand, with just one decision-maker in the Kremlin, Russia was able to make quick and effective decisions (Int-13 2020). Hence, neither Ukraine nor the EU were ready to react quickly to the unexpected and rapid Russian actions in Crimea.

My analysis of Ukrainian leaders' understanding of the resources of the EU, Ukraine, and Russia, clarified the Crimean annexation further. A number of scholars, analysts and decision-makers agree that Ukraine lacked military resources to engage in an open war with Russia during the events in Crimea. The Ukrainian Army was weak, there were numerous acts of betrayal, Russia was much stronger militarily and the population in Crimea was pro-Russian. Additionally, Russia was ready to use its vast resources to reach its goal—to incorporate Crimea—and Ukraine had neither military might, nor the political will of the authorities to resist. On the other hand, Ukrainian policy-makers overestimated the EU's resources and its willingness to use them to save Crimea. The European Union apparently used its standard tools to solve this issue, whilst other mechanisms were not yet available, and/or saving Ukraine's territorial integrity was not its first preference. Russia was also quicker in its decision-making. Counterfactual assumption suggests that Ukrainian civil society potentially might have influenced the situation, but this possibility was missed by the Ukrainian authorities. Although Ukrainian policy-makers were aware of the country's poor resources, they misinterpreted the EU's and Russia's readiness to apply their resources (the understanding of Russia's abilities was better than those of the EU). Therefore, my analysis suggests that Ukrainian decision-makers' poor use of the country's own resources, together with the fact that they lacked a comprehensive assessment of the EU's and Russia's resources, were the final factors in their failure to create a workable strategy to oppose Russia's actions in Crimea.

Conclusion

In this chapter, I have analysed Ukrainian leaders' decision-making process in the country's relations with the EU and Russia during the annexation of Crimea. I discussed information, trust, payoffs, and resources as core factors in Ukraine's foreign policy steps. I have used original data from interviews, policy documents, transcripts of meetings and media reports as my main sources. The key issue which impacted Ukraine's decision-making was the change in power structures after the Euromaidan, which resulted in a deterioration of the new decision-makers' ability to fully take charge and to decide quickly. My core findings suggest that Ukrainian policy-makers misjudged the preferences of their foreign interlocutors, misunderstood the appropriateness of trust in their strategies and failed to fully grasp the payoff structure for all three sides — the EU, Ukraine, and Russia. This was further exacerbated by the Ukrainian leaders' inability to fully employ Ukraine's resources and to correctly estimate the resources of the EU and Russia. Thus, during the rapidly developing events of the annexation, Ukraine failed to construct a robust strategy to meet its objectives, which to some extent helped Russia to take over the Crimean Peninsula.

First of all, the Euromaidan brought about a change in power structures in Ukraine. Although the majority of the new leaders were experienced politicians, they needed time to develop their understanding of the crisis and to build information channels. This was further complicated by the infiltration of Russian agents into Ukraine's core institutions. Secondly, I showed that Russia's core preference was to keep its influence over Ukraine and thus to stop EU-Ukraine integration; although this was understood in Kyiv and Brussels, it was not taken seriously enough. Moreover, Putin's personal preference – to stay in power – should have been part of the analysis (since he was the main decision-maker in Russia), but this was apparently missed in Kyiv. Lastly, the EU preferred to have a stable partner in Ukraine and to have no conflicts in its neighbourhood, which again was not clearly understood by Ukrainian leaders. Thus, through the game theory-based analytical framework, we are able to see that a flawed understanding of others' preferences had a negative impact on the Ukrainian leaders' ability to make rational decisions.

My analysis of trust in EU-Ukraine-Russia relations revealed a few further peculiarities. On the one hand, my empirical evidence suggests that Ukrainian policy-makers trusted the understanding that Russia would not dare to annex Crimea and rejected information which challenged this understanding. On the other hand, they trusted the EU's ability and willingness to protect Crimea from Russia. Trust in the Budapest Memorandum was also high in Ukraine. EU policy-makers had a considerable trust in their Ukrainian interlocutors, but there were some instances of uncertainty about the actions of the new government. Additionally, Russia effectively used bluffing (a staged referendum, threats, denial of the presence of its military in Crimea) during the annexation of Crimea, which deceived both Ukraine and the EU. Thus, Ukrainian leaders' trust in international law – trusting Russia not to attack and the EU to support Ukraine – is considered the biggest miscalculation in their foreign policy analysis during the events in Crimea.

The estimation of all actors' payoffs by Ukrainian policy-makers for this period was overshadowed by Ukraine's desire to integrate with the EU (and to be less dependent on Russia) and later to preserve Ukraine's territorial integrity. To pursue its preference to control Ukraine, Russia first hoped that the 21st February agreement would save the situation after Euromaidan, and this was not taken into account by either Ukraine or the EU. Some Ukrainian decision-makers sensed Russia's further payoff — to stop Ukraine forging closer ties with the EU — but they did not analyse Putin's payoff, which was to boost his domestic support via the annexation of Crimea. Post-revolutionary situation in Ukraine, Russia's interest in Crimea, Russia's losing influence over Ukraine and the need for Putin to increase his popularity — all increased the value of the payoff for the annexation of Crimea for Putin. The EU's payoff for the preservation of the international rule of law was considered to be too high, whilst the EU's actual preferred payoffs were to avoid an outbreak of an open war in Ukraine and to sign the AA with Ukraine. Ukrainian policy-makers confirmed that the EU promised to solve the situation in Crimea, but according to EU officials, the EU viewed itself rather as a mediator, not a party to the conflict. Some of these peculiarities of the structure of payoffs and their formation were missed by Ukrainian decision-makers.

The study of the EU's, Russia's and Ukraine's resources, and their readiness to use them, makes the situation even clearer. As confirmed by both independent observers and actual decision-makers, Ukraine lacked the necessary resources to protect Crimea from Russia by military means. Russia's military groupings on the peninsula were incomparably larger than those of Ukraine, and a number of acts of defections of Ukrainian security services to Russia also took place in Crimea. Additionally, the new leaders in Kyiv were not ready to rule the country in such stormy times; nor did they succeed in reaching out to ordinary Crimeans, who were Russian-oriented. Russia was ready to invest much of its vast resources in this operation. The EU, to Ukraine's disappointment, was not prepared to use its resources to 'save' Crimea. In addition to its greater willingness and more powerful military, Russia had another advantage in resources — time. Ukrainian decision-makers could somehow estimate Russia's resources but did not know what Russia was ready to do in Ukraine. Their awareness of the EU's abilities was even poorer. Thus, Ukraine's own resources were not fully used (the lack of political will to protect the country, a missed opportunity to involve civil society and to reach Crimeans), and the resources of others were not correctly estimated by the Ukrainian leaders. Thus, a number of factors acted against Ukraine and favoured Russia during the annexation of Crimea. Certain issues prevented Ukrainian decision-makers from performing a full foreign policy analysis with a realistic awareness of their own and their opponents' strategies, which is fundamental to any country's success in its foreign relations. What could Ukrainian decision-makers have done differently if they had better perceived the situation? It is hard to write counterfactuals, but a few steps could be done better by the new Ukrainian leaders: no discussion of the cancellation of the language law, dialogue with Crimeans (both online and offline visits of senior officials to Crimea) with the aim to explain the new Kyiv policies and to fight Russian propaganda on the peninsula, clear guidance to soldiers and officials in Crimea in case of Russian provocations, involvement of Euromaidan volunteer groups to support Ukraine's military groupings in Crimea and possible direct talks with Putin so as to try to avoid escalation (as Kuchma managed to do during the Tuzla crisis). The next chapters will look at how Ukrainian decision-making was evolving with the development of this war.

Table 3: The timeline of the annexation of the Crimean Peninsula by the Russian Federation

Date	Event
18-19 February 2014	Mass shootings at Maidan Square in Kyiv
21 February 2014	Agreement on the settlement of the crisis in Ukraine between Yanukovych and opposition leaders under the supervision of Polish, German and French Foreign Ministers and a Russian representative (The agreement on the Settlement of the crisis in Ukraine 2014)
21 February	Yanukovych leaves Kyiv
22 February	Yanukovych leaves Ukraine
22-23 February 2014	Vladimir Putin's night-time meeting with Russian security services regarding the situation in Ukraine (and the decision to start the operation in Crimea) (Kondrashov 2015)
27 February 2014	The Supreme Court of Crimean Autonomous Republic[61] vote on holding a referendum on the status of the peninsula (Resolution of the Verkhovna Rada of the ARC 2014)
4-5 March 2014	Signatories of the Budapest Memorandum met in Paris, no agreement was reached (MFA Briefing 2014)
6 March 2014	The Supreme Court of Crimean Autonomous Republic changed the date of the referendum to 16 March 2014
14 March 2014	The Constitutional Court of Ukraine recognised the resolution on holding a referendum in Crimea as unconstitutional (Constitutional Court of Ukraine 2014)
16 March 2014	The referendum was held in Crimea
18 March 2014	The incorporation of Crimea as a new subject into the Russian Federation (President of Russia 2014b)
26 March 2014	The last Ukrainian military bases were captured by Russia in Crimea (Russian troops captured all Ukrainian military units in Crimea 2014)

---

61   Before the vote, the Supreme Court of the Crimean Autonomous Republic was taken by Russian Special Security Services.

Table 4: Ukraine's decision-making during the annexation of Crimea (February 21st – March 26th)

Information	Trust	Payoffs	Resources
Weak state informational environment	**Position of trust based on international laws**	**"Eyes wide shut" - miscalculation of payoffs**	**Low awareness of resources**
❖ Post-Euromaidan change in power structures ▶ Crimea power vacuum ▶ Broken information channels ▶ Flawed analysis of information ❖ Russian intelligence infiltration in crucial state institutions ❖ Weak understanding of preferences ▶ The EU: no wars + economic cooperation with neighbours ▶ Russia's: control over Ukraine + Putin's preference to stay in power Impact: <u>High</u>	❖ International laws ▶ Trust in legal power of Budapest Memorandum and friendship treaties with Russia ❖ Russia's bluffing and threats ▶ Confused and delayed actions of the EU and Ukraine ❖ EU as a peacekeeper in Europe ▶ Trust in the EU to 'save' Ukraine Impact: <u>High</u>	❖ Flawed perceptions of Russia's payoffs ▶ Perceived: threaten Ukraine, possibly annex Crimea, or start an all-out war ▪ Russia's 'true' payoff: 1st: respect for 21st February Agreement 2nd: reassert regional control through annexation of Crimea 3rd: increase Putin's domestic support ❖ Flawed perceptions of the EU payoffs ▶ Perceived: saving Crimea, integration with Ukraine ▶ The EU's 'true' payoff 1st: avoiding an all-out war in Ukraine 2nd: economic cooperation (AA) ❖ Ukraine's perceived payoffs: integration with the EU, preservation of territory Impact: <u>Medium</u>	❖ Awareness of Ukraine's weaker position in Crimea ▶ In military resources ▶ Crimeans' support for Russia (triggered by possible cancellation of the language law and Russian propaganda) ❖ Lack of the new leaders' 'political will' to fight for Crimea ❖ Misjudgement on the EU's ability to constrain Russia ❖ Russia's advantage on time as a resource Impact: <u>**Medium**</u>

4 Donbas on fire: Improvement of Ukraine's crisis management (April – August 2014)

Introduction

In the previous chapter, we discussed Russia's takeover of all of Ukraine's possessions in Crimea by 26th March; accordingly, it had completed its annexation, despite the condemnation of Ukraine and most of the international community (United Nations 2014). We have also determined that Ukrainian decision-makers failed to thoroughly analyse all of the important elements in their foreign relations with the EU and Russia. For instance, the fact that they did not trust Russia's threats, and relied too much on the EU's support, might have facilitated Russia's success in the annexation. Now we will turn to the situation in the East of the country. This chapter discusses the factors that shaped Ukraine's actions and reactions in its relations with Russia and the EU during the Donbas rebellions in spring, and open war in the summer of 2014 up until Minsk I (26th March – 5th September). Although we might have expected the EU and the Ukrainian authorities to have more experience in dealing with such matters after Crimea, my informants who were involved in EU and Ukrainian decision-making kept referring to their shock and the difficulty they experienced in forming a strategy even in April - May 2014. They recalled growing mistrust towards Russia and a greater understanding of Putin's preferences, but they also mentioned unpredictability and rapid changes as key issues, which hindered the formation of effective foreign policy (Int-1 2020; Int-7 2020; Int-12 2020). During the events in Crimea, the response of Ukrainian leaders was focused on discussions with the EU; however, after the annexation, at least after mid-April, the authorities in Kyiv were more ready to respond militarily to rebellions in Donbas. This escalated into open war in June 2014. Thus, in game theory terms one might say that Russia's increased involvement in Donbas changed the game from a chicken to a prisoner's dilemma[62].

Firstly, it is important to highlight changes to the decision-making of the three actors. In what I present below, we will see that Putin continued to be at the apex of decision-making in Russia, just receiving some advice from a few trusted people. There were also no substantial changes in the EU's decision-making. However, it is relevant to note the developments in Kyiv: post-Euromaidan leaders gained more crisis experience, there were a number of changes in the government (e.g., a new minister of foreign affairs from June 2014), and most importantly, on 25th May, Ukraine elected a new President, Petro Poroshenko. The new President was also recognised by Putin (President of Russia 2014e), which facilitated communication between the countries. As in the previous chapter, the discussion of the strategic decision-making that unfolded in this period is divided into information, trust, payoffs, and resources. I would like to emphasise that in this period, a) Ukrainian decision-makers gradually learned to trust Russia's threats; b) the payoffs structure was changing too fast to be fully grasped; and c) Ukraine was more aware of its own and others' resources (see Table 6). The most decisive element of decision-making was awareness of Ukraine's and other actors' resources and their readiness to use them. Better understanding of the fact that Russia was ready to keep on applying more resources and that the EU was ready to provide Ukraine with only limited support (financial and diplomatic, but not military) helped Ukrainian leaders to concentrate on the development of the country's own resources (in particular its army) and to fight back

---

[62] In a game of chicken, parties see a conflict (defect-defect) as the least desirable payoff, while in a prisoner's dilemma they end in a defect-defect box of a payoff matrix. When the provocative actions of one party makes cooperation less attractive than defection, the game may change from a chicken to a prisoner's dilemma (G. H. Snyder 1971, 92–93). It might be that the EU and Ukraine did not respond to Russia's activity in Crimea and in Donbas in March/beginning of April for fear of a bigger war (a chicken game), but Ukraine introduced the Anti-Terrorist Operation in mid-April after growing rebellions supported by Russia made a defection payoff (counter-attack) greater than cooperation (a prisoner's dilemma).

against Russian-backed insurgents (at least until Russia directly invaded Ukraine in August). Yet until September 2014, Ukrainian policy-makers were not fully aware of Russia's and the EU's intentions to apply their resources in Ukraine.

Secondly, I would like to provide some information about the historical, economic, and social background of Donbas. For centuries, it was a border region between various states on the lands of present-day Ukraine and of Turkic-speaking peoples (Wilson 2016, 633–34). Donbas was sparsely populated before the war of Bohdan Khmelnytskyi in the 17th century. During this war, many peasants escaped Central Ukraine and settled there. After the discovery of natural resources in the region at the time of the Russian Empire, its industrial development connected the region to other parts of the Empire. Apart from the two world wars, the 1932-1933 man-made famine (the Holodomor[63]) had a big influence on the region. After millions of people died, the region was repopulated with settlers from other regions of the Soviet Union (Wilson 2016, 636), which contributed to its ethnic diversity (though Ukrainians remained the majority). In Soviet times, Donbas specialised in industrial development (in particular heavy and military engineering), which had strong connections to Russia. In independent Ukraine, Donbas kept its specialisation and its economic ties with Russia, which created a certain loyalty on the part of Donbas residents to Russia (Mylovanov, Zhukov, and Gorodnichenko 2018) and led to a fear of integration with the EU (Giuliano 2018). This was exploited by the Russian media just as it had been in relation to Crimea. After the collapse of the Soviet Union, the economic situation deteriorated in the region, which led to several miners' protests throughout the years of the country's independence (Mroz and Pavliuk 1996; Sasse 2001). The concentration of resources in the hands of oligarchs, in particular Rinat Akhmetov, was even bigger here than in the rest of Ukraine.

---

[63] Holodomor (death by starvation) is the name given to a man-made famine orchestrated by Stalin's Soviet regime in 1932-1933, which took the lives of 3.3-10 million people (the exact number is disputed). It is considered one of Europe's major genocides and was aimed to repress Ukrainians who rebelled against collectivisation (T. Snyder 2012).

That is why decision-making on the part of local elites, for instance their lack of visible pro-Ukrainian position, was seen by several respondents as a decisive factor in the development of the war in Donbas but not in, for example, Odesa or Kharkiv (Int-14 2020; Int-22 2020; Int-24 2020; Int-27 2020). Having acknowledged the economic and social background of the region, I will now concentrate on the Ukrainian authorities' reactions to the conflict in Donbas and their relations with the EU and Russia between 26th March and 5th September 2014.

4.1. Information: Partial improvement

As I previously explained, information about other actors' preferences (and also their commitment to fight for these preferences) is a crucial part of foreign policy decision-making (Fearon 1995; L. Thompson 1995). After Crimea was annexed by Russia, Ukrainian decision-makers had a better understanding of the whole picture, and in particular they saw that Russia was decisive in following its preferences and that the EU was not. In March-April the Ukrainian authorities were still unable to fully grasp the information environment, which obstructed their quick response to events in Donbas and gave rise to the claim that they had missed the opportunity to stop the war when the first riots took place (Int-1 2020; Int-3 2020; Int-27 2020). In May-June, the understanding of Russia's and the EU's preferences improved, but this was still not as clear as it was to become after Minsk I. I will now explain the Ukrainian leaders' handling of information and shifts in their awareness of others' preferences.

Changes within Ukrainian leadership

Firstly, let us look at changes within the Ukrainian leadership that influenced the country's decision-making. Between 23rd February and 7th June, Oleksandr Turchynov was acting President of Ukraine. On entering office, he fired 42 presidential advisors (Turchynov 2014); this confirms the tendency, I mentioned earlier, of new leaders' dismissal of previous employees, which has a negative impact on information transfer between the changing elites. It is interesting to note that a Polish politician and an expert on Ukraine stressed the EU's awareness of the temporality of Turchynov and the key importance of Petro Poroshenko, Yulia Tymoshenko and Arseniy Yatsenyuk (Int-25 2020). This Arseniy Yatsenyuk was Ukraine's Prime Minister from February 2014 to April 2016, and so he had the opportunity to develop a more durable policy. However, his cabinet had two foreign ministers: the acting one was Andrii Deshchytsia (February - June 2014), and the other was Pavlo Klimkin. From March to September, there were three defence ministers. Andriy Parubiy served as Secretary of National Security and Defence Council of Ukraine in February - August 2014. The Security Service of Ukraine was headed by Valentyn Nalyvaichenko in February 2014 - June 2015 and, as mentioned earlier, he had to create the institution almost from zero due to the disappearance of previous employees (Int-8 2020). On the other hand, my respondents confirmed that old elites within new authorities (Poroshenko, Yatseniuk) were known to the EU (Int-25 2020) and had established political contacts with Russia, while the new ones did not possess those contacts (Int-7 2020). In addition, an advisor to a senior decision-maker in Ukraine recalled that at that time access to information was quite limited and some state organs were misleading, either on purpose or unintentionally (Int-7 2020). The transfer of power, rapid change of ministers, and difficulty in finding new employees for some state organs might have decreased Ukraine's possibilities in the analysis of the required information.

Separatism in Donbas since 2004

With regard to information, I have found evidence of the existence of information about separatist tendencies in Donbas long before March 2014, which, however, was not used for war prevention. Scholars have observed that certain tensions in Eastern Ukraine had started already during the Orange Revolution (Giuliano 2018; Wilson 2016). This claim is supported by a former governor of Luhansk region and a social activist from Luhansk, both of whom call 2004 the start of 'the war', while the separatist congress in Severodonetsk[64] organised people to advocate for the federalisation of Ukraine and fostered powerful propaganda about 'the Russian World' in Donbas (Int-1 2020; Int-3 2020). The attendees of the Congress wanted Yanukovych to become president of Ukraine, and if this did not happen, they supported the creation of an independent South-Eastern Republic (Severodonetsk Congress 2005). Yet the latter could be treated as an offence against the integrity of Ukraine under the country's constitution (Verkhovna Rada of Ukraine 1996). Moreover, investigative journalists argued that if people responsible for separatism in 2004 were brought to justice[65], there would have been no war in Donbas in 2014 (Firsov 2017). This is significant, because it indicates that a certain pro-Russian orientation of some of the Donbas elites existed already from 2004, which in the absence of a state reaction, persisted and contributed to the events of 2014. Building on this, let us now turn to an exploration of foreign influences on these events in Donbas.

Indeed, the separatist tendencies in Donbas were often stirred up by an external actor — namely, Russia. One example of this is the presence of Russian representatives (e.g., the Mayor of Moscow) at Severodonetsk Congress and appeals to Russia from the attendees (Severodonetsk Congress 2005). Another example is the fact that a former deputy of the Russian Duma confirmed Putin's intense involvement in two Ukrainian revolutions, which, according to him, Putin lost, and therefore had to do something to restore his image in the eyes of Russians (Int-17 2020). This was supported by a former governor of Luhansk oblast who said that

---

[64] The first All-Ukrainian Congress of People's Deputies and Deputies of Local Councils took place on 28th November 2004. It was triggered by the Orange Revolution, which cast doubt on the victory of Viktor Yanukovych which was supported by the Congress in the October 2004 presidential elections. The attendees included Yanukovych's allies, e.g,. the governors of Kharkiv and Donetsk regions, but also the mayor of Moscow and an advisor from the Russian Embassy in Ukraine.

[65] In spite of the condemnation of the Congress and its separatist declarations by former Ukrainian President Leonid Kuchma and the Verkhovna Rada of Ukraine, and the opening of an investigation by the Security Service of Ukraine, the people responsible for its organisation were not convicted (Firsov 2017).

the first Russian coordinators appeared in Donbas in November 2013 and "in March 2014, under the guise of tourists, Russian paratroopers were transported to the territory of Slavyanogorsk" (Int-1 2020). To this end, a Luhansk social activist stressed that the appearance of veteran organisations (e.g., veterans of Afghanistan), the receipt of weapons by ordinary people and their participation in insurgences, and the occupation of government buildings in March-April 2014 – all this was coordinated from Moscow (Int-3 2020). These developments could not only be easily identified from open sources, but in addition, local governors transferred this information to Kyiv (Int-1 2020). This highlights the fact that the information about separatism in Donbas and Russia's involvement was available to decision-makers in Kyiv, but no substantial actions were taken during any of the different presidential periods. This shows that the reaction of the authorities to relevant foreign policy information was slow and/or inappropriate.

Foreign policy preferences of Ukrainians

Another point relating to the foreign policy preferences of Ukrainians is that my diverse informants (in particular, Russian journalists) (Int-3 2020; Int-19 2020; Int-22 2020; Int-28 2021; Int-29 2021) noted a certain polarisation of Ukrainian society after the Euromaidan mass mobilisation, which was not openly acknowledged by the new authorities. The former Chief of the Ukrainian Border Guard Service stated that "the way in which the new political class came to power in 2014, it was already a split both within society and within politics" (Int-10 2020). The fact that the *'coup d'état'* was not accepted by residents of the East of Ukraine was also mentioned by Putin in an interview (Seipel 2014). In addition to Euromaidan per se, scholars explain this polarisation as the result of a massive disinformation campaign[66], which further accentuated divisions among Ukrainians living in different regions (Hale, Shevel, and Onuch 2018). At the end of February, anti-

---

66 Later, in spring 2014, Ukraine took retaliatory steps and Russian state TV channels were banned in Ukraine.

Euromaidan and pro-Russian protests started in the East and on 1st March the rebels occupied governmental buildings in Donbas (Pro-Russian protesters 2014). Interestingly, a Russian journalist claimed that protesters in Ukraine's West and East were using the same tactics, and that the only difference was in their flags — the people in Western Ukraine were holding the UPA flag,[67] while in Eastern Ukraine it was that of Russia (Int-19 2020). Confirmation of this perception can be seen in the fact that in April 2014, rebels in Luhansk told the OSCE mission that they would release the occupied building of the Security Service of Ukraine, if the buildings occupied by Euromaidan activists in Kyiv were also liberated (OSCE 2014). This blurring of legality during the protests contributed to the fragile post-revolutionary situation in Ukraine. Knowing this, the new leaders could have tried to calm the population down; however, they failed to do so.

Although, as we already know, Ukrainians had diverse opinions about the country's future, with the majority in the East favouring closer ties with Russia than with the EU (see chapter 3), decision-makers in Kyiv continued to publicly support integration with the EU (Giuliano 2018). An EU official who worked on Ukraine and met with Ukrainian decision-makers on a number of occasions, explained that Ukrainian leaders made it clear to the EU "that their preference was to follow a reform process, which would take Ukraine closer to the EU" (Int-32 2021). The acting foreign minister of Ukraine also referred to closer cooperation with the EU as a key goal for Ukraine (Int-36 2021). On the other hand, a senior EU official dealing with EU-Ukraine-Russia economic relations highlighted the fact that Ukraine aimed at both establishing closer relations with the EU and preserving its important economic ties with Russia (Int-37 2021). Yet the hidden corrupt interests of Ukrainian core decision-makers, for instance their secret business with Russia, was recently revealed by inves-

---

67 UPA (Ukrainian Insurgence Army) was a Ukrainian paramilitary formation, which fought both against Nazi and Soviets in Western Ukraine during the Second World War (Ukrainian Insurgent Army 1993). It remains a symbol of the brave fight for the country's independence and its flag is still used by some in Ukraine.

tigative journalists (BIHUS info 2021a, 2021c). Therefore, it might be that Ukrainian officials' public words about EU integration differed from some of their actual foreign policy steps (maintaining certain business interests with Russia), while at the same time the pro-EU course angered some Donbas residents.

Russia's preferences

Building on the discussion about information flow inside Ukraine (changes within the leadership, the situation in Donbas and the country's preferences), let us now consider awareness on the part of Kyiv decision-makers about Russia's preferences concerning Ukraine. Ukrainian policy-makers confirmed that they had a clearer idea of Russia's preferences after the annexation of Crimea (Int-5 2020; Int-7 2020). Both EU and Ukrainian policy-makers stated that these preferences remained the same — to have control over Ukraine's destiny and to stop Ukraine from further integration with the EU (Int-1 2020; Int-7 2020; Int-11 2020; Int-20 2020; Int-21 2020). Similarly, 'Novaya Gazeta' considered Russia's goal to be "to preserve the maximum possible influence on Ukraine's politics" (Shyriaev 2015). The acting foreign minister of Ukraine explained that Russia's goal (or preference) stayed the same — to get back control over Ukraine — but that its tactics (payoffs) were changing during the war (Int-36 2021). Both analysts (Friedman 2014) and respondents (Int-25 2020; Int-36 2021; Int-37 2021) have confirmed that Ukraine's EU-course was seen by Russia as a threat to its own security. Although this foreign policy preference on the part of Russia was already sensed in Ukraine, Ukrainian leaders did not look at the personal preferences of Russian decision-makers, particularly those of Putin.

Interestingly, both Russian and EU informants stressed that Putin was the sole decision-maker in the Kremlin when dealing with Ukraine (Int-13 2020; Int-17 2020; Int-30 2021) and that his core preference was to stay in power for as long as possible, although his actions did not necessarily reflect the interests of the Russian people (Int-13 2020; Int-18 2020; Int-29 2021). A Russian expert on social attitudes held that originally people were against any Russian intervention, but that Putin managed to convince them by means of stories about the threat to Russian speakers (Int-29 2021). This corresponds with the arguments of those scholars who underscored the possible disjuncture between leaders' and the population's preferences, and thus called for an investigation of the personal preferences of decision-makers in strategic foreign policy analysis (De Mesquita 2006; Morrow 1986; Nye 2005). Thus, although it is hard to wholly separate Putin's and Russians' interests in the country's actions, analysis of Putin's preferences is highly relevant. An advisor to a senior Ukrainian decision-maker said that there might have been some analysis of Putin's preferences by Poroshenko, but for any lower political levels these calculations were too complicated, and were impossible to make due to the rapid tempo of decision-making (Int-7 2020). Interestingly, in their comprehensive analysis of different international conflicts, Snyder and Diesing (1970) came to a conclusion that decision-makers mostly do not do well in analysis of each other's internal politics. Thus, the absence of analysis of Putin's personal preferences by decision-makers in Kyiv could be seen as a limitation to their decision-making.

Another major pattern that came out of my interviews in relation to informational trends driving strategic decision-making in this period was the specificity of Putin's decision-making. Russian respondents stated that Putin used for the most part information coming from special services (Int-16 2020), trusting mostly "what the Security Council prepares" (Int-17 2020), without taking expert opinions into account (Int-26 2020). In addition, a former Russian MP claimed that a Ukrainian politician and a businessman, Viktor Medvedchuk,[68] was Putin's most important informant in Ukraine (Int-17 2020). According to the revealed leaks (of Medvedchuk's phone conversations) from the Ukrainian Security Service, Medvedchuk was chosen as a connector between Putin and Poroshenko, and since May 2014 he was very much involved in all

---

68 Viktor Medvedchuk is a Ukrainian businessman and politician, advocating for better relations with Russia. Russian President Putin is a godfather of Medvedchuk's child.

relevant negotiations on Donbas (BIHUS info 2021b). Putin officially recognised the improvement in his negotiations with separatists thanks to Medvedchuk (President of Russia 2014a). This makes it clear that there were frequent, but indirect, contacts between Poroshenko and Putin in this period. Although my interviewees did not mention any analysis of Putin's decision-making, the leaks I have mentioned reveal that there was contact between Putin and Poroshenko, which may be a sign that core Ukrainian decisions were taken solely by Poroshenko, and that his informational background was somehow better than those of other policy-makers.

The EU's preferences

Turning now to the EU's preferences regarding Ukraine, my research suggests that whilst Ukrainian leaders viewed the EU's aim to be integration with Ukraine and the preservation of the rule of law, the EU actually preferred to have stability near its borders and good economic relations with its neighbours (including Russia). An example of this can be found in the statement by the Head of the Delegation of the European Parliament to Ukraine, that the EU was ready to provide Ukraine with some types of support as long as Ukraine continued with its reforms (Int-25 2020). An EU official also stated that "many in Ukraine had the hope, some would say the illusion, that the EU would make them a member of the EU in the foreseeable future" (Int-35 2021). On the other hand, even having clear facts about Russia's support for insurgencies in Donbas, the EU did not want to fully break off its relations with Russia (Int-13 2020; Int-20 2020), which indicates the importance of cooperation with Russia for the EU. EU policy-makers were in a difficult situation: while they preferred to preserve their relations with both Ukraine and Russia, they also wanted to prevent a conflict near their borders, which led to complicated internal discussions (Int-12 2020; Int-13 2020; Int-20 2020; Int-34 2021). EU policy-makers also explained that the EU had to take into account the views of all of its members both towards Ukraine and Russia (Int-32 2021; Int-34 2021). The acting minister of foreign affairs of

Ukraine also explained that the EU's goal was "to avoid an all-out war on the European continent" (Int-36 2021). Yet despite some understanding of the EU's preference for peace in Europe, Ukrainian policy-makers still did not understand that EU-Ukraine integration was not a priority for the Union and that cooperation with Russia was another important EU preference.

The above discussion provides a few insights. There was information on the preferences of Ukrainians in different regions (e.g., more support for the Russian language[69] and good relations with Russia in the East[70]); there were Ukrainian politicians who were eager to play on separatism sentiments; and there was some understanding of Russia's preferences regarding Ukraine. However, these were not acted on either by previous or by post-Euromaidan leaders. Despite receiving signals from Russia, Ukrainian decision-makers did not conduct a full analysis of Putin's domestic preference, i.e. the strengthening of his power (this understanding could only have been at Poroshenko's level). Yet they already had a better understanding of Russia's geostrategic preference — to preserve Russia's influence on Ukraine. The EU's preferences (economic cooperation and no war near its borders) were not understood in full in Ukraine (in particular, its preference for keeping economic relations with Russia). My analysis has shown that better information management could have provided Ukrainian decision-makers with more possibilities during the military conflict in Donbas. Limited information makes trust more relevant, and we will now explore the role which trust played in Ukrainian leaders' decision-making.

---

[69] In accordance with Pew Research Centre's research on Ukrainians' attitudes in spring 2014, 41% of Ukrainians believed that Ukrainian should be the only official language in the country, while 54% preferred to have both Ukrainian and Russian (66% and 30% in the West; 25% and 73% in the East) (Pew Research Center 2014).

[70] According to the same research, 43% of Ukrainians wanted closer relations with the EU, 18% — with Russia and 27% — with both (68%, 5% and 17% respectively in the West of the country and 21%, 30%, 36% in the East) (Pew Research Center 2014).

4.2. Trust: Gradual decrease

In spring-summer 2014, Ukrainian authorities had developed a better understanding of Russia's and the EU's preferences. However, when it comes to trust, the annexation of Crimea had diminished Ukraine's trust both in Russia and the EU. In an environment of imperfect information, Russia used bluff to change others' perceptions, and continued to deny any involvement in Donbas (even in the face of increasing evidence). The key moments when it comes to trust towards Russia were the actions of Russian coordinators in the spring in Donbas, the appearance of sophisticated military equipment in the hands of rebels, the shooting down of MH17 in July, and the open aggression of the Russian Armed Forces in August 2014 (Int-13 2020; Int-14 2020). During the first weeks of unrest in Donbas (as with the events in Crimea), Ukrainian decision-makers did not trust Russia's threats and overrated the EU's ability to stop the conflict. In May-June, trust was getting more realistic: Russia's aggressive intentions were recognised and the EU's unpreparedness to get more involved was also better understood. Below, I study these features of trust in detail.

Trust issues within Ukraine

Let us start by looking at trust issues within Ukraine that impacted the country's foreign relations and stability in Donbas. Firstly, as with Crimea, there was a confusion about the legality of the new power in Kyiv among Donbas residents and elites (Int-1 2020; Int-3 2020; Int-19 2020). This was also confirmed by an MEP who had visited the warzone in June and said that people "were so confused about this conflict, so they really did not know who is who" (Int-31 2021). Secondly, the attempts of the Ukrainian authorities to build trust with Donbas residents were rather limited. As mentioned earlier, on 18th March, the Prime Minister of Ukraine recorded an appeal to Ukrainians, in particular residents of the South and East, in which he promised not to cancel the language law, to begin decentralization, and to preserve good relations with Russia (Yatseniuk 2014). After the separatists' takeover of Donetsk Regional Administration and the declaration of a referendum on joining Russia which would be held on 6-7 April (see Table 5) (Pro-Russian Group in Donetsk 2014), the acting President Turchynov offered an amnesty to the rebels if they surrendered, future decentralisation and definite rights concerning the use of the Russian language (Turchinov is ready to free the separatists 2014). Apart from these declarations, there was no other major attempt to establish dialogue with Donbas residents and on 15th April, the Anti-Terrorist Operation (ATO) was introduced (President of Ukraine 2014). After the 25th May presidential elections, scholars have identified an even greater alienation of the Donbas population from Kyiv (Marples 2016, 15) and a substantial increase in violence (Alexseev 2016). Additionally, some mistakes made by the Ukrainian military caused a further deterioration in the situation. For instance, on 2nd June, a military aircraft of the Ukrainian Armed Forces launched a rocket into the building of the Luhansk Regional Administration (this was denied by Ukraine, but confirmed by CNN and OSCE), which killed eight civilians (Int-3 2020; Magnay and Lister 2014; Miller 2014). A Luhansk social activist confirmed that this prompted many Luhansk residents to take up arms, while Russian media in the region, and the new Ukrainian leaders' talk about 'Ukrainisation', made them fearful of genocide (Int-3 2020). In an interview to a German TV channel, Putin also suggested that the new authorities could have had a better dialogue with Donbas residents (Seipel 2014). Thus, distrust among Ukrainians not only contributed to Ukraine's failure to regain Donbas (as I show below), but also gave Russia a certain justification for its actions in Ukraine.

(Dis)trust towards Russia

Another relevant issue regarding trust in EU-Ukraine-Russia relations is the initial distrust of Ukrainian and EU policy-makers in the credibility of Russia's threats. In 2008, Putin had declared that he did not see Ukraine as a sovereign state and would not allow it to enter NATO; if it tried, it would lose the Eastern part of the country, and Crimea (NATO is dissolved into packages of blocks

2008). However, although Ukrainian and EU policy-makers were well aware of these threats, the leaders did not take Putin's statements, and his preference to maintain control over Ukraine, sufficiently seriously. A former EU ambassador to Russia confirmed that the EU had intelligence reports and access to research about the possibility that Russia would attack Ukraine (Int-23 2020), but even after the war in Georgia, this possibility was rejected in the EU (Int-14 2020; Int-23 2020; Int-25 2020). Knowing about Russian support for separatists in Eastern Ukraine (as described above), and hearing Putin's threats about a larger scale war, Ukrainian decision-makers could have accepted Russia's aggressive intentions and been better prepared. Timely EU and Ukrainian trust in the credibility of Russia's threats might possibly have mitigated the conflict situation.

Although Ukraine's and the EU's trust in Russia's good intentions decreased after Crimea, it still continued to influence the situation. Some have referred to a mental unpreparedness on the part of Ukrainians for a war with Russia (Int-3 2020; Int-7 2020), while others have claimed that Ukrainian soldiers were only able to shoot at Russians after Russians visibly used their arms against Ukrainians, including shooting at them from Russian territory (Int-11 2020). Ukrainian policy-makers' lack of a clear understanding of the seriousness of the situation can be partly explained by the lack of dialogue with their Russian counterparts. According to Ukraine's foreign minister of that time, the first Ukraine-Russia contacts took place only in April 2014 during the Geneva meeting, and this led to hope for the possibility of negotiations (Int-36 2021). As for EU trust in Russia, it was more nuanced. An EU official confirmed the awareness of a discrepancy between the Russian leadership's words about Ukraine's freedom in its foreign policy and its encouragement of separatism in Donbas (Int-32 2021), and the EU Commissioner on Enlargement also highlighted the decrease in trust in Russia's words after its lies about Crimea (Int-21 2020). Another example of the erosion of trust is that after discussions with Putin, Angela Merkel described him as living in an alternative reality (Baker 2014), since she was apparently shocked that he had lied to her about Donbas and the shooting down of MH17[71] (Int-18 2020). An EU correspondent told me that "very quickly the EU side did not really take what the Russians were saying at 'face value' and realised that they had another agenda in Ukraine" (Int-20 2020). However, he confirmed that EU relations with Russia continued even without trust—"a policy based on necessity" (Int-20 2020)—and a former president of the European Council acknowledged that "after the annexation of Crimea trust was broken, but there were still channels open" (Int-34 2021). Therefore, whilst Ukraine was learning not to trust Russia, the EU retained its contacts with Putin, even with broken trust.

Turning now to the Russian leadership's trust in its EU and Ukrainian interlocutors, my analysis suggests that this trust remained low. Russian informants mentioned Russian decision-makers' distrust in post-Euromaidan politicians in Kyiv due to their perception of Euromaidan as a military coup (Int-17 2020; Int-19 2020), and of Ukrainian leaders as "some enemies, with whom only a zero-sum game [is possible]" (Int-16 2020). Respondents also mentioned that in the view of Russian decision-makers, the new Ukrainian leaders were very dependent on the EU (Int-19 2020; Int-28 2021), while both Ukraine and the EU were dependent on the US (Int-16 2020; Int-17 2020; Int-18 2020). An EU official also suggested that Russia "does not believe in the EU as an organisation and prefers to work with individual countries" (Int-2 2020). Other interviewees held that Russia's strategy comprised of searching for disagreements within the EU, making them bigger and using this to Russia's benefit (Int-16 2020; Int-20 2020; Int-21 2020). Putin's distrust in Ukraine and the EU was influencing relations in this triangle and so should have been part of Ukraine's foreign policy analysis; however, I did not hear this view expressed by Ukrainian respondents.

---

71 On 17 July 2014, Malaysian Airlines flight MH17, flying from Amsterdam to Kuala Lumpur, was shot down over Donbas by pro-Russian rebels with the Russian missile system Buk; this was confirmed by a Dutch-led investigation, but all the same rejected by Russia (Sengupta and Kramer 2016).

Trust between the EU and Ukraine

If we look at trust in EU-Ukraine relations, my informants noted that Ukrainian decision-makers' trust in EU interlocutors diminished after they did not get the requested support during the annexation of Crimea and the first appearance of Russian-backed insurgents in Donbas (Int-7 2020; Int-8 2020; Int-11 2020). This lack of trust was accentuated by the fact that, as an advisor to a senior official in Kyiv explained, due to mistrust towards Ukraine, the EU was sharing information which was not up-to-date (for instance, it provided satellite images that had been taken the previous week) (Int-7 2020). The acting Foreign Minister of Ukraine also felt there was a possibility of EU-Russia negotiations taking place behind Ukraine's back (Int-36 2021). However, EU respondents remembered a quite high level of trust in their Ukrainian interlocutors at that time (Int-2 2020; Int-21 2020; Int-25 2020; Int-35 2021), and that this increased after Poroshenko became president (Int-14 2020; Int-37 2021). Yet a German MP felt that there was a certain distrust towards Ukraine even among its 'friends in Europe', because Europeans did not know about all of the connections between Ukrainian politicians and oligarchs (e.g., Poroshenko did not keep his promise to sell his enterprises, while Kolomoyskiy initially protected Dnipro from separatists but later stole a lot of money from the Ukrainian state and people) (Int-38 2021). Therefore, although EU policy-makers proclaimed trust in their Ukrainian interlocutors, there were certain suspicions on the part of the Ukrainian authorities towards the EU, and *vice versa*. Such distrust might have contributed to more negative outcomes.

Consequences of mistrust

Another point related to trust is the possible failure in reaching common goals due to the actors' distrust in each other (Fearon 1995; Kydd 2000; L. Thompson 1995). This was also reported by my respondents in respect to EU-Ukraine-Russia relations. Although most Ukrainian informants stayed firm in their statement that there could be no common interests with the enemy (Int-1 2020; Int-2 2020; Int-4 2020; Int-11 2020; Int-24 2020), others had different opinions. Many agreed that economic cooperation between the EU, Ukraine and Russia was a shared interest for everyone, but that there was a severe deterioration in this cooperation because of the war (Int-9 2020; Int-16 2020; Int-17 2020; Int-18 2020; Int-21 2020). Moreover, such tactical goals as the prevention of ecological catastrophe in Donbas and the spread of infectious diseases from the warzone were also considered to be common interests which had not been achieved (Int-7 2020). Others argued that peace and security in Europe was a shared goal for the three sides (Int-12 2020; Int-21 2020). Even an advisor to one of the highest decision-makers in Ukraine stated that peace was a common interest for everyone, although Russia's conditions for peace differed from those of Ukraine (Int-7 2020). A foreign journalist in Ukraine also mentioned stability as a common goal, though acknowledging that "stability [was] defined in three different ways" (Int-15 2020). This confirms that the three sides shared certain goals which could possibly have been achieved with more trust between them. While the highest level of mistrust was detected between the EU-Ukraine and Russia, the latter's mistrust towards the others and their mistrust towards Russia resulted in failure to meet everyone's joint interests.

Thus, we see major differences in relation to trust (the predictability of others' actions) in this period, and specifically a marked decline in Ukraine's trust both in Russia (due to its aggression) and the EU (due to its failure to provide the expected help). Firstly, trust was not established between the Ukrainian authorities and Donbas residents, which stirred up the conflict and helped Russia to succeed. Secondly, mistrust in the credibility of Russia's threats in March-April meant that there was no rapid reaction to the unrest in Donbas. Thirdly, towards the summer, Ukrainian decision-makers understood better that the EU's words of support did not turn into significant actions, while Russia's threats to protect Russian-speakers beyond Russia's borders did turn into actions, not only in Crimea, but also in Donbas. Fourthly, Putin's trust in the EU's and Ukraine's interlocutors remained low in spring, but later he recognised Poroshenko as the president of Ukraine, which was positive for trust-building. Lastly, I have discovered certain common interests on the part of the three parties which were not achieved due to the lack of trust (mainly towards and from Russia). These findings support scholarly views on the relevance of trust in conflict prevention and resolution (Fearon 1995; Hoffman 2002; Larson 1997; Wheeler 2018). To better understand how these changes in trust and these shifts in information altered the scope of strategic decisions, we must consider the expected payoffs.

4.3. Payoffs: Limited awareness

The period between March and September 2014 is marked by major and rapid shifts in payoffs, and their limited understanding by Ukrainian leaders. Generally, I found that most interviewees believed that after its success in Crimea, in spring 2014 Russia was trying to implement the Novorossiya plan—to gain control of almost half of Ukraine. This payoff on the part of Russia was apparently recalibrated due to the lack of local support for Russia and the successes of the Ukrainian military. The latter meant that Russia had to use its Army directly in Ukraine in August, which changed the payoffs' structure substantially. The EU's preferred payoffs were to develop economic cooperation with Ukraine (which was partly achieved by the signing of the Association Agreement) and to avoid and later stop the war in Ukraine, which was not fully understood by Ukraine. Ukrainian decision-makers saw Ukraine's preferred payoff as protection of the country's territorial integrity (which overshadowed the aim of EU integration); at that time there was no real awareness of the possibility of defeat. Below, I analyse these shifts in payoffs and perception about them in Ukraine.

Russia's payoffs

At first, it is important to point out that in March-April hardly anyone could predict Russia's subsequent actions, which could be partly explained by Putin's spontaneous decision-making. While some in Ukraine and Russia could not believe that the Russian leadership would start this war (Int-8 2020; Int-16 2020; Int-18 2020), others (e.g., the acting Foreign Minister of Ukraine) had anticipated a bigger war (with Russia's occupation of the South of Ukraine up to Transnistria) (Int-36 2021). Some politicians in European capitals even feared Russia would attack EU countries while "the Kremlin and Putin are in a grabbing mood" (Int-14 2020), while others made "the assumption …, perhaps naively, that Russia would be satisfied with taking back Crimea" (Int-35 2021). Interestingly, a former deputy of the Russian Duma stated that the conflict in Donbas started out of "a competition between different groups of influence" on Putin, with Putin supporting the proposed idea about Donbas on the grounds "that it would then be a bargaining chip over Crimea" (Int-17 2020). Thus, payoffs on Donbas could be bound up with those on Crimea, which is in line with scholarly assumptions about the possibility of starting a war with the aim of improving one's payoffs for future negotiations (Wagner 2000, 470). Putin's last-minute decisions were also pointed out by other respondents. As one EU analyst put it: "Putin is a genius when it comes to tactics, ad hoc decision-making in order to punch above his weight" (Int-13 2020). A Russian analyst, in similar vein, explained that "in general these were opportunistic decisions [by Russia], without any grand plan" (Int-16 2020). Likewise, an EU official noted that "[Putin] was content to support separatists in the East and … to keep everyone guessing about Russian intentions" (Int-32 2021). Yet while unpredictability in Putin's decision-making had an impact on the development of the conflict, Ukrainian respondents did not mention taking this into account.

My analysis shows that the unpredictability of Putin's actions puzzled the EU and Ukraine so much in spring 2014 that they could not make any clear forecasts. We already know that Putin's preference was to stay in power and thus his gambling on Russia's foreign policy could be seen as his involvement in nested games (domestic and international arenas) aimed at the best combined payoff, as explained by Tsebelis (1990). This uncertainty obstructed Ukrainian decision-makers from making any strategy. One example can be found in the words of an advisor to one of the highest decision-makers in Ukraine, that "it was hard not to think about the possibility of everything getting even worse, [we did not see] any further perspectives" (Int-7 2020). Another example is that the Head of Luhansk region mentioned that "the situation was changing so rapidly, no one knew what Russia planned in Donbas" (Int-1 2020). An EU official said this period was like "a flammable gas", pointing out the EU's concern that "Donbas could potentially spread to other regions" (Int-2 2020). According to an EU analyst, a good-case scenario for that time would be the withdrawal of Russia from Donbas with negotiations on Crimea, and the worst case scenario would be a total Russian-Ukrainian war with the occupation of Novorossiya[72] (Int-13 2020). What happened, according to him, was something "in between these two extremes" (Int-13 2020). Therefore, Putin's unpredictable actions in Donbas in spring 2014 and his nested games (aiming for the best payoff from international and domestic arenas) made it hard for Ukraine and the EU to see everyone's payoffs clearly.

Now, let us study Russia's possible payoff — the creation of Novorossiya. My EU, Ukrainian and Russian interviewees all mentioned that starting from spring and going into summer, Russia was considering the annexation of 7-10 Ukrainian regions of the so-called Novorossiya (Int-2 2020; Int-4 2020; Int-9 2020; Int-11 2020; Int-16 2020; Int-17 2020; Int-18 2020). According to an EU official, this was the main issue the EU had to deal with in this period (Int-2 2020). As suggested by respondents, Russia could possibly gave up this plan, because the failures of separatist protests in Kharkiv and Dnipropetrovsk convinced the Russian leadership that the required local support was absent (Int-16 2020; Int-17 2020; Int-18 2020; Int-25 2020). This overreliance on large-scale support for the 'Russian World' in Ukraine was considered to be a big mistake on the part of Russia by Ukraine's acting Foreign Minister (Int-36 2021). On the other hand, according to a Russian politician, the plan to establish Novorossiya was aban-

---

[72] Novorossiya was a region in the Russian Empire, which included the South and East of present-day Ukraine (Kharkiv, Luhansk, Donetsk, Kherson, Zaporizhzhya, Mykolaiv, Dnipro and Odesa regions plus Crimea).

doned because it would have involved too many deaths (Int-17 2020). Here we can see Ukrainian leaders' understanding of the Novorossiya payoff. Let us now look at the situation in these Eastern regions in Ukraine, and the government's policy there, in more detail.

Ukraine's payoffs

My data reveals that although Ukrainian leaders aimed to restore the country's territorial integrity, the situation in Donbas was more complicated than that of other Eastern regions. Some Ukrainian policy-makers saw the possibility of restoring state power in Donbas in the same way as had been done in Kharkiv, for instance (Int-3 2020; Int-7 2020). The end result for Ukraine was seen by some to be stopping Russian aggression and "regaining control over the border of Ukraine" (Int-11 2020), returning Crimea to Ukraine and liberating the East (Int-8 2020). The acting Foreign Minister of Ukraine explained that Ukraine aimed to save the rest of the territory (both by military means, and by the creation of a diplomatic international coalition) and to make reforms in the country (Int-36 2021). However, my data suggests a few shortcomings in the actions of the Ukrainian state (I have also mentioned above the unintentional murder of civilians in Luhansk by the Ukrainian Army). For instance, two Russian journalists thought that the tragedy in Odesa on 2nd May[73] (the death of pro-Russian protesters) was crucial to the decision of some of Donbas residents to rebel against Kyiv (Int-19 2020; Int-28 2021). This is significant, since it confirms the diverse perceptions and interests of Donbas residents, which influenced the achievement of Ukraine's payoff. The Kyiv authorities did record video appeals to the residents of Ukraine (mentioned above) and organised round-table peace talks in Kyiv on 14th May (Ukraine crisis 2014), to which, however, separatist leaders were not invited (unless they

---

[73] On 2nd May 2014, there were anti- and pro-Euromaidan demonstrations in Odesa. They clashed, and a coincidence of misfortunes resulted in a fire in a building occupied by anti-Euromaidan protesters, which caused the deaths of 48 people, and 208 serious injuries (the victims were primarily anti-Euromaidan protesters) (Hale, Shevel, and Onuch 2018).

would agree to lay down their arms), because they were defined as 'terrorists' by the Ukrainian authorities (Ukraine crisis 2014). Later, on 20th June, the new President Poroshenko offered a 15-point peace plan (Poroshenko unveils peace plan 2014), which was criticised by the Russian Foreign Minister for not including discussions with separatists (Lavrov criticizes Poroshenko's peace plan 2014). Therefore, Ukrainian decision-makers sought to regain Ukraine's territory, but overlooked the interests of some residents of Donbas, which possibly contributed to their failure in Donbas.

The new President's approach to Donbas was harsher — it approached the payoff of regaining Ukraine's territory, but it was considered to have caused too much bloodshed. Elected on 25th May, President Poroshenko was recognised by both Western leaders and Putin (President of Russia 2014e). He declared his aim to restore the territorial integrity of Ukraine and to end separatism in Donbas (Verkhovna Rada of Ukraine 2014). From the game theory perspective, Russia's ever greater involvement in Donbas might have changed 'the game' from a chicken to a prisoner's dilemma, which, as explained by scholars (Snyder 1971, 92–93), made the war more probable. Thus, Poroshenko counter-attacked in June and stated that ATO could be finished in a few hours, rather than lasting for months (Poroshenko 2014). However, the predicted fast removal of separatists from Donbas involved waging a war also against sections of the Ukrainian population who had rebelled against Kyiv for the reasons explained above. According to a Russian journalist, "Ukraine wanted to subjugate everything by force" (Int-28 2021). Another respondent, a Baltic diplomat, viewed this option as too bloody and having little practical benefit, because there was not enough support for Ukraine from locals in Donbas (we will come back to this in the next section) (Int-14 2020). According to him, "the start of the war was Russia, was Putin. But this [Poroshenko's] more populist, more nationalist, revolutionary approach in Donbas also helped in this" (Int-14 2020). Additionally, an independent foreign journalist described the chaotic, uncontrollable environment in Donbas, in which separatist leaders were fighting with each other; this led him to consider that the best-case scenario would be a frozen conflict (Int-15 2020). This approach on the part of Poroshenko was successful in regaining Donbas, but only up until the end of August 2014.

A number of Ukrainian, Russian and EU observers (politicians, journalists and military commanders) are in agreement that the Ukrainian military had the chance of regaining control over all of the territory of Donbas at the end of summer 2014 (Int-1 2020; Int-3 2020; Int-4 2020; Int-11 2020; Int-13 2020; Int-19 2020). The Governor of Luhansk region stated: "I already saw the end of this war. Luhansk was liberated. Even on the outskirts of Luhansk, our national flag was raised." (Int-1 2020). Consequently, my respondents assumed that the tangible victory of Ukraine in Donbas was prevented by Russia's use of direct military force (Int-3 2020; Int-4 2020; Int-11 2020; Int-13 2020). Therefore, the near achievement of Ukraine's preferred payoff—the liberation of Donbas—inclined Russia to take a more assertive attitude. The arrival of the Russian Regular Army resulted in the bloody Ilovaisk battle and the defeat of Ukrainian forces, which changed the payoff structure significantly.

The EU's payoffs

While Ukrainian-policy makers could hardly follow Russia's payoffs due to the fact that they were rapidly changing, they could also not identify those of the EU due to their ambiguity. First of all, the payoff of the AA was achieved, since the political part of the EU-Ukraine Association Agreement was signed on 21st March 2014, and the economic part on 27th June 2014 (The European Union and Ukraine 2014). Secondly, since the EU preferred not to have wars in its neighbourhood, it aimed to avoid and later to stop the war in Ukraine. An EU correspondent characterised the EU policy-makers as being shocked and unsure about how to respond; they did not want "to be dragged into this war" and preferred to isolate it in Eastern Ukraine (Int-20 2020). EU officials working on Ukraine also confirmed that there was no clear EU goal, since some countries were eager to give more help to Ukraine, while others did not want to destroy their business with Russia (Int-32 2021; Int-34 2021). A former president of the European Council confirmed that the EU's goal was to stop the war (Int-34 2021) and a Ukrainian politician argued that the EU wanted to do this in the least aggressive way (Int-11 2020). For their part, Ukrainian officials were trying to convince the EU to respond more strongly to Russian aggression in Donbas (Int-11 2020; Int-20 2020). An EU official confirmed this, saying: "Ukraine at that time wanted to make sure that the European Union understands the magnitude of the crisis, as seen from the Ukrainian point of view… given that international laws were quite clearly broken" (Int-12 2020). The success of Poroshenko's diplomacy in impacting EU policy-makers was also mentioned (Int-8 2020; Int-20 2020). However, the EU's indecisive reaction could be explained by its complicated and slow decision-making process, the different opinions of the member-states, and Ukraine not being considered a priority (Int-20 2020). Thus, since the EU's payoffs were not well defined, Ukrainian leaders could not see them clearly, but tried all the same to influence them to Ukraine's benefit.

My analysis has revealed that the complicated period of spring-summer 2014 made it hard for Ukrainian leaders to see others' payoffs clearly. Putin's spontaneity in decision-making, his 'nested games' and his worldview (weak EU and Ukraine, both dependent on US) puzzled the EU and Ukraine. Ukrainian decision-makers, seeking to end separatism in Donbas, might have missed the others' payoffs: Russia's (to destabilise Ukraine), the EU's (to stop the war), and that of part of the Donbas population (to receive respect for their views). In June, the newly elected President of Ukraine started a counterattack to clear 'terrorists' from Donbas, which resulted in many deaths and the further alienation of Donbas residents from Kyiv. When the victory of Ukraine was tangible, Russia used its regular Army in August 2014, thus showing its commitment to maintaining its influence over Ukraine. By the end of August, the payoff structure was different. Russia abandoned the idea of Novorossiya due to Ukraine's military response and weak local support. Ukraine had to accept that the full liberation of Donbas was impossible due to Russia's strong assistance to separatists. Explaining strategic rationality in decision-making, scholars have argued that countries are not able to follow their best strategy without taking into account others' choices (Snidal 1985, 39), and an inaccurate understanding of pay-off structure may result in worse outcomes for all (Snyder 1971, 80). This could explain the fact that Ukraine ended up with a worse outcome by the end of summer — uncontrolled Donbas. However, for the full picture of Ukraine's decision-making in its relations with the EU and Russia, we will look in more detail at resources and their use by the three sides.

4.4. Resources: Development of Ukraine's resources and learning about those of others

We have discussed the role of information, trust, and payoffs in Ukrainian leaders' decision-making in spring-summer 2014. Now we will explore how knowledge about Ukraine's, Russia's and the EU's resources influenced Ukrainian policy-makers' foreign policy decisions. My empirical data have shown substantial shifts in resources, their significance in decision-making during this period and the Ukrainian leaders' better understanding of everyone's resources. For this reason, I consider resources to be the key element in this period. For instance, with the volunteers' help, the Ukrainian military had improved and was able to fight back from June 2014. Russia was prepared to constantly use more resources in Ukraine, which culminated in the arrival of the Russian Regular Army in August 2014. The EU already had better understanding of what was going on in Ukraine, and by mid-summer (after the downing of MH17) applied economic sanctions against Russia. Below, we will learn more about everyone's resources and the Ukrainian leaders' awareness of them.

Russia's resources in Ukraine

To start with Russia's resources, Ukrainian leaders were well aware that Russia possessed incomparably greater resources than Ukraine in the first months of unrest in Donbas. As explained by the acting Minister of Defence of Ukraine on 11th March 2014, Russia placed 220 thousand soldiers in Crimea and near the Eastern border of Ukraine, while Ukraine could manage only six thousand (Tenyukh 2014). An astonishing point is made by an advisor to one of the highest decision-makers in Ukraine: he said that there was such a scarcity of resources in Ukraine that commanders had to move small military groups back and forth near the frontline to create an impression of thousands of soldiers (Int-7 2020). Other respondents highlighted Russia's readiness and Ukraine's unpreparedness for this war (Int-1 2020), Russia's stronger military and energy resources (Int-16 2020; Int-35 2021) and the Ukrainian government's inability "to match Moscow's political club, its military abilities or its economic connections to Europe" (Int-15 2020). On the other hand, a Russian investigative journalist argued that it was not so much Russia's special military or economic resources, but the fact that Ukraine's position (with no Army) was so much worse than Russia's, that enabled Russia to succeed in the war's first stages (Int-18 2020). Similarly, Novaya Gazeta wrote that "for the clearance from Donbas of bands of adventurers who had turned the region into a 'bloodbath', one combat-ready unit would have been enough, but the Ukrainian Army did not possess this in April 2014" (Polukhina 2020). Additionally, a foreign journalist in Ukraine stressed that until 2014 Ukraine did not have any experience of 'real' foreign policy-making (Int-15 2020). Thus, Russia was better equipped for this war in the first stages, and Ukrainian decision-makers were to some extent aware of this.

However, not only did Russia possess more resources, but it was also more ready to apply them, which is crucial. A Russian journalist explained that although being weaker than the EU and the US, Russia was more ready and able to deploy its resources (including people's lives), since it is a less democratic country (Int-18 2020). This supports scholarly arguments that autocracies are more inclined to involve themselves in wars than democratic countries (De Mesquita 2006). A former Baltic ambassador to Ukraine also stressed that the willingness to commit resources was more important than their amount (Int-14 2020). My respondents confirmed that although there was no direct intervention in spring 2014, Russia was supplying military equipment and arms to the rebels (Int-11 2020) and using its soldiers in Ukraine (as was proven by the Russian independent investigative agency "Insider"[74] (Int-18 2020) and later also by Glazyev tapes and Surkov leaks (Censor.net 2018; Surkov leaks 2016). A Ukrainian Interior Minister also acknowledged that Russian coordinators were seen during pro-Russian protests in the East of Ukraine (Butusov 2016). However, officially Russia was sending different signals. It accepted the law on the use of the Russian Army in Ukraine (The Federation Council 2014); yet Putin did officially acknowledge the involvement of the Russian military in the Crimean referendum (President of Russia 2014c). All the same, he publicly continued to claim that 'they are not there' (Int-16 2020). By May-June, Ukraine's understanding of Russia's readiness to use its resources in Ukraine had improved (Int-11 2020; Int-16 2020). However, a Ukrainian military commander and politician expressed the view that people must protect their land and that only cowards count the enemy's resources (Int-22 2020); this could serve as evidence that not all policy-makers saw an analysis of Russia's resources as relevant. Another point was made by a foreign journalist in Ukraine, that Ukrainian politicians could not understand Russia and its capabilities well, since Ukraine had previously only had transactional relations with Russia (Int-15 2020). As confirmed by my empirical data, Russia was ready to invest its varied resources (military technique, coordinators, soldiers) in rebellions in Donbas, and some Ukrainian policy-makers had gained better understanding of this by the end of spring.

In addition to Russia's military resources, I have also discovered its advantage in hybrid and informational warfare. An EU analyst explained that this war was a hybrid, "which by definition involves military, economic, technological, cultural, and social media-based instruments in combination" (Int-13 2020), while a Russian analyst underlined Russia's "technology of information/psychological influence" (Int-16 2020). That this was hybrid warfare, with informational campaigns preceding military

---

74 According to the founder of "Insider", investigators in "Insider" were in contact with a Russian soldier when he was recruited to fight in Ukraine, when he was in Ukraine and then when he was back in Russia. In this way, they proved Russian presence in Ukraine already in spring 2014 (Int-18 2020).

campaigns, was also recognised by Ukrainian policy-makers (Int-8 2020; Int-27 2020). Moreover, according to a person involved in Ukraine's decision-making, Russia was using institutional particularities in Ukraine (e.g., the legal inability of special services to conduct operations in the presence of civilians) to achieve its goals (Int-7 2020). The role of Russian foreign intelligence, Russia's special forces and information warfare in this war were also highlighted by scholars (Galeotti 2015). However, some scholars (Hutchings and Szostek 2015) and an advisor to a senior official in Ukraine (Int-7 2020) pointed to Ukraine's fight with Russia's information warfare, for example by means of the ban on Russian channels in the country in spring 2014. Thus, although Russia succeeded in hybrid warfare, Ukraine was taking certain steps to deal with it.

Ukraine's resources

Looking further into Ukraine's resources, it is necessary to mention the development of one crucial resource — volunteers. Ukrainian and EU policy-makers pointed out the importance of volunteers, who were not only supplying everything to the Ukrainian Army, but also creating voluntary battalions to protect the country (Int-1 2020; Int-7 2020; Int-11 2020; Int-13 2020; Int-14 2020; Int-33 2021; Int-36 2021). One of the Baltic Ambassadors to Ukraine noted that in the beginning, "the Ukrainian Army and defence ministry were very much old, old-minded generals, who simply were not capable of any long-term military operation" (Int-14 2020). However, over time, "the volunteer wave" helped to build the Army day by day (Int-1 2020; Int-8 2020; Int-14 2020; Int-20 2020) and became an important resource for Ukraine (Int-16 2020). An advisor to one of the highest decision-makers in Ukraine perceived voluntary battalions and the change of psychology in the Army as "game changers" (Int-7 2020). An acting foreign minister of Ukraine said that neither Russia nor the EU, nor even the Ukrainian government, expected such a huge contribution from volunteers (Int-36 2021). An MEP and an MP from Germany both referred to Ukraine's ability "to build up a fully functioning Army in the period of aggression" as a miracle (Int-31 2021), as was preventing Russia from going further in its aggression (Int-38 2021). Thus, the self-organisation of Ukrainians became an important resource for the country, which contributed to its foreign policy capabilities.

Another important factor in respect to Ukraine's resources is the role of local elites in the development of this war. For instance, to fight the separatism in Kharkiv, Ukraine's interior minister Arsen Avakov (from Kharkiv elites) applied a tough approach — an assault on the occupied regional state administration building, blocking off the subway, introducing armed patrols and using Ukraine's special security forces (subdivisions of the special forces "Jaguar") (Butusov 2016). On 8th April, separatists were imprisoned and the situation calmed down in the city (Butusov 2016). One of the Baltic Ambassadors in Kyiv also highlighted the fact that Ukraine in those days was almost 100% decentralised and that only the support of the Kharkiv governor for Kyiv helped the region to remain within Ukraine (Int-14 2020). Additionally, the acting Foreign Minister of Ukraine confirmed that the Ukrainian authorities often delegated decision-making to local elites, since those in Kyiv could not react so quickly and effectively (Int-36 2021). However, a German MP stated: "We know about the mayors in Kharkiv, in Odesa and other cities, who had seemingly made agreements with the Kremlin" (Int-38 2021). All these different decisions made by local elites (either in favour of or against the Kyiv authorities) were explained by the acting Foreign Minister of Ukraine as their attempts to save their assets (Int-36 2021). Thus, we see how local elites were playing a separate role in these events.

Turning now to Donbas, one view is that the protests in Donbas were initially financed by Yanukovych's son (Separatism in Donbass 2018) and supported by an oligarch Rinat Akhmetov, who fully controlled Donbas (Int-22 2020; Int-24 2020). A Ukrainian volunteer and politician explained that Rinat Akhmetov originally supported separatism due to his aim to get concessions from Kyiv (Int-22 2020). This kind of role on the part of local elites was analysed by scholars, and Kudelia (2014, 1), for example, argued that Donbas insurgencies were "primarily a home grown phenomenon" which was triggered by "state fragmentation, violent regime change, and the government's low capacity" together with "resentment and fear emotions of Donbas residents". On the other hand, respondents have underlined Russia's greater support for rebellions in Donbas than in the above mentioned regions (Int-22 2020; Int-24 2020; Int-36 2021; Wilson 2016). This is in line with Wilson's (2016) argument that the alienation of Donbas residents from Kyiv created a background for the conflict, which, however, could not develop into a full-scale war without the support of both local elites and Russia. Thus, the acting Foreign Minister of Ukraine explained that Russia's military support for Donbas, the difference in the actions of local elites (Akhmetov playing with and losing to Russia[75]), but also the difference in the support of the population led to different outcomes in these regions (Int-36 2021). Therefore, apart from the direction of local elites and Russia's role in Donbas, the loyalty of Ukrainians to Kyiv was different in the South-East of Ukraine than in the rest of the country.

Let us look more closely at the attitudes of the Ukrainian population in Donbas. We already know that support for EU integration was much lower and positive feelings towards Russia were higher in Donbas. According to a Russian analyst, Putin's idea was "to seize Ukraine largely with the hands of Russian-speaking Ukrainians" and Russian coordinators and militants were meant only to support and coordinate the process (Int-9 2020). More social statistics are helpful in understanding the situation. In February 2014, 33% of residents of Donetsk and 24% of those of Luhansk region wanted Ukraine to unite with Russia, with the average for Ukraine being 12% (KIIS 2014a). Pro-Russian residents of Donbas did not constitute the majority, but their substantial number was dangerous enough (taking into account the situation after Euromaidan and Russia's goals in Ukraine) for Kyiv politicians to be more cautious in their decisions. Moreover,

---

[75] Akhmetov allegedly wanted to agree with Russia that he would control Donbas but remain loyal to Russia, but Russia preferred to control the territory without him in the end (Int-36 2021).

around 70% of Donbas residents (Luhansk and Donetsk oblasts) did not see the acting president Turchynov and prime-minister Yatseniuk as legitimate in April 2014 (KIIS 2014b). Even the volunteer battalions were viewed differently in the East and the West of Ukraine, with 51% in the West but only 19% in the East, and 8% in the liberated territory of Donbas, viewing them positively (Petro 2015, 30). A Chief of the Border Guard Service of Ukraine (who served for 11 years and worked with four presidents) stressed that Ukrainian leaders did not preserve a big, balanced, and multinational country and through their policies helped foreign actors to easily interfere in the country's affairs (Int-10 2020). Thus, Ukrainian leaders did not invest enough in turning Donbas residents from antagonists into supporters of Ukraine, and to a certain extent this helped Russia to succeed.

In August 2014, when Ukraine was about to re-take the whole territory of Donbas, Russia used its Regular Army, which set back the previous gains of the Ukrainian forces. Several international organisations (EU, OSCE, and NATO) confirmed the entrance of Russian troops into Ukrainian territory in August (M. R. Gordon 2014). This was also documented by a commander of a voluntary battalion when Russian paratroopers were captured (Int-11 2020). Pictures and interrogations of captured Russian soldiers were made available by the Security Service of Ukraine (Security Service of Ukraine 2014). As an EU analyst told me, NATO had satellite photography and "the decision-makers in Brussels knew that the Russian military was officially involved" (Int-13 2020). This changed the alignment of forces and prevented Ukraine from regaining control over its territory (Int-11 2020; Int-14 2020). A former MEP told me that without robust Western help Ukraine could not win the war, and so had to sign the Minsk Protocol (Int-31 2021). Thus, in August 2014, Russia's use of resources in Ukraine culminated in the entrance of its Regular Army, which became the biggest game changer in this war (up until 2022).

Ukraine's hopes for the EU's support

As during the events in Crimea, in spring-summer 2014 Ukrainian policy-makers also thought they could rely on the EU's support against Russia's aggression, for instance because the Euromaidan won under the EU flag (Int-7 2020; Int-14 2020; Int-15 2020). The EU did introduce sanctions against certain Russian individuals after the annexation of Crimea (The European Council 2020), but it did not help militarily. Only a few months later, some Ukrainian policy-makers had developed a better understanding of the EU's readiness to use its resources in Ukraine, while many continued to show surprise and anger about the lack of anticipated EU support (Int-4 2020; Int-15 2020; Int-16 2020; Int-22 2020). For instance, the acting Foreign Minister of Ukraine argued that if the EU had been tougher in its reaction, this could have resulted in a withdrawal of Russian forces from Donbas (Int-36 2021). Other Ukrainian statesmen blamed the poor work of Ukrainian diplomacy in this respect (Int-1 2020; Int-22 2020). On the other hand, an EU correspondent argued that Ukrainian leaders had misunderstood the EU's role as a foreign policy actor (Int-20 2020). Similarly, an EU official described the difference between Russian hard power (military and political influence) and the EU's soft power (norms and democracy promotion) (Int-35 2021). A Russian investigative journalist suggested that Russia would not have attacked Ukraine, if Russian leaders thought that the EU would involve militarily (Int-18 2020), while the president of the European Council stressed: "we never envisaged sending NATO troops or helping Ukraine militarily" (Int-34 2021). While Ukraine was asking for military support, what it received was financial and technical help, and consultancy advice about transforming Ukraine's political and economic structure and fighting corruption (Int-7 2020; Int-11 2020; Int-14 2020; Int-20 2020; Int-37 2021). EU officials explained that "the EU stepped up gradually" (Int-37 2021), and that only in the course of time did it develop its foreign policy mechanisms and come to understand that "we had to think outside the box" (Int-12 2020). In fact one international effort to reach peace in Ukraine had already taken place in the spring, when the EU, the

US, Ukraine and Russia issued the Geneva Statement, in which the parties "agreed on initial concrete steps to de-escalate tensions and restore security for all citizens" (Geneva Statement on Ukraine 2014). However, only after the downing of MH17 did the EU adopt hard economic sanctions against Russia (The European Council 2020). Thus, in April-August, the EU was gradually involving itself more in Ukraine, and Ukrainian policy-makers, although with certain misperceptions, could understand the EU's abilities better in summer than in spring 2014.

The major obstacle within Ukraine

Having discussed the impact of resources on Ukrainian decision-makers' actions, we will now look at the principal domestic obstacle in Ukraine—corruption. A Baltic diplomat in Ukraine argued that although Ukrainian decision-makers directed many of the country's resources to this war, they were still using the opportunity to enrich themselves (Int-14 2020). A Russian politician also explained:

> After the volunteers defended the country, they [Ukrainian politicians] largely returned to the state of affairs of the Yanukovych times, when they began to extract what is called administrative rent from their power position in the country, and in every possible way to parasitise on this war. (Int-17 2020).

Corruption amongst Ukrainian key decision-makers, their unwillingness to protect the country, and even their betrayal of national interests, were also pointed out by Ukrainian former MPs (Int-22 2020; Int-24 2020). An EU official explained that "some of them [Ukrainian decision-makers], like Poroshenko, have some interests: personal, business, economic interests in Russia" (Int-35 2021). An MEP also claimed that there could have been a more effective fight against corruption, e.g., in the Army (Int-31 2021), and several EU officials saw corruption as a major issue in Ukraine (Int-32 2021; Int-34 2021; Int-35 2021). Moreover, a commander of a volunteer battalion (and an MP) explained that the Ukrainian leadership had allowed a military column under the command of the Russian GRU officer Igor Girkin to leave Sloviansk in July 2014[76], and did not give the command to shoot at it, which further fuelled the war (Int-22 2020). He also stressed that the senior military leadership ignored the threat of Russian invasion in August 2014 and was in cahoots with Russia over the murder of soldiers who were leaving the Ilovaisk trap (Int-22 2020). This was also confirmed by a former Ukrainian MP, who gained access to secret documents concerning the state investigation against former military commanders (Int-24 2020). Further confirmation comes from leaks from the Security Services of Ukraine, which showed that Poroshenko was receiving financial benefits from Medvedchuk's business with Russia, for instance from his ownership of the oil pipeline "Samara - Western direction" (BIHUS info 2021a). A German MP also noted that "most Ukrainian politicians had hidden agendas and it was not clear who would be playing on which side" and mentioned "quite a few personal decisions and money decisions [on the part of Poroshenko], which are very disappointing" (Int-38 2021). This attitude of Ukrainian decision-makers is an important issue, since it led to the deterioration of the country's resources and its ability to confront Russia.

The period of April-August 2014 showed a visible change in resources and in the understanding of these resources by Ukrainian decision-makers. Ukraine developed its Army with the unprecedented help of a volunteer movement. Russia was showing its increased readiness to use more hard power in Ukraine – consultancy and military equipment, which had been provided to rebels in Donbas in spring, escalated into the entry of the Russian Regular Army into Ukraine in August 2014. Although the former was more or less understood in Ukraine, the latter was very unexpected and was the biggest game changer in this war (up until the 2022 Russian full-scale invasion of Ukraine). The EU, due to its complicated decision-making procedures, was reacting slowly and

---

76 Igor Strelkov-Girkin, GRU officer, led a group of militants from Russia to Ukraine in the end of spring-beginning of summer 2014. According to him and several experts, the leaving of his group from Slovyansk and its entrance into Donetsk in July 2014 was decisive in the further escalation of the war (Polukhina 2020; Strelkov 2014).

hard economic sanctions against Russia were introduced only after the downing of MH17 in July. Under the new president, Poroshenko (who was elected on 25th May), Ukraine was in a better position to fight both on the diplomatic and military fronts. However, the liberation of Donbas caused an enormous death toll, which was also due to the population's alienation from Kyiv. The mood of Donbas residents, but also the EU's readiness to help Ukraine, was not correctly assessed by Ukrainian decision-makers. Additionally, the corruption of the Ukrainian leadership, as described by several respondents and confirmed by the Security Service's leaks, helped Russia to succeed.

Conclusion

This chapter has dealt with Ukraine's foreign policy actions concerning the country's relations with the EU and Russia between 26th March and 5th September 2014. The Crimean annexation made the EU and Ukraine understand that Russia 'is playing a big game'. However, Putin's unpredictable decision-making fooled his interlocutors in Ukraine and the EU, many of whom could not believe in the possibility of a war in Donbas in March-April. Disagreement with Kyiv's policies on the part of some Donbas residents was used by Russia to start the conflict, which made a cooperation payoff less attractive for Ukraine (and is likely to have changed the game from a chicken game to a prisoner's dilemma). Thus, although Ukraine did not respond militarily to the annexation of Crimea (a game of chicken), it did so to the Donbas rebellions (a prisoner's dilemma), and this led to an open war. At the end of August, Russia used its regular forces, pushed back the Ukrainian military, and changed the alignment of forces once again. Below, I provide my main findings regarding Ukraine's strategic decision-making during this period.

With regard to information, respondents mentioned the existence of pro-Russian elites in Donbas and Russia's support for them since 2004. This, however, was not addressed by Ukrainian decision-makers in time. When the situation deteriorated in spring 2014, the information about Russia's actions in Donbas and the preferences of its residents was available through open sources and local authorities, which again was not properly used by the leaders in Kyiv. Russia's preference stayed the same—to control Ukraine—and this was already understood in Ukraine. My evidence has also shown that decisions in Russia were taken solely by Putin and so not only his personal preferences, but also his decision-making process was crucial in understanding Russia's actions. My Ukrainian respondents did not mention analysis of this issue but assumed that Poroshenko would have had more access to this kind of analysis, which would have been reinforced by his indirect contacts with Putin (confirmed by recent leaks). The EU's preferences were to avoid a war near its borders and to have economic cooperation with its neighbours. On the whole, it can be said that certain specificities of Russia's decision-making and the EU's preferences were not fully grasped by Ukrainian decision-makers. By concentrating on their own preferences (EU integration and Ukraine's territorial integrity) Ukrainian leaders turned a blind eye to the preferences of other actors (both inside and outside Ukraine).

This period was marked by a substantial decrease of trust in EU-Ukraine-Russia relations. It is important to point out that originally both the EU and Ukraine did not trust the credibility of Russia's threats to attack Ukraine, though the respective signals had existed for years. In spring 2014, with more evidence of Russia's actions in Ukraine (military personnel and equipment in Donbas), Ukrainian and EU officials started to comprehend the Russian aggression, which reduced their trust in Russia. Ukraine's trust in the EU's readiness to save Ukraine from Russia also decreased, although the EU placed high hopes on Ukraine's new leaders. For its part, Russia did not trust the EU and Ukraine, partly due to the broken 21st February agreement, and partly because Putin did not see Ukraine and the EU as independent foreign policy actors, preferring to negotiate with EU member-states or the US. I have also shown that the three sides had certain common interests (economic cooperation and security), which were not met due to mutual mistrust. On the other hand, trustful relationships were not built within Ukraine — Ukrainian politicians failed to reach Donbas residents as they did not reach Crimeans. Having preferences for keeping ties with Russia and listening to Russian propaganda, some of Ukrainians in Donbas turned into pro-Russian protesters, which helped Russia.

Looking at Ukrainian decision-makers' analysis of the payoff structure, my analysis showed that they were mostly unaware of Putin's personal goals and his tactical decision-making but had better understanding of Russia's foreign policy payoffs. Although in March-April Russia's payoffs on Donbas were not grasped in Kyiv, Russia's further goal to build Novorossiya was already understood. After the 25th May elections in Ukraine, the new President developed the country's foreign policy, but also counter-attacked in Donbas with the aim of restoring the territorial integrity of Ukraine. Although it was bloody, this approach almost succeeded (according to my respondents), but the situation changed after the entrance of the Russian Army at the end of August. The EU apparently did not have a clear goal regarding Ukraine (apart from having the AA signed) but wanted to stop this war and to keep economic relations with both Ukraine and Russia. One can say that in an analysis of the payoffs of all three actors, Ukrainian decision-makers concentrated too much on their preferred outcome (to restore the territorial integrity of Ukraine), did not pay enough attention to Russia's payoff to destabilise Ukraine through Donbas, and the EU's payoff to stop this war; in particular, they did not realise that this was not a priority for the EU. As predicted by game theory, flawed perceptions about others' payoffs could have contributed to worse outcomes for Ukraine (uncontrolled parts of Donbas and the war).

Speaking of resources, I have found that Ukrainian decision-makers' awareness of everyone's resources improved in comparison with the previous period. Volunteers contributed to the development of Ukraine's resources (e.g., by support for the Army, and by forming voluntary battalions). Russia was ready to continually invest more resources into the war in Donbas; the Ukrainian authorities were mostly able to analyse these changes but did not predict the arrival of the Russian Regular Army in August. Ukraine's understanding of the EU's readiness to apply its resources, although this was better than in February-March 2014, was still based on their hopes as to how the EU 'should' react. Both the EU and Ukrainian interviewees thought this could be explained by Ukrainian policy-makers' poor awareness of the EU's mechanisms and abilities as a foreign policy actor. In addition, the key role of local elites was almost totally missed by decision-makers in Kyiv. Lastly, even with the vast mobilisation of Ukraine's resources for the war in Donbas, Ukrainian politicians were still able to extract administrative rent through corruption, which also helped Russia to achieve its aims in Ukraine. When the alignment of forces changed at the end of August 2014, Russia, and Ukraine, with the OSCE as facilitator, agreed on peace talks on 5th September. Thinking about more beneficial ways of action for Ukrainian decision-makers, I would like to mention better communication with Donbas residents, avoiding further mistakes that could alienate them from Ukraine (talks about the cancellation of the language law, some military mistakes, failure to both counterattack Russian propaganda and explain benefits of EU integration for Donbas) and fighting corruption within senior officials. The period between the Minsk I and Minsk II Peace Agreements is analysed in the next chapter.

Table 5: The timeline of key events between 26th March and 5th September 2014

Date	Event
12 April	Unmarked forces take over the cities of Slavyansk, Kramatorsk, and Druzhkivka
15 April	Ukraine's introduction of the Anti-Terrorist Operation in Donbas
17 April	Geneva talks between the US, Russia, Ukraine, and the EU; acceptance of Geneva Statement on de-escalation steps
11 May	Referendum on the independence of the Donetsk and Luhansk People's Republics
25 May	Presidential elections in Ukraine and the victory of Petro Poroshenko
3 June	Counter-attack of the Ukrainian military; liberation of North of Donetsk region
20 June	Poroshenko announces 10 days' unilateral ceasefire
1 July	A full-scale military counteroffensive of Ukrainian forces along the entire frontline
5 July	Igor Girkin's group leaves Slovyansk and later enters Donetsk
17 July	Downing of a civilian airplane MH17
7 August – 2 September	Battle of Ilovaisk
5 September	Minsk Protocol signed by OSCE representative Heidi Tagliavini, Ukraine's representative Leonid Kuchma, Russian ambassador to Ukraine Mikhail Zurabov, and separatist leaders Alexander Zakharchenko and Igor Plotnitsky

Table 6: Ukraine's relations with Russia and the EU during the events in Donbas (26th March– 5th Sept 2014)

Information	Trust	Payoffs	Resources
Minimal improvement of informational capacity	**Trust decreased following the escalation**	**Recalibration of perception of payoffs**	**Medium awareness about resources**
❖ Limited analysis of information ➢ Underestimation of separatist tendencies in Donbas + missed preferences of local elites ➢ Awareness of Russia's geostrategic goals, but not of Putin's preferences ❖ Incomplete awareness of the EU's preferences ❖ Improved information background ➢ New President, but weak information transfer between changing officials ➢ Ban on Russian State TV	❖ No trust in Russia's threats (March-May) ❖ Decrease of trust between Ukrainian government and Donbas residents ❖ Russian hardware and personnel cross border/fighting breaks out ➢ Decrease of trust towards Russia and the EU – Ukraine's fight back in Donbas ➢ Downing of MH17 (core critical juncture for the EU) ❖ Russia's mistrust in the EU and Ukrainian interlocutors – hardship in reaching any compromise	❖ Recalibration of perception of the payoffs structure post-annexation ➢ Crimean question overshadowed by Donbas ➢ Poor analysis of Kremlin tactical decision-making ➢ Understanding that Russia would not give up on Donbas ▪ Novorossiya plan paused (weak local support for Russia) ❖ Limited awareness of the EU's payoffs: to stop/localise the war ❖ Regaining Donbas up until the end of August – change of payoffs after entrance of Russian military	❖ Improvement of Ukraine's resources ➢ The new President in May - improvement of foreign policy (counter attack in Donbas) ➢ Development of Ukrainian military (volunteers' help) ❖ Deterioration of Ukraine's capacity due to its elites' corruption ❖ Inattention to the role of Donbas elites and residents ❖ Improvement of awareness of Russia's readiness to use any resources ❖ No full understanding of the EU's ability to use its resources
Impact on decision-making: **Medium**	Impact: **Medium**	Impact: **Medium**	Impact: **High**

5 Efforts in reaching peace: The post-Minsk crystallised image (5th September 2014 – 12th February 2015)

Introduction

We already know that in the period between April and August 2014, decision-makers in Kyiv learned not to trust Russia and gained a better awareness of their own and others' resources and readiness to use these resources in Ukraine. Thus, after Ukraine's liberation of Donbas was stopped by the Russian Regular Army at the end of the summer, the Ukrainian authorities were determined to end the bloodshed and after negotiations with Russia, peace talks were agreed for 5th September. They resulted in the signature of the Minsk Protocol, with the promise of an immediate cessation of violence in Eastern Ukraine. In spite of this, a few days later the war resumed (OSCE Special Monitoring Mission to Ukraine 2014). Periodic fighting took place in autumn/winter 2014-2015, and there were major battles over Donetsk airport and Debaltsevo. Consequently, on 11-12 February 2015, Ukrainian, Russian, German, and French heads of states negotiated a new peace deal: the Minsk II Agreement. Minsk I and II remained the core references for the settlement of the conflict up until 2022 Russian full-scale invasion of Ukraine. In this chapter we will study the Ukrainian leaders' decision-making in their relations with the EU and Russia between the Minsk Agreements I and II. The actions of Ukrainian policy-makers which I analyse here include discussions with the EU and Russian counterparts, reactions to the escalations in Donbas, and the peace negotiations. My game theory-based analytical framework helps me to determine what shaped the responses of Ukrainian decision-makers in their relations with Russia and the EU between 5th September 2014 and 12th February 2015.

My analysis makes it clear that after Minsk I was signed, Ukrainian decision-makers gained a much better understanding of the whole situation (see Table 7). There were certain changes in all four elements of Ukrainian leaders' decision-making, but I found that the understanding of payoffs influenced Ukraine's decision-making the most (for instance, there was a certain acceptance of the new *status quo*). These changes were as follows. Firstly, Ukrainian decision-makers' understanding of other actors' preferences improved, which was partly because interlocutors from the EU, Ukraine and Russia were able to meet on a few occasions and to share their views on the situation. While the parliamentary elections in Ukraine resulted in new politicians coming onto the stage, the core Ukrainian decision-making remained in the same hands, those of the President and his allies. Secondly, the Ilovaisk tragedy and consequent disadvantageous Minsk Protocol reduced Ukrainian decision-makers' trust in Russian and EU interlocutors. Ukrainian leaders developed a better feeling for a mismatch between the EU's words and actions and became more aware of Russia's misleading signals. Thirdly, I would argue that the payoff structure and Ukraine's understanding of it is the most interesting feature of this period. Both Russia and the EU had achieved their preferences to an acceptable extent via the frozen conflict: Russia — to control Ukraine, and the EU — to stop the fighting. While the EU and Russia were mostly satisfied with the new *status quo*, Ukraine's payoff to regain the territory of Donbas was becoming less likely. The discrepancy between Ukraine's and Russia's goals during the Minsk negotiations resulted in a compromise, which was both imperfect and difficult to implement. Later, on 12th February 2015, Minsk II froze the conflict, something acknowledged by Ukrainian decision-makers. Fourthly, there were fewer changes in resources during this period. Some policy-makers blamed Ukrainian leaders for the signing of the Minsk agreements, and there was even a suggestion that the Ukrainian decision-makers had betrayed national interests, though others praised the coherence of the work of the Kyiv authorities. Although the EU helped Ukraine financially and with the implementation of reforms (my EU informants acknowledged the development of its foreign policy in this respect), it did not support Ukraine militarily and was not present during Minsk I, although France and Germany both participated in the Minsk II negotiations. Below, I go into more detail about my findings.

5.1. Information: Good awareness

In comparison with previous periods, I found that Ukrainian decision-makers developed far better awareness of the EU's and Russia's preferences after Minsk I. One could frame this time period as one in which conflict reduced asymmetries of information. Once the conflict was partly frozen by the Minsk Protocol, there was some understanding that Russia wanted to control Ukraine's domestic and foreign policy (which to a certain extent was achieved by Minsk I). My analysis suggests that President Poroshenko and those around him were aware that it was impossible for Ukraine to join the EU and NATO, and of the Russian threat if Ukraine continued its integration attempts. Ukrainian leaders also realised that the EU preferred to have any kind of stability in Ukraine, but also to maintain economic relations with Russia. However, their understanding as to how the EU wanted to achieve this stability was still limited (this will be explained in the section about payoffs). The Ukrainian leaders' perceptions about the country's own preferences changed from integration into the EU, which prevailed in public discourse in the beginning of 2014, to a closer partnership with the EU. Thus, the goal of EU membership was not abandoned, but better understanding of the situation moved this to the distant future. In the following section, I will discuss how Ukrainian decision-makers' understanding of Russia's and the EU's preferences was changing in accordance with the available information, its analysis and how it influenced their decision-making.

Peace Agreements

Let us start by tracing the various attempts to achieve peace in Donbas. Already on 23rd June 2014, Ukraine's former President Kuchma, Russian Ambassador Zurabov, OSCE representative Taliani, Ukrainian politician Medvedchuk and separatist leaders Tsarev and Borodai met in Donetsk and agreed to a ceasefire starting from 27th June (Peace negotiations 2014). However, all of the sides did not accept Poroshenko's peace plan, which included, among other things, disarmament of the insurgents (Poroshenko's peace plan

2014). Later, on 27th July, Poroshenko asked the Belarusian President for help in organising peace negotiations in Minsk on 31st July (Poroshenko decided to hold peace talks in Minsk 2014). Finally, on 26th August, Presidents Putin and Poroshenko met in Minsk, but almost no information about the results of the meeting was made public (The meeting between Poroshenko and Putin 2014), with only the Putin-Poroshenko handshake appearing in the news (Poroshenko and Putin shook hands 2014). On 3rd September, the two presidents allegedly agreed to a permanent ceasefire and de-escalating steps in Donbas, which was published on the Ukrainian President's web-site (Poroshenko reached an agreement with Putin 2014). However, the Russian President's press secretary denied that there had been agreement on a ceasefire, since Russia was supposedly not involved in the conflict (Poroshenko reached an agreement with Putin 2014). On 5th September, the Minsk Protocol, which included peace initiatives on the part of both Putin and Poroshenko, was signed by Ukraine's former President Kuchma, Russian Ambassador Zurabov, OSCE representative Taliani and separatist leaders Plotnitskyi and Zakharchenko (Protocol on the results of consultations of the Trilateral Contact Group 2014). That there had been such a long road to the peace agreement could be explained by persistent misunderstandings between the Ukrainian and Russian leaders, which also contributed to the need to negotiate Minsk II in February 2015.

However, after the 5th September Minsk Protocol, peace did not come to Donbas, so there was a further search for a settlement. As early as 7th September, OSCE observed the violation of the ceasefire (OSCE Special Monitoring Mission to Ukraine 2014). By the end of November, the Ukrainian side reported more than 3000 shellings by insurgents in violation of the Minsk Agreement (Terrorists violated the Minsk agreements 2014). Russia and Ukraine each claimed that the other had started the shooting, and an EU official in Kyiv complained that the fact that neither side would accept responsibility for the shelling created a major difficulty for the EU (Int-2 2020). In January-February 2015, the war resumed with new intensity, with major battles for Donetsk airport and Debaltsevo. Thus, peace had to be renegotiated and the leaders of Ukraine, Russia, France, and Germany met in Minsk on 11th-12th February 2015. This resulted in the signing of Minsk II, which confirmed the parties' commitment to the Minsk Protocol and also proclaimed that the constitutional reform in Ukraine, including the "adoption of permanent legislation on the special status of the stated districts of Donetsk and Luhansk regions", was to be completed by the end of 2015 (The full text of the new Minsk document 2015). It is important to point out that the Minsk II discussions highlighted once again the fact that decisions about the war in Donbas on Ukraine's side were taken for the most part by Poroshenko, along with his close allies. Below, I study the Ukrainian leaders' awareness of the other actors' preferences during this period.

Improvement of Ukrainians' awareness about Russia's preferences

My data suggest that Russia's preference—to preserve control over Ukraine—stayed the same, and some Ukrainian policy-makers already comprehended this in autumn 2014. For instance, Putin, in his interview in November 2014, mentioned that he saw the EU-Ukraine Association Agreement as a new dividing line in Europe (Seipel 2014); this confirms Russia's rejection of EU-Ukraine integration and its desire to be involved in any decisions on the subject. Although this preference stayed unchanged, the ways of achieving it (payoffs) were changing, and the freezing of the conflict by Minsk I might have helped Russia to achieve its aim. This was somehow understood in Ukraine, with an advisor to one of the highest decision-makers in Ukraine stating that Russia achieved its aim of stopping Ukraine's integration with the EU and NATO by means of this war (Int-7 2020). This was also confirmed by EU policy-makers. As a Baltic Ambassador to Ukraine noted, Russia wanted to ensure that Donbas continued to function as a lever of pressure on Ukraine and its leaders (Int-14 2020). A former President of the European Council highlighted the fact that Russia achieved its aim of destabilising Ukraine and stopping it from becoming "a fully-fledged independent country" (Int-34 2021), while a senior EU official stated that by the end of 2014, the Russian preference to have influence over Ukraine became very clear to the EU (Int-33 2021). Thus, a better understanding of Russia's preference characterises the post-Minsk I period.

Two further examples elucidate the communication between Ukrainian and Russian leaders in this period. On 17th October, Putin and Poroshenko met face-to-face in Milan (with Merkel, Holland and EU representatives), and the sides subsequently reported that there had been difficult but productive discussions and that they had established mutual support for the implementation of the Minsk Protocol (Putin and Poroshenko 2014). On the other hand, after the Putin-Merkel meeting, the Russian President's official web-site reported the existence of "still serious differences in views on the genesis of the intra-Ukrainian conflict, as well as on the root causes of what is happening there at present" (President of Russia 2014d). On 27th November, Ukrainian media reported a phone call between Putin and Poroshenko, in which Putin allegedly threatened that Russia would attack Ukraine, requested that Ukraine recognise the separatist republics, and that it stop attempts of joining NATO and the EU (Poroshenko received an ultimatum from Putin 2014). It was also reported that Poroshenko and his colleagues argued against acceptance of the law on Ukraine's integration into the EU/NATO (although this law was supported by the other parties), because the EU and NATO would not have accepted Ukraine in any case, but this would still anger Russia (Poroshenko received an ultimatum from Putin 2014). However, later both the Russian and Ukrainian presidents' press offices denied the reports of Putin's threats in his conversation with Poroshenko (Kremlin 2014; Poroshenko and Putin 2014). These two events show the existence of communication between Putin and Poroshenko and a certain understanding by Poroshenko and his close allies of Russia's preference for Ukraine not to join NATO and the EU. This might even have influenced Ukraine's slowdown of EU/NATO integration attempts. Thus, I conclude that through the communication of senior Ukrainian officials with their Russian interlocutors, Ukrainian decision-makers gained a better understanding of Russia's preferences.

Better understanding of the EU's preferences

As we already know from the previous period, Ukrainian policy-makers had partial awareness of the EU's preference for achieving stability in Ukraine, but only after Minsk I did they start to comprehend the important fact that Ukraine was not a priority in the EU's foreign policy. On the one hand, as mentioned above, there are media reports about Poroshenko's understanding of the impossibility of entering the EU in the near future (Poroshenko received an ultimatum from Putin 2014). On the other hand, on 17th October Poroshenko told Bild magazine that there was a possibility of Ukraine joining the EU, but integration with NATO would take longer due to the need for reforms in Ukraine (Ronzheimer 2014). This inconsistency in Poroshenko's position could be explained by a general difference between his public statements and personal opinions. The understanding of the EU's preferences was further confirmed by an advisor to a senior official in Kyiv, who claimed that although Ukraine "was standing for joining the EU and NATO", the EU did not want to offer Ukraine a membership perspective because of Russian pressure (Int-7 2020). A Ukrainian MP in 2014 assumed that the EU wanted to help Ukraine, and only in 2016-2017 did he understand that "the goal of the European Union is to do nothing, to protect its borders, not to interfere in any military conflicts, to get richer and tell everyone about its moral and democratic values" (Int-22 2020). An advisor to a senior decision-maker in Ukraine also mentioned that achieving peace was the EU's priority (Int-7 2020). The EU's interest in having fewer conflicts near its borders was further confirmed by a Russian scholar (Int-26 2020). Therefore, although this was not reflected in their electoral statements, I could detect a better understanding on the part of Ukrainian officials of the EU's preferences in Ukraine—stability, no conflict, and no membership perspective.

Parliamentary elections in Ukraine

This period also marked important changes within Ukrainian politics which had an influence on the country's foreign policy-making. Parliamentary elections were held on 26th October 2014. Firstly, 56%

of deputies were elected for the first time (Ukrainians renewed the Rada by 56% 2014), and this, together with the high number of former soldiers entering parliament as new MPs, was seen by experts as a threat to the new Rada (2014 Parliamentary elections 2014). Secondly, the largest proportion of votes was received by the then Prime Minister Yatseniuk's Party and the then President Poroshenko's Party (44% altogether) (The CEC processed 100% of the protocols 2014). A leading Polish politician saw these two Ukrainian politicians as key, and referred to the EU's experience of cooperation with them (Int-25 2020). Thirdly, the Opposition Party (considered pro-Russian) gained 9,5% of votes (The CEC processed 100% of the protocols 2014), which signifies both a persistence of Russian supporters in Ukraine, and Russia's continued influence on the country's politics. With regard to information, those of my informants who were elected into the Rada for the first time reported access to better information (including secret information), which they did not have in their previous positions as members of the military, local leaders or journalists (Int-11 2020; Int-24 2020; Int-27 2020). However, a former MP and soldier stressed that 95% of decisions by Ukrainian MPs were taken on the orders of oligarchs (directly or via fraction leaders), so he considered that MPs' information background was not that relevant (Int-22 2020). The same politician also reported that more experienced deputies made it difficult for the new ones to access information (Int-22 2020). Therefore, although new policymakers came onto the stage in Ukraine, they had less influence on the country's decision-making than the old elites, partly due to the fact that the President and the Prime Minister strengthened their power by retaining almost half of the seats in the parliament for their own parties.

The above analysis reveals an important confirmation of game theory's assumptions — the unchanged nature of preferences. My data confirmed that the preferences both of the EU (preservation of stability in Ukraine) and of Russia (influence over Ukraine) stayed the same during the whole first year of the conflict. The preservation of Ukraine's territory and a closer partnership with the EU were seen as Ukraine's key preferences by leaders in Kyiv (Int-7 2020; Int-11 2020). However, it was only after Minsk I that Ukrainian core decision-makers understood better the Russia's and the EU preferences, as mentioned above. Better access to and use of information by Ukrainian leaders could be explained by the development of their competences and war experience, but also by the change of events after the entrance of the Russian Regular Army into Donbas in August and the Minsk Protocol in September. Another crucial factor in the creation of a better information environment is the closer communication between Ukrainian decision-makers with their Russian and EU interlocutors. I will now look in more detail at the changes in trust in this period.

5.2. Erosion of trust

We already know that after Minsk I, Ukrainian decision-makers' assessment of others' preferences improved. The same factors also contributed to changes in their trust in the actions of the EU and Russia. Given that agreement was reached, and that the Minsk Protocol was signed following the negotiations between OSCE, Ukraine, Russia, and pro-Russian insurgents, it can be assumed that a certain level of trust was developed. Nevertheless, my respondents reported that Ukrainian leaders now had less trust in their foreign partners. Firstly, the EU was not present during the peace discussions, and its support for Ukraine was only diplomatic, financial, and technical, and did not include military help. Moreover, it also continued its economic cooperation with Russia. For these reasons, policy-makers in Kyiv had diminished trust in the EU's willingness to help Ukraine. Secondly, Russia's deceitful actions and the continuation of fighting in Donbas further reduced trust in Russia's words. I will now explain these changes in trust in EU-Ukraine-Russia relations in September 2014 – February 2015.

Decrease of trust in the EU

Since Ukrainian leaders had requested the EU's help against Russian aggression, but the EU's pronouncements about its support to Ukraine did not turn into anything substantial, my informants reported that Ukrainian leaders now had a better understanding of the

EU's words and actions and the discrepancy between them. For instance, as a Ukrainian MP pointed out, in deciding between cooperation with Russia and greater support to Ukraine (e.g., harder sanctions, more financial help), the EU inclined more towards the former, although it did not publicly acknowledge this (Int-27 2020). In the same vein, an EU correspondent explained:

> There was a worry in many European capitals, especially further West, that we should not let the Ukraine crisis damage our … economic business too much, nor our political business with Russia (Int-20 2020).

He also recognised that this could be perceived as dishonesty on the part of the EU towards Ukraine (Int-20 2020). Moreover, an advisor to a senior Ukrainian official[77] confirmed the orientation of certain EU member-states towards business with Russia rather than helping Ukraine (Int-7 2020), while one of the Crimean Tatar leaders said that while Ukraine hoped for much support from the EU, the EU did not meet its own standards (Int-6 2020). However, according to a former EU Ambassador to Russia, the EU stopped all further development of cooperation with Russia (visa liberalisation, free trade agreement, Four Spaces etc.) after Russia's aggression against Ukraine (Int-23 2020). This was also confirmed by the president of the European Council (Int-34 2021). All the same, a former MEP suggested that "the whole situation with Ukraine was always weakened by the idea of the West that continuing economic relations with Russia would serve in the end to convince Russia that fighting is not the right way" (Int-31 2021). Regarding the EU's trust in Ukraine, there was uncertainty about the honesty of Ukrainian politicians in their commitment to democratic and economic reforms (Int-32 2021), or their desire to fulfil the EU-Ukraine Association Agreement fully rather than just adopting the parts of it which were useful to these politicians (Int-25 2020). This shows a clear misperception of EU-Russia relations by Ukrainians and Europeans: whilst the freezing of further political relations was seen as a significant step by the EU,

---

77 He also perceived the EU's 'Ukrainian fatigue' as being the "hiding of its real position, that is, orientation towards Russia as a resource", and Ukraine was seen as a factor that negatively influenced the relations of some of the EU member-states with Russia (Int-7 2020).

Ukrainians were dissatisfied with the continuation of the EU's economic ties with Russia. Thus, better awareness of the EU's interest in maintaining business links with Russia contributed to Ukraine's diminished trust in the EU's words of support.

Another reason for Ukraine's distrust in the EU could be confusion on the part of some Ukrainian policy-makers of the OSCE with the EU. Two Ukrainian politicians (from local and national levels) confirmed that Ukraine's trust in the EU had diminished due to a perception that the OSCE's work was biased (due to Russian influence) and inefficient (Int-1 2020; Int-22 2020). A former Ukrainian military commander and MP characterised the OSCE as "an extremely useless organisation, which showed concern in every situation when people were dying", while acknowledging that they (the soldiers) did not understand that this was a monitoring organisation, thinking that it possessed some instruments by which to influence Russia (Int-22 2020). Therefore, poor knowledge on the part of some Ukrainian policy-makers about the EU's (and the OSCE's) functioning also decreased their trust in the EU.

Distrust in Minsk Agreements

Turning now to the processes of negotiating and implementing of the Minsk Agreements, my evidence shows a substantial amount of misleading tactics here. For instance, a Russian analyst viewed Minsk negotiations as "some kind of dances between Russia and Ukraine", whilst neither side could openly proclaim that they were against the negotiations, but each side "tried to set conditions that would be unacceptable to the other, or that would be extremely difficult to monitor" (Int-16 2020). He saw the EU's role as mediator to be a positive one, with the help of which at least a limited ceasefire was being honoured (Int-16 2020). Yet an advisor to a senior official in Ukraine explained that high level negotiations are always a game of some kind, in which the sides always mislead each other (Int-7 2020). As an example, he mentioned the EU's attempts to force Ukraine to hold elections on the occupied territory of Donbas in order to achieve the EU's goal of ending the war (Int-7 2020). A former green MEP working on Ukraine did not support this EU's position and suggested that mistrust in the Minsk process was coming from "unfair requirements made for Ukraine" (Int-31 2021). According to a leading Polish politician who was also working on Ukraine, there was always a suspicion that Russia "was not honest when it declared that it was in favour of a peaceful resolution of the conflict", and that Putin was able to intimidate the Western countries by making it clear that he was ready to do anything which would weaken Ukraine (Int-25 2020). In his interview in November, Poroshenko said that Russia would be doing things one day which were the opposite of promises made the day before (Ronzheimer 2014). A Ukrainian MP viewed the Minsk Agreements as a positive development, but, in similar vein, felt this should not be overestimated due to the instability of Russia's promises (Int-27 2020). Thus, my respondents considered that in the Minsk Agreements all of the parties were in some ways misleading the others. This contributed to the limited functionality of the Agreements, which was understood to a certain extent by Ukrainian decision-makers.

In addition to the above, a number of my respondents described a certain deadlock in the implementation of the Minsk Agreements. For instance, a former member of the Russian State Duma saw the Minsk Agreements as an important stabilisation factor, which, although written badly and incorrectly, became, after their acceptance by the EU, UN and everyone else, "the track which it is not possible to jump out of", thus making everyone "hostages of that night in Minsk" (Int-17 2020). A Russian expert on Ukraine supported this view, saying that "the conflict was still going on due to inertia, the inertia of previously adopted decisions, and all parties were already in a narrow corridor, in which there were very few opportunities" (Int-26 2020). Russian analysts argued that it would be impossible for Putin to follow the Minsk Protocol (and leave Donbas), since in this way he would 'lose face' in the eyes of his electorate in Russia (Int-18 2020; Int-26 2020). Interestingly, Ukrainian interviewees did not mention the fact that Putin would find it difficult to implement Minsk I for this reason, but they reduced their trust in Russia after it broke the Agreement by continuing to support the insurgents in Donbas. However, it was not only Russia who could not implement the Minsk Agreements because of concern about domestic support, but Ukraine as well.

The perception of the Minsk Agreements in Ukraine was rather negative, which also influenced the way in which they functioned. As well as calling them unacceptable (Int-1 2020; Int-22 2020; Int-24 2020), some Ukrainian policy-makers also saw them as illegitimate, since there was no information, no discussion and no vote on them in the Ukrainian Parliament (Int-22 2020; Int-24 2020). One of Ukraine's leading politicians, Yulia Tymoshenko, blamed Poroshenko for endangering the territorial integrity and sovereignty of Ukraine by means of Minsk I (Tymoshenko criticized the Armistice Protocol 2014). Even an advisor to one of the decision-makers in Kyiv stated that "changing the Geneva format to a European one was wrong" (Int-7 2020). Not only politicians, but also the public disliked the Minsk Agreements. For instance, the unexpectedly low support for the President's Party in the parliamentary elections in October (23% in comparison to 55% in the presidential elections in May) (The CEC processed 100% of the protocols 2014) was seen by scholars as a sign of declining trust in Poroshenko because of the Minsk Protocol (Shevel 2015). According to the sociological research conducted by the Razumkov Centre in March 2015, 34% of all Ukrainians evaluated the Minsk Agreements positively, 22% negatively, and 26% neutrally (Razumkov Center 2015). However, when we look at these data by region only in the Donbas (Donetsk and Luhansk regions), a majority (57%) had a positive view (Razumkov Center 2015). All the same, we can see that dissatisfaction with the Minsk Agreements both on the part of some Ukrainian elites and ordinary people led to the decline of trust in decision-makers and also contributed to a deadlock in the agreements' implementation.

The existing distrust in EU-Ukraine-Russia relations was also a reason for the failure to reach their common goal – peace. According to an EU official who had access to the EU's decision-making on Ukraine, "in an ideal world, we would have found a solution to the conflict and then that solution would have been implemented" (Int-12 2020). This official explained that although parts of the Minsk Agreements had a clear timeline, they could not be implemented mainly because of the lack of trust that existed then in Russian-

Ukrainian relations (Int-12 2020). An advisor to a Ukrainian senior official also mentioned that although everyone wanted peace, "Peace is Russia's method of war. Peace is a method of imposing bad political decisions on the enemy, so that he destroys himself from within." (Int-7 2020). In addition, an EU analyst supposed that "some decision-makers in Brussels" had "a suspicion that there is lack of a good will on the Ukrainian side" to fulfil Minsk I and II (Int-13 2020). Thus, although everyone was supposedly aiming at peace, mistrust between the sides contributed to the failure of this aim.

The period between the Minsk I and Minsk II Agreements showed the persistence of the previous tendency of declining trust on the part of Ukrainian politicians towards both Russia and the EU. Although the Minsk Protocol was signed, it was broken in two days. Russia continued to deny its involvement in Donbas and to give out misleading signals. This was understood by the core Ukrainian decision-makers, which is why Russian pronouncements were not trusted in Kyiv. The lack of support from the EU and its continued business with Russia also reduced Ukraine's trust in European interlocutors. Mutual bluffing, distrust in each other, and lack of acceptance of the Minsk Agreements on the part of the population of both Ukraine and Russia, contributed to a deadlock in their implementation. Due to this mutual distrust, peace, although supposedly a common interest, was not achieved. All in all, it can be argued that in this period Ukrainian decision-makers were more careful about trusting their foreign interlocutors. To further analyse the Ukrainian leaders' decision-making, we will now consider their awareness of everyone's payoffs in this period.

5.3. Payoffs: 'Eyes wide open'

Having studied the changes in the information background of Ukrainian leaders and their trust in their EU and Russian interlocutors, we will now turn to the analysis of the role of payoffs in Ukraine's decision-making after Minsk I. Based on my findings, I would argue that the shifts in payoffs and their understanding by Ukrainians is the major development between the Minsk I and Minsk II Agreements. After the Russian Regular Army prevented the

Ukrainian military from regaining the whole territory of Donbas at the end of August, the payoffs changed significantly. The possibility of Ukraine restoring its territorial integrity had faded away and the probability of a bigger war made all sides more inclined towards peace talks. Therefore, prior to the discussions in Minsk on 5th September, the EU aimed to stop the fighting, Russia aimed to maintain its influence over Ukraine, while Ukraine had the two core goals — to regain Donbas, and to stop the bloodshed. The signing of the Minsk Protocol cemented the existing alignment of forces and led to a freezing of the conflict. The EU achieved its aim of ensuring some stability in Ukraine (a frozen instead of a hot conflict) and Russia maintained control over Ukraine through its influence over the occupied areas of Donbas. Between Minsk I and II, some political forces in Ukraine still hoped to regain the territory of Donbas. The renewed clashes, in particular the battles for Donetsk airport and Debaltsevo in January 2015, brought the sides back to the negotiating table and resulted in the signing of Minsk II. After this, the substantial part of Ukraine's establishment understood the impossibility of regaining Donbas in the near future. Below, we will look at these changes in payoffs and how they were understood in Kyiv.

Ukraine's payoffs

My analysis of Ukraine's payoffs suggests that some policy-makers thought it would be possible to regain Donbas (and perceived the Minsk Protocol to be an opportunity to do so), while others still aimed to maintain Ukraine's cooperation with Russia. An advisor to a core decision-maker in Ukraine told me that while in the summer "the Ukrainian appetite [for regaining Donbas] grew over time" due to the improvement of the situation, "the Minsk Protocol was very bad and limiting for the country, although possibly the best that was available" (Int-7 2020). Thus, after the hard situation at the end of August, there were fewer options for Ukraine. However, one of the Crimean Tatar leaders pointed out that "Minsk I was Ukraine's weapon", which helped it to gain time and to develop the Ukrainian Army (Int-6 2020). In the same vein, both a Ukrainian social activist from Luhansk and an MP (a former commander of a voluntary battalion) noted that Minsk I gave Ukraine a chance of strengthening the country, so that to win back the lost territories later (Int-3 2020; Int-22 2020). These "illusions" existed up to 2015 (Int-22 2020). On the other hand, an independent foreign journalist in Ukraine claimed that after successive defeats, the Minsk Agreements looked like capitulations, although Ukrainian decision-makers presented them in a different light (Int-15 2020). Interestingly, in defiance of claims on the part of Ukrainian policy-makers about their pro-EU course, several EU officials pointed out that in addition to integration with the EU, Ukraine aimed to preserve economic relations with Russia (Int-33 2021; Int-37 2021). Thus, we see different and changing understandings of Ukraine's payoffs by Ukrainian decision-makers. While some of them rejected Minsk I, as I mentioned above, others perceived Minsk I as a way of gaining time so that Ukraine could get stronger and regain Donbas. Ukraine's desire to maintain business activities with Russia, as described by EU officials, reveals a discrepancy between Ukraine's proclaimed aim to achieve EU integration (as discussed in the section on preferences) and the practical steps it apparently took to maintain economic relations with Russia.

The EU's payoffs

We will turn now to the EU's payoffs. Following its preference to have stability in Ukraine, the EU amended its previous payoff—to stop the war—and was satisfied with the ceasefire which came about after the Minsk Protocol. When this was not respected, the EU aimed to stop the fighting once again. EU officials and diplomats confirmed that the EU's core aims were to end the bloodshed, to stop the fighting and to bring all sides to the negotiating table (Int-12 2020; Int-14 2020; Int-23 2020). One of the European diplomats explained that the EU understood that Minsk I was very hard to fulfil, both from the Russian and Ukrainian perspectives (e.g., pressure from right-wing members of the population would not allow changes to the Ukrainian constitution) (Int-14 2020). All the same, an EU official claimed that the EU called for the implementation of the Minsk Agreements, made its tools available to support this, and accepted the agreed parameters (Int-12 2020), and a former MEP also reiterated that "when Minsk was signed it was clear that there was no room for renegotiation" (Int-31 2021). An EU correspondent described that the EU's goals in this period were to provide Ukraine with political and symbolic support and to contain the conflict in Eastern Ukraine so that it did not reach and did not cause suffering to the EU (Int-20 2020). An EU Commissioner on Enlargement explained:

> At that time, it was not really us [the EU] who were running the show… Our role was limited to kind of interested and involved observer. We started to prepare sanctions … but nothing has stopped Putin from completing the annexation process, nothing stopped Putin from supporting the forces in Eastern Ukraine, … and nothing stopped him from direct intervention there (Int-21 2020).

It is clear, then, that the EU saw itself as a mediator with only minor influence on the conflict in Ukraine. Some Ukrainian policy-makers understood the EU's preferred payoff to be stopping the fighting in Ukraine (Int-7 2020; Int-24 2020), but also in "helping Ukraine to withstand the pro-European choice of its citizens" (Int-24 2020). According to the acting Foreign Minister of Ukraine, the EU wanted to avoid an all-out war, but some countries still maintained cooperation with Russia (this was understood by him after he had left his post, so 6-12 months after Crimea) (Int-36 2021). Therefore, although the EU did aim at stopping the war in Ukraine, this goal was not a priority for the EU (also due to its preference for business with Russia). This was already better grasped in Ukraine during this period, and this also contributed to the decline of Ukrainian leaders' trust in the EU.

Russia's payoffs

With regard to Russia, the country changed its desired payoff from supporting intense fighting in Ukraine to keeping a frozen long-lasting conflict going. This helped Russia to achieve its preference of maintaining an influence over Ukraine's destiny. A Russian scholar told me he thought that a protracted conflict in Ukraine served Putin's domestic goals since he presented it as an internal conflict with Russia playing the role of a mediator (Int-26 2020). This was also the view of an EU correspondent who pointed out that "Russia had accomplished what it wanted — to control the future destiny of

Ukraine" (Int-20 2020). Russia's satisfaction in holding Donbas as leverage over Ukraine and the EU was also mentioned by an EU official (Int-32 2021). Russia's goal "to control Ukraine politically" by means of an "eternal instability zone" inside the country was further confirmed by a Ukrainian politician and military commander (Int-22 2020). On the other hand, a Russian state correspondent (with pro-Putin views) explained that "Minsk I and II Agreements are Russia's attempts to get back to agreements with Yanukovych (on 21st February 2014), to get everybody to the negotiating table and to agree on the rules of the game" (Int-19 2020). In respect to Minsk II, France's former President Hollande understood that during Minsk II negotiations, Putin wanted to win time, let separatists gain more territory and force the surrender of the Ukrainian Army in Donbas, in order to maintain Putin's influence on pro-Russian regions and weaken the Ukrainian leaders (Lazareva 2018; The long night in Minsk 2018). Later, Putin proposed granting autonomy to separatist regions, which was rejected by the other participants (Lazareva 2018; The long night in Minsk 2018). This opportunity to talk with the Russian leader certainly contributed to a better understanding of Russia. As I have also mentioned in the section on information, Ukrainian decision-makers were already aware that Russia's preference to keep control over Ukraine was achieved via the payoff of the frozen war in Donbas.

How was the conflict's development foreseen in Ukraine? My empirical evidence indicates that there was no common view on the part of Ukrainian leaders on possible developments in Donbas at the end of 2014 – beginning of 2015. Discussing the most probable outcome at the end of 2014, an advisor to one of the highest decision-makers in Ukraine said that many former soldiers, who became deputies in the new parliament, assumed that they would soon be fighting against Russia again, but this time in Kyiv (Int-7 2020). In the same vein, the leader of one of the volunteer battalions explained that in December 2014, politicians (he was an MP by then) were getting ready for a prolonged military conflict and were trying to create a functioning Ukrainian state (Int-11 2020). Thus, some of Ukraine's leaders thought it possible that there would be a renewed war with Russia at the end of 2014. This might also be explained by their desire to regain Donbas. However, according to a leading EU analyst, "the Western sanctions were very successful in stopping the Russian military from moving forward", and so "the likelihood of a total war between Russia and Ukraine decreased"; "by early 2015, it was clear that the most likely outcome would be some kind of frozen conflict, though including some exchange of fire" (Int-13 2020). Therefore, it appears that some Ukrainian decision-makers thought it possible that there would be a larger war in winter 2014-2015, and this could be explained by their desire to change the *status quo* and regain Donbas.

Ukrainian decision-makers' awareness about the payoffs structure is considered the most significant aspect of their decision-making between the Minsk I and II Agreements. My analysis clearly indicates rough shifts in payoffs for the EU, Ukraine, and Russia. The equilibrium which was achieved — the frozen conflict — was apparently satisfactory for everyone apart from Ukraine. Yet an EU correspondent thought the frozen conflict in Donbas was "not 100% satisfactory for anyone [the EU, Ukraine, Russia], but was ok for all of them" (Int-20 2020). He explained that although costly for Russia, the conflict helped to control Ukraine's destiny; for the EU it was convenient since there was no need to offer membership to Ukraine, but at the same time it amounted to failure of the EU's diplomacy; and Ukrainian policy-makers could postpone the solution of the war, although it could turn into a hot war at any time (Int-20 2020). In achieving its preference to control Ukraine, Russia chose an unsolvable frozen conflict over the previous goal of supporting an open war in Donbas. In this way, Russia retained leverage over Ukraine and continued to support insurgents but presented itself as a mediator in this conflict. Russia's strategy was now better understood by Ukrainian leaders. As for the EU, it accepted the frozen conflict as a way of achieving a certain stability in Ukraine. Ukrainian policy-makers were able to understand this but did not fully grasp the EU's view of itself as a mediator with limited influence over the situation in Ukraine. Ukraine's own payoff was seen by some policy-makers as becoming a stronger country and later regaining Donbas. That this was impossible was understood in full only after Minsk II. The payoffs of all of the actors were confirmed by their readiness to employ their resources to achieving them, which is described in the following section.

5.4. Resources: Good awareness

Now that we know about the changes in the Ukrainian leaders' understanding of the others' preferences, the continuing decrease in trust and substantial shifts in the payoffs structure, we will look at Ukrainian leaders' ability to analyse Ukraine's, Russia's, and the EU's resources together with their willingness to apply their resources. My findings suggest that their awareness of Russia's resources in Ukraine was fairly good, while their understanding of the EU's resources was still imperfect. Although EU policy-makers stressed that there was substantial improvement in the EU's foreign policy mechanisms in Ukraine by this time, Ukrainian leaders asked for more support (e.g., harder sanctions against Russia and military assistance for Ukraine). While some Ukrainian politicians claim that the state was functioning well in that period, others mentioned corruption and weak diplomacy as issues that prevented Ukraine from achieving its aims. My analysis, as detailed below, reveals these peculiarities in resources between the Minsk I and II Agreements.

Ukraine's resources

Let us first look at how the different actors within Ukraine assessed the effectiveness of the functioning of the Ukrainian state. On the one hand, an advisor to one of the highest decision-makers in Kyiv underlined the coherence and conceptual unity of Ukrainian decision-makers during the war and stated that "the fact that Poroshenko, even at the cost of the Minsk Agreements, managed to keep the state as it is, is strange in its own way" (Int-7 2020). Compared to fights between parliament, government, and president in previous years (see chapter 2), this was indeed a surprising development. Moreover, the changes in society, de-communisation, the development of the Ukrainian language and patriotism were seen as Ukraine's new resources (Int-6 2020). The EU's pressure on Ukraine to fight corruption and its pledge to provide financial assistance only after certain reforms had been carried out was also praised as a tool in the fight against corruption and the oligarch lobby (Int-7 2020). In addition to the war, the new parliament and government in November 2014 had to deal with the country's exhausted financial resources, which were allegedly a consequence of Yanukovych's rent-seeking (Int-11 2020; Shevel 2015). Another of my informants—a Russian social activist—pointed out that although Ukraine was in a weaker position, it was trying to demonstrate that it had the power to re-take Donbas and Crimea (Int-16 2020). This is supported by the fact that in November Poroshenko told Bild newspaper that Ukraine was ready for an all-out war, and that the Ukrainian Army was in far better condition than it had been five months previously (Ronzheimer 2014). This falls in line with Fearon's (2005, 381) arguments about leaders' incentives to misrepresent private information in order to bargain more effectively. Therefore, my findings suggest that there were some positive changes in relation to Ukraine's resources, and that Ukrainian decision-makers were demonstrating the country's strength in their public foreign communications.

In contrast to the above, other informants referred to the failures in Ukrainian foreign diplomacy in this period. One example is the perception of a former politician and military commander about the betrayal of the Ukrainian authorities before Ilovaisk and consequently the humiliation of Ukraine by Minsk I, and a subsequent betrayal during Debaltsevo, and even more humiliation in relation to Minsk II (Int-22 2020). In his view, Ukraine's leaders, in particular Poroshenko, gave these concessions to Russia in exchange for "the right to further rob this territory—Ukraine—and guarantees for their [Ukrainian politicians'] possessions in Russia" (Int-22 2020). Another Ukrainian MP claimed that "after Ilovaisk, it became clear that Ukraine's military leadership was not ready to effectively counter the Russian Regular Army and that the war became a trench war on Ukraine's territory" (Int-24 2020). A former governor of Luhansk oblast underlined the fact that Poroshenko's diplomacy and the Ukrainian Parliament did not work effectively; in the summer she could already envisage an end to the war, but after Minsk I it turned into a frozen conflict without the prospect of peace (Int-1 2020). The possibility of Ukraine's diplomacy working better and convincing the EU to give more help to Ukraine was also referred to by Ukraine's former Foreign Minister (Int-4 2020). Moreover, the leaking of Medvedchuk's phone conversations suggests that Poroshenko was involved in secret corrupt business with Russia; for example, after October 2014 he had supported Ukraine's purchase of coal from separatists, in spite of his public rejection of this purchase (BIHUS info 2021c). From the previous chapter, we already know about corruption amongst Ukrainian high officials, and this was recognised by senior EU officials (Int-31 2021; Int-33 2021). Accordingly, a number of high-level respondents criticised the flawed work of Ukraine's diplomacy and even mentioned betrayal on the part of senior officials. This is significant, since it shows that Ukrainian leaders did not use the country's resources properly (similarly to the previous periods), which reduced Ukraine's capacity to deal effectively with the EU and Russia.

Russia's resources

Turning to Russia's resources, various empirical sources support the view that Russia continued to give substantial support to the insurgents in Donbas, and that Ukrainian decision-makers were well aware of this. It should be noted that in accordance with Minsk I, all foreign troops had to be withdrawn from Ukraine (Protocol on the results of consultations of the Trilateral Contact Group 2014). Speaking to Ukraine's Parliament on 10th September, Poroshenko told MPs that 70% of Russian troops had already been withdrawn from Ukraine (Russian troops in Ukraine 2014). However, when the ceasefire was not adhered to, Poroshenko's strategy was to convince the world that Russia could be a threat to any country. Commenting on Putin's claim that Russia could capture Kyiv in two weeks, Poroshenko said that Russia would be able to capture any European city with its strong army, and for that reason it was crucial for the world to unite against Russia (Poroshenko: Russia can take any city 2014). In his interview with Bild in November 2014, Poroshenko stated that there were "thousands of Russian soldiers, hundreds of tanks, heavy artillery" in Ukraine (Ronzheimer 2014). Moreover, Ukraine officially reported that Russian-backed insurgents were shelling their own territory to create the impression that this was being done by the Ukrainian Army (The National Security and Defense Council 2014). Since Russian involvement was documented and to some extent acknowledged by Russia, the Ukrainian decision-makers' understanding of the situation was close to reality. One example is that in his memoirs, France's former President Hollande mentioned that during the Minsk II negotiations (February 2015) Putin became so angry that he started shouting at Poroshenko that he would destroy Ukraine's forces in Donbas, which, according to Hollande, was confirmation that the Russian Army was actually present in Donbas (Lazareva 2018; The long night in Minsk 2018). Another example is an interview given by Putin, in which he mentioned his communication with separatists in Donbas and his determination not to let Ukraine destroy pro-Russian separatists there (Seipel 2014). Hence, it is in this period that Ukrainian leaders learned more about Russia's readiness to employ its resources in Ukraine. For instance, a Ukrainian MP referred to the Ilovaisk battle (at the end of August 2014) as "a cold shower" for Ukrainians, bringing them to an understanding of Russia's readiness to use all of its resources in Ukraine and the EU's unwillingness to help Ukraine more (thus leaving Ukraine alone against Russian aggression) (Int-27 2020). Therefore, more confirmation of Russian involvement in Donbas, including Putin's acknowledgement of it, resulted in Ukrainian leaders' better awareness of Russia's resources in Ukraine.

The EU's resources

Looking at the EU's resources in this period, my European informants pointed to the adjustment of the EU's foreign policy in relation to the war in Ukraine, and Ukrainian informants mentioned their better (but not full) understanding of what the EU was and was not ready to do for Ukraine. Whilst a former MEP mentioned that EEAS was at that time "in the making" and "not ready to cope with the challenge" (Int-31 2021), an EU official said that at around the same time (2014-2015), the EU had developed new mechanisms in its foreign policy and that "it was a very critical period not just for EU-Ukraine or EU-Russia relations, but also for the EU's foreign policy-making" (Int-12 2020). On the other hand, an advisor to a senior decision-maker in Kyiv pointed out that "the EU is a peacetime institution that is incapable of coping with crises like the Russian-Ukrainian war" (Int-7 2020). He also mentioned that Ukraine hoped for more financial support, such as an EU Marshal plan for Ukraine, which did not happen (Int-7 2020). According to an EU official, in precisely 6-8 months Ukrainian leaders were able to understand what resources the EU was and was not ready to invest in Ukraine (Int-32 2021). Speaking to Bild, Poroshenko said that it was clear to Ukrainians that the EU would not send soldiers to Ukraine, but it could still help with technical and military support (Ronzheimer 2014). Although Ukrainians were rather unsatisfied with the amount of help from the EU, the facts show substantial financial (e.g., €365 million only from the European Neighbourhood Instrument in 2014), institutional (e.g., the creation of the Support Group for Ukraine) and restrictive (sanctions against Russia) support (EU-Ukraine relations - factsheet 2021). A leading EU analyst confirmed that EU officials were well aware of Russian official involvement in Donbas, but he assumed that they lacked the political will to fully confront Russia (Int-13 2020). However, he stressed the crucial role of the combined EU resources — "phone diplomacy, the Minsk process, political sanctions against Russia (e.g., excluding it from G8), economic sanctions" (Int-13 2020). This politico-diplomatic support from the EU in reaching peace agreements was also underlined by Ukraine's former Foreign Minister (Int-4 2020). Therefore, Ukrainian policy-makers developed a better understanding of what kind of resources the EU was ready to employ in Ukraine — limited diplomatic and financial, but no military, help.

One more interesting peculiarity regarding the EU's actions in Ukraine was mentioned by a number of respondents — the EU's absence as an actor during the peace negotiations. Indeed, there were OSCE representatives during the Minsk I negotiation process, and the German and French heads of states took part in Minsk II, in a way representing the whole of the EU. An EU correspondent remembered that he was surprised about "how France and Germany came to dominate the discussion fairly quickly in the EU" (Int-20 2020). A former EU Commissioner on Enlargement and Neighbourhood Policy expressed his disapproval of France's and Germany's domination; he felt that the EU as a united organisation would be able to deal with the conflict in Ukraine better, and that this division of EU member-states served Russia's goals precisely (Int-21 2020). Not only were these two countries taking the role of the EU, but other EU countries such as Poland and the UK were excluded (Int-20 2020), which was also criticised by a former MEP (Int-31 2021). Regarding the role of the US, the same former MEP explained that the US was busy with other things, so it was happy to let the EU deal with the conflict in Ukraine and agreed to the France/Germany format (Int-31 2021). Therefore, the EU 'missed' Minsk I negotiations and was not involved as a unified actor in Minsk II, which, as was confirmed by EU policy-makers, might have served Russia's goal of weakening the EU by dividing it.

To sum up, I have discovered certain (but not crucial) shifts in the resources of all three actors, and a change in the perception of Ukrainian policy-makers about these resources, during the period under study. While some in Ukraine praised the unity and efficient work of the Ukrainian authorities, others criticized them for corruption and poor foreign diplomacy, which they felt could decrease Ukraine's capabilities. Although EU policy-makers stressed the development of EU foreign policy, Ukrainian politicians still wanted more support, though they now understood better (but not fully) the EU's abilities as a foreign policy actor. The EU also did not take part in the negotiations of Minsk I, and only France and Germany joined the Minsk II negotiations. Decision-makers in Kyiv were also well aware of Russia's use of resources in Ukraine. This was probably easier to comprehend during this period, since even Putin to some extent acknowledged Russia's involvement in Donbas on a number of occasions. My informants told me that the battle of Ilovaisk in August 2014 was 'a cold shower' for Ukrainians, because it helped them to understand Russia's readiness to employ any resources in Ukraine and the EU's unpreparedness to give more support to Ukraine.

Conclusion

This chapter dealt with Ukrainian leaders' foreign policy decision-making between Minsk I and II Agreements (5th September 2014 – 12th February 2015). Viewing the decision-making process as a combination of four elements — information, trust, payoffs, and resources — I have shown that the role of payoffs (Ukrainian leaders' improved understanding of payoffs and major shifts in them) was particularly significant, with slight changes in other components. Thus, my data indicated the improved awareness of Ukrainian policy-makers about the EU's and Russia's preferences, which may be explained by better communication due to peace talks and other meetings among the leaders. Concerning trust, even the signed Minsk Protocol did not help to develop trustworthy relations between Russia and Ukraine, since, according to Ukrainian politicians, the pronouncements of Russian officials always diverged from Russia's actions. The payoff of the frozen conflict helped to serve both Russia's preferences (control of Ukraine) and the EU's (stability in Ukraine), and so brought about a fairly stable equilibrium. Many in Ukraine still hoped to liberate Donbas, and only after Minsk II did they realise the impossibility of doing so. These actors' payoffs were reflected in their readiness to employ their resources in Ukraine. Russia was prepared to invest its vast resources in Donbas, and this was well understood in Ukraine due to better information. The EU was ready to support Ukraine financially, but not militarily, which was also comprehended by some (but not all) Ukrainian leaders. I will now explain these findings in more detail.

Concerning others' preferences, Ukrainian decision-makers now had more information about these in comparison to previous periods. They became aware that Russia wanted to preserve control over Ukraine and understood that this had been achieved by means of a frozen conflict that could be unfrozen by Russia at any time. The EU's preference of having stability in Ukraine was also seen more clearly now in Kyiv. Moreover, the impossibility of Ukraine gaining membership in the EU in the near future was comprehended by some, but not all policy-makers in Ukraine. After parliamentary elections, new politicians came to power, but decision-making stayed in the hands of Poroshenko and his close allies (at least in part due to the President's and Prime Minister's parties gaining 44% of the votes). The development of Ukrainian leaders' competences and crisis-management experience, but also their contacts with EU and Russian interlocutors, contributed to the creation of a better information environment in Ukraine's decision-making.

Trust in EU-Ukraine-Russia relations continued to decline in this period. Although Minsk I was signed, Russia continued to support insurgents in Donbas and to deny this. However, Ukrainian decision-makers were already more aware that the Russian leadership's words could not be trusted. Limited financial and the absence of military support from the EU, the EU's continued business with Russia, but also Ukrainian leaders' misunderstanding of the EU's foreign mechanisms, further decreased their trust in the EU. Uncertainty regarding the willingness of Ukrainian politicians to fully implement the EU-Ukraine Association Agreement negatively influenced EU policy-makers' trust in their Ukrainian counterparts. Apart from this, a number of respondents also mentioned mutual bluffing during the Minsk negotiations and a deadlock after all parties had committed to them. Failure to accept Minsk I on the part of the Ukrainian public and some of the elites was a further obstacle for Ukrainian decision-makers. Similarly, Russian respondents pointed out that it would have been impossible for Putin to follow the Minsk Agreements and so 'to lose face' in front of his electorate. Thus, in this period, the trust of Ukrainian leaders in their Russian and EU interlocutors further declined, and this had a negative effect on the possibility of stable peace in Donbas.

Changes within payoffs structure and the Ukrainian leaders' awareness about them was found to be the most relevant factor during this period. After the Ilovaisk battle in August and the consequent peace agreement on 5th September, the payoffs' structure had changed significantly. The conflict was frozen, and the possibility of Ukraine regaining the separatist-controlled territory of Donbas faded. Following the preference of keeping control over Ukraine, Russia switched from its previous payoff of keeping a hot war in Donbas to that of a frozen conflict (with the possibility of heating it up at any time), which meant that Russia had leverage over

Ukraine's foreign and domestic policy. With its aim of achieving stability in Ukraine, the EU was ready for any peace, and so also accepted a frozen conflict. Ukrainian leaders had good, but not full, understanding of the others' payoffs. Many of them were able to grasp that the EU and Russia had achieved their payoffs and that changing the situation for Ukraine (i.e. for it to get Donbas back) was not an option. Others initially still aimed at regaining Donbas, and only after Minsk II had to admit that this was impossible.

In September 2014 – February 2015, the resources of the three actors, and the Ukrainian leaders' understanding of them, did not undergo major changes, but certain developments were detected. Politicians in Kyiv were better informed about Russia's involvement in Ukraine, and there was ever more confirmation of this, in addition to Putin acknowledging it to some extent. Moreover, Ukrainian decision-makers started to understand that the EU was ready to support Ukraine financially to a certain extent (but not as far as setting up a Marshal plan) and also by means of sanctions against Russia, but it would not help militarily. The EU did not take part in Minsk I negotiations, and France and Germany took the lead in Minsk II, which diminished the EU's role in the conflict settlement. Awareness about others' resources varied among different Ukrainian policy-makers, but still was better during this period than it had been in the past. On the subject of Ukraine's own resources, some informants mentioned a coherence amongst the Ukrainian authorities and their good management of the country, while others stressed their corruption (even betrayal) and weak diplomacy. Although Ukrainian decision-makers gained a better understanding of the resources of all sides after the Minsk Protocol, it was already hard to change the frozen alignment of forces, while all parties agreed to follow the agreement. Minsk II resulted in the permanent cementing of the existing situation and left very limited options for manoeuvres on the part of Ukraine. Further, in the conclusion I will highlight the core findings of the whole book.

Table 7: Ukraine's decision-making in relations with Russia and the EU between Minsk I – Minsk II (5th September 2014 – 12th February 2015)

Information	Trust	Payoffs	Resources
Improvement of informational capacity	Trust shifted to low or no trust	'Eyes wide open' - understanding and certain acceptance of payoffs	Good awareness of resources
❖ Interactions with foreign interlocutors ❖ Better understanding of the EU's preference (cooperation, but no membership + business with Russia) ❖ Improved understanding of Russia's commitment to stop EU/NATO-Ukraine integration	❖ Peace agreements, but no peace ➢ No trust in Russia's words ➢ Further decrease of trust in the EU ❖ Minsk Agreements - mutual bluffing and distrust between the sides, but everyone's acceptance – deadlock in implementation	❖ 'Eyes wide open' – a frozen conflict as oppose to a 'hot' war is a second order payoff for both the EU and Russia ❖ Little hope to regain Donbas disappeared after Minsk II - compromise for 'peace'	❖ Ilovaisk battle - "cold shower": ➢ Russia ready for any use of resources ➢ the EU not ready to give more support ❖ Development of the EU's foreign policy, but still limited financial and diplomatic support
Impact on decision-making: Medium	Impact on decision-making: Low	Impact on decision-making: High (acceptance of new *status quo* after Minsk II)	Impact on decision-making: Low

Conclusions

Introduction

This book has examined Ukrainian policy-makers' crisis management, their perceptions of foreign relations and their consequent interactions with their Russian and EU counterparts in the first year of the war in Ukraine (February 2014 – February 2015). The book demonstrated how the employment of the game theory-inspired analytical framework allows to explain foreign policy decision-making during the times of conflict. This novel four-dimensional (information, trust, payoffs and resources) framework could be of further usage both for policy-makers and scholars of foreign policy analysis and international relations. My core empirical findings uncovered the Ukrainian decision-makers' weak foreign policy analysis and poor experience in crisis management, which led to their misperceptions both about the EU's and Russia's preferences and actions. Certain drawbacks in Ukrainian decision-makers' response to these challenging events could be explained by a number of factors. These are pre-existing issues in Ukraine's politics (corruption amongst elites that impacted the country's preferences and resources; East-West integration fluctuations), post-revolutionary changes in power structures, the leaders' unwillingness to take responsibility for their war decisions, the unpredictable situational steps of the Russian leadership, and both the EU's and Russia's intentionally/unintentionally misleading signals. Following the development of Ukraine's decision-making during the whole first year of the war, I have albeit noticed the improvement of Ukraine's foreign policy: better understanding of others' preferences, distrust in good intentions of foreign partners and certain development of the country's resources. Thus, my findings can become a useful source for Ukraine's aim to build a more professional foreign policy.

The main research question of this research was: *What factors shaped the response of Ukrainian policy-makers in their interactions with*

Russia and the EU during the first year of the conflict in Ukraine (February 2014 - February 2015)? I approached this question using an innovative four-dimensional game theory analytical framework for decision-making in foreign relations. The game theory literature outlined elements that were considered crucial for a foreign policy decision-maker: information about other countries' preferences, trust in words and signals coming from those countries, the payoff structure for all participants, and the resources they had available in any particular interaction. This analytical framework was employed with the help of four research sub-questions: *1. What was the type and quality of information available to Ukrainian policy-makers regarding the preferences of the EU and Russia during different points of escalation/de-escalation in the first year of the conflict? 2. To what extent was trust towards their interlocutors in Russia and the EU important in determining the strategy of Ukrainian policy-makers during different moments of the escalation/de-escalation of the conflict? 3. How did Ukrainian policy-makers perceive Ukraine's, Russia's, and the EU's payoffs in different periods during the first year of the conflict in Ukraine? 4. How aware were Ukrainian leaders of Ukraine's (and others') resources and readiness to use them at different points of escalation/de-escalation of the conflict?* In this conclusion, I provide my core empirical and theoretical findings, while answering these research questions.

The book uses elements of game theory in order to provide a framework for the analysis of Ukrainian policy-makers' perceptions, decisions and interactions with Russia and the EU during the first year of the Russo-Ukrainian war. The book contributes to the literature on foreign policy analysis and Area Studies in three main domains. Firstly, I fill a gap of a limited application of game theory to the conflict in Ukraine, as well as developing the use of the theory beyond formal modelling. Secondly, the novelty of my approach lies in its focus on individual actors' perceptions, thinking and decisions, when most scholars look at countries as single actors in IR and foreign policy analysis. Thirdly, I study EU-Ukraine-Russia relations during the war from the perspective of Ukraine's decision-making, while the majority of scholars have concentrated on relations between Russia and the EU, paying less attention to Ukraine's own actions. Thus, the book has not developed a new theory, but, using game theory literature, it has constructed a decision-making analytical framework with the aim of explaining the foreign policy decision-making of individual leaders. The methodological contribution is my design of the interview guide and interview items that apply the game theory elements of my analytical framework. Using this interview guide, I conducted 38 elite semi-structured interviews with EU, Ukrainian and Russian policy-makers, who were encouraged to think within the game theory-based framework and to reflect on EU-Ukraine-Russia relations in 2014-2015. In addition, official documents, transcripts of meetings and media outlets from the three sides were analysed to triangulate data from the interviews. The data were processed by means of thematic analysis structured around four game theory themes and three periods in the first year of the conflict.

This conclusion is comprised of three sections. I start with the discussion of my theoretical and methodological contributions. I then move on to my core empirical findings, which are connected to the role of information, trust, payoffs, and resources in Ukraine's foreign policy decision-making. I finish by looking at the broader implications of my work—themes which were outside the parameters of this project, but which emerged from my analysis and could be pursued in further research. These include a discussion of the EU as a foreign policy actor, and the roles of Russia and the US in this conflict. I conclude with a number of counterfactuals and recommendations for the improvement of Ukraine's foreign policy.

Theoretical and methodological contribution

Theoretical contribution

The major theoretical contribution of this book is the development of a decision-making analytical framework based on core game theory elements, and its diligent employment for the explanation of Ukrainian leaders' perceptions and interactions with the EU and Russia in February 2014 – February 2015. In this way, I contribute to Area Studies (EU-Ukraine-Russia relations from Ukraine's perspective) and foreign policy analysis (the employment of the game theory-based analytical framework to foreign policy analysis of Ukrainian leaders' decision-making). This book does not attempt to produce a new theory, but rather 'consumes' existing theoretically-driven concepts from game theory in order to produce a theoretically informed explanation of how individual Ukrainian policy-makers made decisions about interactions with their foreign interlocutors based on their perceptions and analysis of the situation. By building this analytical framework from concepts prevalent in game theory and employing it in the Ukrainian case, I aimed both to widen the use of game theory beyond formal modelling and to offer a novel view on the first year of the armed conflict in Ukraine. To do this, I utilised themes that appear in different parts of game theory literature (information, trust, payoffs, and resources) and used them in tandem with one another, hence developing a more holistic and comprehensive way of explaining the evolution of Ukrainian leaders' decision-making and their interactions with their EU and Russian counterparts over the course of the first year of this armed conflict.

Since the war in Ukraine in 2014 caused a substantial deterioration in European security, many scholars from IR and Area Studies have tried to explain how and why it evolved, offering a range of perspectives. Let us briefly remind the core views. Some placed responsibility on the West, because of its assertive policy in Ukraine – democratisation, the EU-Ukraine Association Agreement, and support for Euromaidan, which, in combination, threatened Russia's 'traditional' influence over Ukraine (Charap and Colton 2017; Kissinger 2014; Lukyanov 2016; Mearsheimer 2014; Sakwa 2015b). Several scholars also pointed to the EU's policy of normative hegemony over Russia and how this developed a negative attitude in Russia (Gretskiy, Treshchenkov, and Golubev 2014; Haukkala 2015, 2016; Lukyanov 2016; Wiegand and Schulz 2015). These scholars send a clear message that Russia's 'rules of the game' were missed by the West. Another group of scholars placed their attention on the illegality of Russia's annexation of

Crimea and the country's military support for pro-Russian insurgents in Donbas (Averre and Wolczuk 2016; Gehring, Urbanski, and Oberthür 2017; Haukkala 2016). Interestingly, but a few others (R. Allison 2014; Dubinsky and Rutland 2019) explained how Russia interpreted international law in favour of the steps it took in Ukraine. This again shows the crucial role of perceptions and subjective analysis in international relations. Other research highlighted flaws in the EU's weak and indecisive approach (which was partly due to internal divisions) to relations with Ukraine and Russia (Averre 2016; Haukkala 2016; Pastore 2014; Rasmussen 2014; Sobczyk 2015), and to drawbacks in Ukraine's policy of integration with both Russia and the EU (Dragneva and Wolczuk 2014; Dragneva-Lewers and Wolczuk 2015; Haukkala 2016). Thus, while scholars have covered chronic issues in Russia's, Ukraine's and the EU's foreign policies and pointed to different misperceptions in their relations, they have paid less attention to how these policies were developed by individual decision-makers and how their interactions with their foreign counterparts directed relations between states. In particular, Ukraine's crisis management during the war was poorly studied.

Indeed, most of the literature regarding the war in Ukraine in 2014-2015 has looked at the actions of 'major actors' and paid limited attention to Ukraine's own policies (sometimes implying that the country has no agency). In particular, the role of policy makers' (mis)perceptions, decisions, actions, and interaction is relatively understudied. Scholars have studied the interactions between the EU (and the West in general) and Russia regarding Ukraine (Alcaro 2015; Birchfield and Young 2018; Charap and Colton 2017; Haukkala 2015, 2016; Kudelia 2019; Mearsheimer 2014; Sakwa 2015a), while only a few have looked at Ukraine's relations with Russia and the West (Averre and Wolczuk 2016; D'Anieri 2019; Dragneva-Lewers and Wolczuk 2015a; Samokhvalov 2015) or at the country's domestic issues leading up to the war (Katchanovski 2017; Kudelia 2014, 2016; Wilson 2016). There have been a few applications of game theory to the conflict in Ukraine, which have concentrated on Western-Russian relations as well (Ericson and Zeager 2015; Veebel and Markus 2016). Yet these have not provided us with a systematic understanding of how different players perceived the war, nor a theoretically informed way of understanding Ukraine's foreign actions and reactions.

To fill the gaps of the limited research on both Ukraine's own actions during the war and policy-making by individual politicians, this book offered a nuanced study of Ukrainian leaders' decision-making and their interactions with their foreign counterparts. My analysis was facilitated by the employment of an analytical framework based on elements which are more widespread and better conceptualized in game theory. First, these scholars argue that foreign policy actors require information about the preferences of all actors involved in a given international interaction (Bennett 1995; Khumalo and Baloyi 2018; Michel 2013; Milner 1997; Snidal 1985; L. Thompson 1995). Additionally, an examination of the 'leadership factor' (Kydd 2000, 352; Morrow 1986, 1133; Nye 2005) and a state's internal power dynamics (Bueno de Mesquita 2006; Pahre and Papayoanou 1997; Putnam 1988; G. H. Snyder and Diesing 1977) are important parameters for the analysis of any conflict. Accordingly, I have studied the type and quality of information available to Ukrainian policy-makers regarding the preferences of their interlocutors. Secondly, scholars have discussed possible failure in reaching best outcomes because of mistrust in the opponent's intentions (Booth Wheeler 2008; Devetak, George, and Percy 2017; Fearon 1995, 401; Lieberman 1964, 272; Michel 2013, 884). To address this issue, I have looked at the extent to which trust towards their EU and Russian interlocutors was important in determining the strategy of Ukrainian decision-makers. Thirdly, the game theory literature underlines the importance of studying how states' preferences are reflected in their anticipated payoffs (Snidal 1985, 40) and describes how different perceptions may lead to misperceived payoffs (Bennett 1995, 30–31; Snidal 1985, 42) and worse outcomes for everyone involved (G. H. Snyder 1971, 80). The book discussed how the Ukrainian authorities perceived Ukraine's, the EU's, and Russia's payoffs in different moments of that first year. Lastly, scholars argue that available resources and readiness to use them may determine the outcome of conflicts in international relations (Clausewitz, Howard, and Paret 1976; Moravcsik 2010; G. H. Snyder 1971). The book analysed Ukraine's awareness of its own and others' resources and their readiness to use them. In this context, I have proposed a game theory-inspired framework for the analysis of Ukraine's decision-making during the first year of the armed conflict.

In addition to taking the four themes from the literature on game theory, the book has also systematically traced their evolution and relevance in relation to Ukraine's decision-making in different phases of the armed conflict. In my empirical findings, I show the shifts in the four themes' evolution and explain how they shaped the crisis management of Ukrainian decision-makers. This has allowed me not only to detect persistent gaps in senior Ukrainian officials' analysis, but also to provide evidence that they were learning how to better manage the situation. The game theory-based analytical framework developed here is an innovative approach to the analysis of foreign policy; it combines different elements which are crucial for decision-makers, but also presents them in a consistent structure. Certain components of G. Allison's (1971) famous work on the rational actor, the organisational process and governmental politics models, which was used to explain US-USSR interactions during the Cuban missile crisis, also appear in my work. I also consider actors' rationality (Model 1), issues related to crisis management and limited resources (Model 2), the preferences of individual policy-makers, and poorly coordinated post-revolutionary actions at central and regional levels (Model 3). I have sorted all these elements into four themes, which has helped me to structure and guide my analysis. Based on this analysis, the theoretical answer to my core research question is: *to a different extent in different moments in time, Ukrainian decision-makers' perceptions and operation with the four elements – information, trust, payoffs and resources – shaped their interactions with the EU and Russia in February 2014 – February 2015.*

In this way, the book makes a contribution to the literature on Area Studies, in particular European and Ukrainian Studies, and foreign policy analysis. Novel empirical data on EU-Ukraine-

Russia relations complement other scholars' studies of this region and a focus on Ukrainian decision-making fills a persistent gap in understanding Ukrainian actions during this war. My concentration on individual policy-makers (and not countries as actors in IR) and employment of the game theory-based analytical framework offers a novel approach to foreign policy analysis. The development of this coherent analytical framework from game theory concepts, instead of formal modelling, is an alternative application of the theory in foreign policy analysis. It offers a particularly helpful tool for analysis of state relations in times of external conflict, when a rapid change of events and interdependency on foreign actors require decision-makers to show robust strategic thinking and scrutiny. The case study of relations between the EU, Ukraine and Russia during the Russo-Ukrainian war also relates to IR literature in a broader sense.

Although I consider my game theory-inspired analytical framework appropriate and helpful in the explanation of foreign policy decision-making, it is also important to highlight some of its possible shortcomings. First of all, the (im)possibility of rational calculations by state actors (or even individuals) is a popular critique of rational choice based theoretical approaches. In my discussion on information, I have mentioned this critique of game theory due to the impossibility of achieving perfect information (but also limitations of people's cognitive abilities[78]) for a 'fully rational' decision-making (Lindblom 1959, 84; Sen 1977; Snidal 1985, 26; Tingley and Walter 2011). On the other hand, according to Simon's (1997) 'bounded rationality'-driven humans aim at satisfying rather than maximizing outcomes in the world of imperfect information. Tsebelis (1990) also shows how a seemingly irrational behaviour may be a sign of nested games, which, if analysed in a combination, contextualises actors' rationality, and Guzman (2008) clarifies how a deeper study of states' behaviour reveals rationality in their strategies. Thus, decision-makers often

---

78 In their laboratory experiments, Tingley and Walter (2011) discovered wrong strategies of some individuals even after the possibilities of learning in repeated games.

do follow rational calculations, based on the best available information, but as scholars highlighted there may be a challenge for a researcher to recognise everyone's preferences across the full picture (Guzman 2008; Moore 1995; Tingley and Walter 2011; Tsebelis 1990).

In the case of the Russian-Ukrainian war, the role of disinformation was substantial. I have described how Russia used disinformation strategies by lying about its involvement in Ukraine, but also by challenging the legitimacy of the new Kyiv government in its media in Crimea and Donbas. This did not only complicate actions of Ukrainian and EU decision-makers but helped to increase pro-Russian mood of the population in these regions. I have also mentioned Ukraine's counter measures to fight the Russian propaganda via the ban of Russian state TV in spring 2014. Consequently, in periods with limited information (February-May 2014), trust played an even bigger role. I have explained how original distrust in Russia's threats in respect to Crimea and Donbas obstructed Ukrainian and EU leaders from timely response to these threats. In addition, uncertain environment allowed Russia to use misleading strategies, e.g., staged referendum in Crimea, its contradictory signals (rejection and confirmation of the presence of Russian military on Ukraine's territory on different occasions). Therefore, the proposed game theory-based analytical framework assumed decision-makers both to analyse different pieces of information carefully and to estimate what is worth trusting.

In turn, complicated real-life environment creates a challenge for scholars in conducting research on these matters. Indeed, approaches which focus on strategic interactions require heavy empirical data, which Sen (1977) calls the requirement of "ideal observational conditions". This could be seen as a limitation given the hardship in access to decision-makers in different countries. For this book, I have conducted 38 elite interviews (and several of my interviewees are high officials). However, I do not claim that I talked to every important person in this respect and in particular, getting respondents from Russia was challenging. To overcome this, I triangulated my interview material with official documents and information from media outlets. This enabled me to make more robust analysis and conclusions.

Another usual critique of rationality-based approaches is a so-called constructivist counter argument. For instance, actors' estimation of payoffs or interests of their countries are based on their individual perceptions, which could be dependent on cultural, historical, or educational backgrounds. However, in this book, I had to make some choices, which entailed a degree of empirical compromises. For example, I did not cover a number of important things such as the process of construction of national ideas and I made assumptions about how people viewed Ukraine's (and other countries') national interests etc. This, in turn, enabled me to present a nuanced analysis of actors' decision-making during the studied events. Otherwise, some may argue that the division of the whole decision-making process during the war into four game theory concepts was overly simplistic. In my view this was a good way to approach my analysis, which allowed to simplify complex processes to an acceptable extent and to provide certain insights, which would not have been possible otherwise. In the same way, Mueller (2003, 674) acknowledges the critique of rational choice approaches, but states that its opponents offer less structured and less powerful explanations. Whilst I acknowledge the limitations of my analytical approach, I still maintain that this has allowed me to analyse complicated inter-state relations during the times of war and to engage with as much empirical data as it was possible, given the available resources.

The theoretical framework I have used in my research has also enabled me to move away from 'macro' understandings of the conflict (realism vs liberalism) or normative conclusions about virtue or guilt (i.e. whether certain actions were illegal or morally questionable) and to go deeper into the details of the armed conflict and to discover how Ukrainian leaders were making state decisions in their relations with the EU and Russia. In this sense, the analysis provided here focused on the meso level, albeit with references to the macro picture or to the level of individual decisions where appropriate. Additionally, my analysis is systematic and covers a major period of the conflict — the turbulent first year with its escalation and de-escalation phases.

Lastly, I hold that my innovative game theory-based analytical framework to the explanation of leaders' decision-making during the conflict can be of further usage for both policy-makers dealing with foreign relations and scholars studying interactions between states. This analytical framework was used for the first time in the study of the armed conflict in Ukraine and in Eastern Europe more generally. I argue that the proposed analytical framework would be of further use in explaining other conflicts in the region, for instance in Georgia and Moldova, where there is also involvement on the part of Russia and the EU, as in the case of Ukraine. Since my book helps us to understand how actors engage with each other, it suggests that stable communication between all actors, which uncovers their preferences and strategies, may also help to de-escalate conflicts. Thus, this game theory-based analytical framework for crisis decision-making and foreign policy interactions can be further applied to studies of other conflicts and international interactions in different parts of the world.

Methodological contribution

The core methodological contribution of this research lies in the design of the interview guide and interview items that apply game theory elements of my game theory-based analytical framework. I then used this interview guide for the collection and analysis of 38 semi-structured elite interviews. I have interviewed EU, Ukrainian and Russian policy-makers (13 Ukrainians, 16 from the EU, eight Russians and one American) — among them 14 were officials, 10 - politicians, 9 - analysts, 5 - journalists in 2014. I contacted the respondents directly or used snowball sampling. The choice of the interviewees reflected my goal of hearing the views of people from different levels of policy and decision-making and different political backgrounds. This helped me to obtain very diverse opinions on the conflict, its evolution and the actors' decision-making. This further confirmed one of my core empirical findings: the diversity of actors' perceptions, which may lead to misunderstanding and conflicting situations.

In addition to the novel and fascinating data, which was collected, another methodological contribution of this book is the adherence to the game theory-based analytical framework in my interviews. The structure of questions was designed to provoke respondents into thinking about what took place within my studied period and in terms of the four game theory elements. When the discussion started going in a different direction, I was able to lead interviewees back by means of supporting questions. This enabled the novel application of my game theory-inspired framework also via the data collection. Moreover, I triangulated my interview data with other materials. I collected official documents, transcripts of meetings, and interviews with decision-makers in the media and news from the EU, Ukraine, and Russia. Such triangulation helped me to overcome some of the limitations of interviewing (human memory or positional bias) and to develop more robust conclusions. Thematic analysis of the four themes and three periods of the first year allowed me to structure the findings in accordance with how events were understood by Ukrainian decision-makers. These perceptions were compared with factual information about the studied events and in certain places with other academic literature.

Empirical findings

This book has shown how the employment of a game theory-inspired analytical framework has helped us to understand the Ukrainian leaders' crisis decision-making (and its evolution) in their relations with the EU and Russia during different escalation/de-escalation moments of the first year of the armed conflict in Ukraine. Looking at Ukraine's decision-making in this way has provided us with the perspective of the most concerned side of the war and has also enriched the existing literature, most of which focused on the relations between the West/EU and Russia. In the following section, I go into a detailed description of my major empirical findings. In each of the four sections, which correspond the four elements of my game theory-based framework for analysis, I first describe the element's evolution in the studied periods, then point to the period in which it was most relevant, then finally explain its general influence on decision-making and the escalation/de-escalation of the conflict. I present a compressed table of my major empirical findings in the beginning and extended tables for each of the elements at the end of each of the respective sections. Based on my findings and analysis, I have considered the relevance of each of the elements in each period (low, medium, and high). Although, as I described in detail in the introduction, my division of the first year into three periods was justified by a number of factors (critical events, agreements, decisions), my respondents were not sure about the precise division of this year into these periods. This could be partially explained by selective and limited memorisation of past events (which took place six to seven years ago in this case).

Table 8: Ukrainian leaders' decision-making in relations with Russia and the EU in February 2014 – February 2015

	Annexation of Crimea	Insurgency and war in Donbas	Peace Agreements
Information	Weak state informational environment Impact: High	Minimal improvement of informational capacity Impact: Medium	Improvement of informational capacity Impact: Medium
Trust	Trust in international law and agreements Impact: High	Trust decreased following the escalation Impact: Medium	Trust shifted to no or low trust Impact: Low
Payoffs	'Eyes wide shut' - miscalculation of payoffs Impact: Medium	Recalibration of perception of payoffs Impact: Medium	'Eyes wide open' - understanding and acceptance of payoffs Impact: High
Resources	Low awareness about everyone's resources Impact: Medium	Medium awareness about resources Impact: High	Good awareness about everyone's resources Impact: Low

Moreover, live interviewing (without prior familiarisation with the questions) provides limited time for self-reflection. However, many of the respondents recognised the critical junctures: the annexation of Crimea, the tragedy in Odesa on 2nd May (crucial for pro-Russian insurgents), the downing of MH17 (the most important event for the EU), the entrance of the Russian Regular Army in Donbas in August 2014, Minsk I and Minsk II. Therefore, crucial changes during the enfolding of the conflict influenced my decision to stay with the chosen division. Namely, my periods are: the annexation of Crimea (21st February - 26th March 2015), the insurgencies and the war in Donbas (26th March – 5th September 2014) and the Minsk Agreements (5th September 2014 – 12th February 2015).

Information about interlocutors' preferences

In my explanation of the factors that shaped Ukraine's response in relations with the EU and Russia in February 2014 – February 2015, I started with an analysis of the type and quality of information available to Ukrainian policy-makers regarding the preferences of the EU and Russia. My empirical data showed restricted access to information and also its poor analysis by Ukrainian officials, which together had an adverse effect on their foreign policy capabilities. Certain limitations, for example, the presence of Russian agents within some of the crucial state institutions, and also the fleeing of some of their employees after the fall of the Yanukovych regime (e.g., from the Security Service of Ukraine), reduced the possibility of acquiring reliable information. In addition, although the new decision-makers were well-established politicians (some were previously in the opposition and Poroshenko was minister of the economy during the Yanukovych presidency), they had to act in a new conflict environment. Furthermore, in the moment of instability during the transfer of power, channels that would have normally been used broke down and the new decision-makers had weak informational network ties, especially at the informal level. This resulted in a deterioration in decision-making, specifically during the annexation of

Crimea. In respect to the war in Donbas, Ukrainian decision-makers did not try to deal with the separatist tendencies there from 2004, although they did have the required information. When the protests erupted in March-April 2014, the regional authorities were transferring the information to Kyiv (as my respondents confirmed in the interviews), which apparently was not taken into account by the country's decision-makers. However, Ukrainian leaders managed to mitigate the Russian misinformation landscape in the region by means of a ban on Russian channels in spring 2014. From another perspective, the rapid change of events during the annexation of Crimea, rebellions in Donbas and an open war in the summer of 2014 required fast decision-making, which further worsened the normal process of information collection and analysis. Respondents confirmed that with the development of Ukrainian state institutions (e.g., changes within the government after Poroshenko's election), access to and analysis of information was getting better and it substantially improved during post-Minsk I stabilisation.

The restricted access to information and its flawed analysis mentioned above meant that Ukrainian decision-makers' understanding of others' preferences was limited. First of all, the authorities did not pay enough attention to the diversity of the preferences of the Donbas residents, and in particular its local elites, who played a crucial role in the unfolding of the war in Donbas. Secondly, the understanding of Russia's preferences changed from having a vague sense of Russia's desire to control Ukraine (specifically its foreign policy) to being convinced of this after Minsk I. However, there was no or very limited analysis (possibly only at Poroshenko's level) of Putin's personal preferences (to stay in power and to use foreign policy to enable this). Thirdly, the perception of the EU's preferences in the eyes of Ukrainian policy-makers changed from an overoptimistic conviction that the EU would welcome Ukraine's integration into the club and was ready to defend the rule of law in the country at any cost (in February-March 2014), to a more realistic understanding (after Minsk I): namely, the EU prioritising cooperation with its neighbours and avoiding having wars near its borders. Consequently, Ukrainian elites realised the impossibility of achieving Ukraine's preference of integration with the EU in the near future. On the other hand, in certain circumstances, the preferences of decision-makers also had influence on their countries' foreign policies in the case under study.

My analysis has revealed how the preferences of key decision-makers, in my case those in Russia and Ukraine, impacted their countries' preferences. One example of this is the fact that my respondents pointed out that although Yanukovych wanted EU-Ukraine integration, his desire to stay in power was greater; this resulted in him not signing the AA after Russia put pressure on him to not do so and provided him with financial help in his re-election campaign. Speaking of Russia, Putin managed to achieve his key preference of staying in power by convincing the population, by means of state propaganda, that he was following their foreign policy preference ('powerful Russia confronting the West and a protector of Russian-speakers) (Int-29 2021). Similarly, several respondents argued that Ukrainian decision-makers did not protect the country properly because of their hidden corrupt preferences; this was confirmed by the recent leaks of Medvedchuk's phone conversations (BIHUS info 2021b, 2021a, 2021c). Therefore, the private and/or corrupt preferences of decision-makers could have had an impact on their countries' foreign policies.

Another consequence of a flawed information background is the creation of actors' perceptions about each other. For instance, some in Russia (its decision-makers and the public) apparently perceived the US to be the core decision-maker regarding Ukraine, and Russian propaganda also justified the country's support for pro-Russian insurgents in Donbas as a way of constraining American influence. On the other hand, many in Ukraine (its decision-makers and the public) perceived this war as a struggle for EU-Ukraine integration and a stand against dependence on Russia, although the prospect of EU membership was never actually offered to Ukraine. Whilst Ukrainian decision-makers expected more EU support (greater financial, but also military help), EU officials confirmed that the EU was not a side in the conflict, but a supporter of reforming Ukraine. In addition, Ukrainian leaders and the public perceived the EU's foreign actorness as that of a nation state. Therefore, all of the actors' differing perceptions meant that they somehow lived in parallel realities, which added another difficulty in finding a settlement to this armed conflict. This is relevant, since it shows how individual policy-makers' analysis of the situation and (mis) perceptions can direct foreign relations.

My empirical data have shown how Ukrainian leaders' use of information about their interlocutors' preferences was shaping Ukraine's foreign policy during the period I have studied. Thus, while during spring - summer 2014 Ukrainian decision-makers were acquiring knowledge about the EU's and Russia's preferences, it was not until autumn 2014 that they were finally able to develop a more realistic understanding of them. After Minsk I, better personal communication between Ukrainian leaders and their EU and, in particular, Russian interlocutors made a positive contribution to a better understanding of their preferences in autumn 2014. Improved awareness of the others' preferences might have contributed to de-escalation of the conflict in autumn 2014. For instance, Poroshenko's and his party's alleged disapproval (as described in the media, but denied by Poroshenko later) of the law on Ukraine's EU/NATO course (because these organisations would not accept Ukraine, but all the same, if Ukraine expressed desire to join them, this would anger Russia) could be interpreted as a move towards de-escalation by Ukrainian decision-makers due to their better awareness of others' preferences in the autumn.

Thus, my core findings in response to the first sub-question are: *during the first year of the conflict, Ukrainian policy-makers suffered an 'information vacuum' and flawed analysis of the available information, which led to a misunderstanding of Russia's and the EU's preferences. This can be attributed to both a lack of professionalism and an unstable conflict environment, and also to 'hidden' (often corrupt) preferences on the part of key Ukrainian players that diverged from those put forward in their public appeals. The situation partly improved after Minsk I due to a substantial change of circumstances and increased communication between Ukrainian, EU and Russian leaders.* In the table below, I summarise my main empirical findings regarding the role of information in Ukrainian leaders' decision-making. After this, we will see what role trust played, in particular in periods in which there was limited information.

Table 9: The role of information in Ukrainian leaders' decision-making in relations with Russia and the EU in February 2014 – February 2015

Annexation of Crimea	Insurgency and war in Donbas	Peace Agreements
Weak state informational environment	**Minimal improvement of informational capacity**	**Improvement of informational capacity**

❖ Post-Euromaidan change in power structures
   ➢ Crimea power vacuum
   ➢ Broken information channels
   ➢ Flawed analysis of information
❖ Russian intelligence infiltration in crucial state institutions
❖ Weak understanding of preferences
   ➢ Those of the EU: no wars + economic cooperation with neighbours
   ➢ Those of Russia: control over Ukraine + Putin's preference to stay in power
 	
Impact: **High**
	❖ Poor analysis of information
	   ➢ Underestimation of separatist tendencies in Donbas + missed preferences of local elites
	   ➢ Awareness of Russia's geostrategic goals, but not of Putin's preferences
	   ➢ Incomplete awareness of the EU's preferences
	❖ Improved information background
	   ➢ New President, but weak information transfer between changing officials
	   ➢ Ban on Russian State TV
	
	Impact: **Medium**
		❖ Interactions with foreign interlocutors
		❖ Better understanding of the EU's preference (cooperation, but no membership + business with Russia)
		❖ Improved understanding of Russia's commitment to stop EU/NATO-Ukraine integration
		
		Impact: **Medium**

Trust in interlocutors' signals

If we look at my empirical findings regarding the role of trust in Ukrainian leaders' foreign policy analysis, we will see that trust had a substantial influence on their decision-making and that there was a drastic change from high to low trust during the studied period. Originally Ukrainians had high trust in international agreements and the rule of law (e.g., the Budapest Memorandum and friendship agreements with Russia), but with time this decreased to almost no trust either in the EU or Russia. While Ukrainians trusted that Russia would surely not attack, but if it did so, the EU would stop Russia during the events in Crimea, this trust decreased when the annexation took place, and there was a gradual destruction of trust in spring-summer 2014 following Russia's greater involvement in Ukraine and the EU's weak reaction to this. After Minsk I, many decision-makers in Ukraine understood that Ukraine could only rely on itself, since Russia always cheats, and the EU is reluctant to provide more support (some of the new politicians understood this only after Minsk II). On the other hand, trust between Kyiv officials and the Donbas population was decreasing in spring and was destroyed in summer 2014. It is important to note that the leaders in Kyiv missed the opportunity to build this trust within Ukraine, and that this contributed to Russia's success in Donbas. Additionally, Russia was better equipped to influence others' perceptions by means of threats and misleading information (the staged referendum, threats of a bigger war, claims that its military was not involved). Russia did not trust its EU and Ukrainian interlocutors, for instance, because of the breaking (by both Ukraine and the EU) of the 21st February agreement with Yanukovych, and the perceived dependence of both the EU and Ukraine on the US. While these were core characteristics of trust during the whole first year, they had different degrees of importance at different times.

My analysis has shown that trust played the core role in Ukraine's decision-making during the annexation of Crimea, while Ukrainian leaders' decision not to act was for the most part influenced by a pre-existing trust in the EU and Russia. My respondents explained that Russia's threats to attack Ukraine (and the available information about this possibility) were not trusted due to greater trust in the Budapest Memorandum and bilateral friendship agreements with Russia. Several interviewees who had been involved in Ukraine's decision-making also confirmed that their EU interlocutors asked Ukraine not to provoke Russia over Crimea and promised to solve the situation. It appears that Ukrainian decision-makers trusted the EU's promise, which contributed to their decision not to try to deter Russia. A number of other interviewees suggested that these EU requests might have been used by Ukrainian leaders to justify their inaction in relation to Russia. However, if decision-makers in Kyiv trusted in the possibility of Russia's annexation of Crimea and the EU's inaction in this respect, they might have reacted differently, e.g., using the Ukrainian Army and volunteers in Crimea or getting involved in direct diplomatic negotiations with Russia. This could possibly have led to different outcomes for Ukraine, but these counterfactual assumptions would need to be evaluated in further research.

Scholars highlighted the importance of trust in cooperation between countries, and my empirical findings also confirmed that Ukrainian leaders' differential trust in their counterparts had an effect on the escalation/de-escalation of the conflict. Unjustified trust in the EU and Russia in February-March 2014 'blinded' Ukrainian decision-makers and they did not respond to Russian actions in Crimea, which led to the loss of the peninsula. The same misplaced trust is likely to have contributed to Ukraine's delayed response to pro-Russian insurgencies in March-April in Donbas. Russia's greater involvement in Ukraine and the fact that it lied about this, together with the EU's words of support but weak actual support (as perceived in Ukraine), destroyed the Ukrainian leaders' trust in most of the words and signals coming from the EU and Russia. This mistrust resulted in Ukrainian decision-makers relying on the country's resources and developing them, but also making an escalation move — starting anti-terrorist operation in Donbas in April and full counteroffensive in June. The trust in good intentions of both Russia (not to attack Ukraine) and the EU (to save Ukraine) was fully destroyed after Russia entered

Ukraine with its regular Army in August. This escalation reached such an extent that all sides agreed for peace negotiations. With regards to the game theoretic assumptions about possible failure in achieving common interests due to distrust, my respondents viewed peace in Donbas as a strong core common interest, which was not achieved mainly due to the erasure of trust between Ukraine and Russia. In respect of the Minsk Agreements, the respondents described actors misleading each other during the negotiations (e.g., Ukrainians and Russians each pretended to want peace, but imposed impossible requirements on one another) and in their expression of commitment to the agreements after signing them. Since the agreements were poorly designed, this commitment (trust in the agreements, but not in each other) resulted in a kind of deadlock in their implementation.

Therefore, in respect to my second sub-question regarding the role of trust in Ukrainian decision-makers' relations with the EU and Russia, *my evidence suggests diverse understandings of international laws and of each other's words, both purposefully and unintentionally misleading, which together decreased trust. Unreasonable trust in the EU's and Russia's actions in February-May 2014 decreased Ukraine's chances of reaching a more beneficial outcome in Crimea and Donbas. Thus, Ukrainian leaders switched from trust in the good intentions of the EU and Russia at the beginning of the conflict, to suspicion of the words and intentions of both of them at the end of 2014 – beginning of 2015.* My core empirical findings with regard to trust are presented in the table below. These shifts in trust also had an impact on Ukrainian leaders' understanding of all of the actors' payoffs.

Table 10: The role of trust in Ukrainian leaders' decision-making in relations with Russia and the EU in February 2014 – February 2015

Annexation of Crimea	Insurgency and war in Donbas	Peace Agreements
Trust in international law and agreements	Trust decreased following the escalation	Trust shifted to no or low trust

❖ International law
   ➤ Trust in legal power of Budapest Memorandum and friendship treaties with Russia
❖ Russia's bluffing and threats
   ➤ Confused and delayed actions of the EU and Ukraine
❖ EU as a peacekeeper in Europe
   ➤ Trust in the EU to 'save' Ukraine
 	
Impact: **High**
	❖ No trust in Russia's threats (March-May)
	❖ Decrease of trust between Ukrainian government and the population in Donbas
	❖ Russian hardware and personnel cross border – fighting breaks out
	   ➤ Decrease of trust towards Russia and the EU – Ukraine's fighting back in Donbas
	   ➤ Downing of MH17 (core critical juncture for the EU)
	❖ Russia's mistrust in the EU and Ukrainian interlocutors – hardship in reaching any compromise
	
	Impact: **Medium**
		❖ Peace agreements, but no peace
		   ➤ No trust in Russia's words
		   ➤ Further decrease of trust in the EU
		❖ Minsk Agreements – mutual bluffing and distrust between the sides, but everyone's acceptance – deadlock in implementation
		
		Impact: **Low**

The payoff structure

Due to the improvement in Ukrainian leaders' understanding of others' preferences, and the adjustment of trust in foreign interlocutors, their awareness about the payoffs structure was also developing. The total miscalculation in February-March 2014 changed into a better understanding of reality, even if this was still a blurred image, in the summer, and to a so-called 'eyes wide open' position after Minsk I. During the annexation of Crimea, policy-makers in Ukraine had diverse perceptions of Russia's possible payoffs: threatening Ukraine without annexation, actual annexation, or the start of an all-out war. However, Russia's 'real' preferred payoffs were: that all parties would respect the 21st February Agreement, that Russia would reassert regional control through the annexation of Crimea, and that there would be an increase in Putin's domestic support. The EU's preferred payoffs were considered by Ukrainians to be EU-Ukraine integration and the saving of Crimea from Russia (protection of the rule of law), while in reality the EU aimed to avoid a war in Ukraine and to foster economic cooperation with the country. When events were unfolding in Crimea, Ukrainian decision-makers concentrated on saving the country's territorial integrity. The consequent annexation of Crimea at the end of March was a shock for Ukrainian politicians (and for those in the EU). After the escalation of insurgencies in Donbas, the Crimean issue was moved into the background and Ukrainian leaders concentrated on saving Donbas. In spring-summer, Ukrainian policy-makers were able to comprehend Russia's payoff — the creation of Novorossiya out of half of Ukraine. However, Putin's fast tactical decision-making (grabbing an opportunity without having a grand plan) puzzled both Ukraine and the EU, and their policy-makers could not foresee a substantial part of Russia's actions. The EU's payoffs — of localising the war in Donbas and having economic cooperation with both Ukraine and Russia — were not understood by Ukrainians until the autumn. After Russian direct intervention in August, the payoffs structure for all parties experienced a huge shift, which was understood by Ukrainian policy-makers only after Minsk I.

The ability (or inability, as may have been the case) to understand the payoffs structure contributed to the capacity of Ukrainian leaders to make decisions in their relations with Russia and the EU. Without being able to anticipate Russia's and the EU's payoffs, Ukrainian leaders were 'stepping into the dark' both in the spring and summer of 2014. And after the signing of the Minsk Protocol, Ukrainian leaders' decision-making was influenced by their perception of payoffs the most. It was at this time that the payoffs for all three actors shifted substantially, and their image crystallised for Ukrainian decision-makers. Ukraine's perception of the Minsk Protocol is also interesting: whilst certain policy-makers viewed it as a way of gaining time so they could build a better economy and enable the Army to regain Donbas (which still had not happened by 2023, when this book was being written), others blamed decision-makers for a betrayal of national interests. Although with better knowledge about everyone's payoffs Ukrainian leaders could have fought more effectively for the country's interests, the Minsk Protocol did not leave them this option. After Minsk I, Ukrainian leaders started to comprehend that a frozen conflict as opposed to a 'hot' war was a second order payoff for both the EU and Russia, while it helped them to achieve their preferences to an acceptable degree (for Russia to control Ukraine and for the EU to stop this war). In this way, a frozen conflict with periodic small battles became the new equilibrium, which was hard to change. This clear understanding of payoffs and the equilibrium deescalated the war to a certain extent. In the course of time, Ukrainian leaders also started to call it 'a compromise for peace'. Thus, my analysis has confirmed that in order to achieve a country's preferred outcome, a decision-maker needs to understand all of the actors' payoffs, and that once a game reaches an equilibrium, which is satisfactory to the majority, it is hard to change it.

Table 11: The role of payoffs in Ukrainian leaders' decision-making in relations with Russia and the EU in February 2014 – February 2015

Annexation of Crimea	Insurgency and war in Donbas	Peace Agreements
'Eyes wide shut' - miscalculation of payoffs ❖ Flawed perceptions of Russia's payoffs ➤ Perceived: threat Ukraine, possibly annexation of Crimea or the start an all-out war ➤ Russia's 'true' payoffs ▪ 1st: respect for 21st February Agreement ▪ 2nd: reassertion of regional control through annexation of Crimea ▪ 3rd: increase Putin's domestic support ❖ Flawed perceptions of the EU payoffs ➤ Perceived: saving Crimea, integration with Ukraine ➤ The EU's 'true' payoffs ▪ 1st: avoiding an all-out war in Ukraine ▪ 2nd: economic cooperation (AA) ❖ Ukraine's perceived payoffs: integration with the EU, preservation of territory Impact: **Medium**	**Recalibration of perception of payoffs** ❖ Recalibration of perception of the payoffs structure post-annexation ➤ Crimean question overshadowed by Donbas ➤ Poor analysis of Kremlin tactical decision-making ➤ Understanding that Russia would not give up on Donbas ▪ Novorossiya plan put to test and paused (due to weak local support for Russia) ❖ Limited awareness of the EU's payoffs: to stop/localize the war ❖ Regaining Donbas up until end of August – change of payoffs after entrance of Russian military Impact: **Medium**	**'Eyes wide open' understanding and acceptance of payoffs** ❖ 'Eyes wide open' – a frozen conflict as opposed to a 'hot' war is a second order payoff for both the EU and Russia ❖ Little hope to regain Donbas disappeared after Minsk II – 'compromise for peace' Impact: **High** (acceptance of the new *status quo* after Minsk II)

To summarise my core findings regarding the role that an awareness of payoffs played in Ukrainian leaders' decision-making (my third sub-question), *my analysis clarified Ukrainian decision-makers' struggle in uncovering the payoffs' structure and also the Minsk deadlock, which could not be changed easily once everyone had committed to the Minsk Agreements. At the beginning of 2014, Ukrainian leaders viewed the EU's payoffs through the lens of Ukraine's payoff — 'to save Ukraine' — and could not grasp all three actors' payoffs until Minsk I. Misjudgement about the EU payoffs could be explained by Ukrainians' poor comprehension of the Union's foreign actorness. At the same time, it was hard to uncover Russia's payoffs due to Putin's tactical decision-making (grabbing opportunities without a grand plan). Moreover, Ukrainian leaders often concentrated on the country's goals (and/or their personal goals) without analysing the whole payoffs structure of the key participants.* The payoffs of all actors were affirmed by their readiness to use their resources to achieve these payoffs.

Resources

Lastly, we will look at how Kyiv-based leaders' understanding of everyone's resources (all their available means) evolved over the period under study and influenced their decision-making. My analysis has revealed that Ukrainian policy-makers lacked full knowledge of Ukraine's, Russia's and the EU's resources in February-March 2014, but by the summer, and in particular after Minsk I, they had a much-improved estimation of the resources. In February-March, Ukrainian leaders understood that Russia had larger resource provision, but did not grasp Russia's readiness to use these resources in Ukraine. They also misjudged the EU's willingness and ability to stop Russia from annexing Crimea. In addition, decision-makers in Kyiv did not have the political will (as stressed by several interviewees) to protect Crimea. In the summer of 2014, Ukraine strengthened its Army, received much help from volunteers (e.g., financial support to soldiers, creation of voluntary battalions), and the key decision-makers became more experienced in conflict management. In this way, the Ukrainian military was better prepared to fight with pro-Russian insurgents in Donbas. However, after Ukraine's military successes, Putin decided to invest even more resources in Ukraine and to use the Russian Regular Army in August 2014. Hence Russia started by misusing international law (in staging a referendum in Crimea); later, in the spring, it supported Donbas insurgents with consultancy and unmarked military groups; then, in August, it sent its Regular Army to Ukraine. The EU's use of resources in Ukraine also developed. It introduced different sanctions targeting Russia and provided Ukraine with more financial and diplomatic assistance. However, with no understanding of the EU's role as a foreign policy actor, Ukrainian policy makers expected more substantial help — direct military support, a Marshal plan for Ukraine and even tougher sanctions against Russia. Since even the presence of the Russian Army in Donbas did not convince the EU to stop economic relations with Russia and to support Ukraine militarily, Ukrainians finally had a better understanding of the EU after Minsk I. Respondents saw the Ilovaisk battle (at the end of August) as a 'cold shower' for Ukrainians, since it made them aware that Russia was ready to use almost any resources it had, and the EU was not ready to give Ukraine any more help.

My data analysis suggests that resources as an element in decision-making played the most crucial role in April-August 2014. It was during the spring and summer that the development of Ukraine's own resources, and the country's understanding of those of the EU and Russia, had the greatest influence on Ukrainian leaders' decisions and on the development of the conflict. During the spring protests in Donbas, the authorities in Kyiv were careful in their use of the country's resources, but they used the Ukrainian Army there in June, which respondents saw as a factor contributing to the increase of violence and the alienation of Donbas residents. This lack of attention on the part of Ukrainian decision-makers to residents of the East and, in particular, to the role of local elites in Donbas, and their failure to turn them into supporters of the Kyiv government, was crucial. For instance, the role of oligarch Rinat Akhmetov's original bargaining with Russia (and his lack of a pro-Ukrainian position) was seen as a core factor in the unfolding of this war (Int-22 2020; Int-27 2020; Int-36 2021). At the same time, Russia was continually investing more resources into Donbas, which culminated in the use of its Regular Army and the defeat of Ukraine after a close victory in August 2014. If Ukrainian decision-makers could have predicted that Russia would use its Army, and that the EU would not react to the deployment of Russian regular forces on the territory of Ukraine, then they could have used a different strategy in relation to the country's resources, e.g., through negotiations with insurgents and local elites, communication with Putin, etc.

Thus, Ukrainian decision-makers' awareness of everyone's resources was important in the escalation and de-escalation of the conflict. For instance, without proper knowledge about the resources of the others, Ukrainian decision-makers found it hard to make any decisions during the events in Crimea. Later, in June, with the development of Ukraine's resources and the EU's diplomatic support, Poroshenko decided to counterattack. However, such decisive action on the part of Ukrainian leaders may be explained by their lack of full awareness of Russia's readiness to invest its resources in Donbas and the EU's reluctance to provide more substantial support for Ukraine. This ended in the Ilovaisk battle and, as many have argued, resulted in disadvantageous Minsk I. Having better knowledge of everyone's resources and their ability to employ them in Ukraine after Minsk I, Ukrainian decision-makers were more careful in their actions.

On the other hand, a number of my respondents from different backgrounds mentioned that corruption on the part of the Ukrainian authorities (or even their betrayal of the country's national interests) enabled Russia to achieve its goals more easily. For instance, during the events in Crimea, a lack of political will on the part of Ukrainian decision-makers was considered one of the core reasons for Ukraine's failure to save Crimea. Some also argued that the larger war in Donbas could have been stopped in July or in the middle of August if Ukrainian core decision-makers had not surrendered to Russia (if a small group of Russian militaries led by Girkin had been prevented from entering Donetsk in July, and if intelligence reports about Russia's possible attack had been trusted in August). The recent leaks of Medvedchuk's phone calls also confirmed the substantial involvement of Poroshenko and those surrounding him in corrupt business with Russia (e.g., trade in coal, gas and electricity) (BIHUS info 2021b, 2021a, 2021c). While the increasing number of scholars argue about the necessity of analysing states' internal politics when we try to explain states' foreign actions (e.g., Bueno de Mesquita 2006 and Putnam 1988), corruption is an important aspect to look at. In countries where the ruling class is mired in corruption, this should be taken into account, while applying the game theory analytical framework, as a factor that diminishes these countries' resources.

Therefore, in respect to the role of the analysis of resources in Ukrainian leaders' decision-making (fourth sub-question), I can state that *the story of Ukrainian decision-makers' understanding of Ukraine's, Russia's and the EU's resources can be considered a bitter lesson, showing that Ukraine was 'left alone' against Russian aggression; this resulted in the move from an idealistic to a more realistic awareness of others' readiness to apply their resources in Ukraine. Hence a sense of Russia's ability 'to play a big game' in Ukraine in February-May 2014 changed to an accurate post-Minsk I awareness that Russia was ready to use almost any resources to achieve its preferences in Ukraine. However, an understanding of the EU's abilities and tools was always based largely on an idea of how the EU 'should' react to the war in Ukraine. The gap between hopes and reality did lead to Ukraine developing its own resources; however, corruption among senior decision-makers reduced these mediocre resources and Ukraine's capabilities.*

Table 12: The role of resources in Ukrainian leaders' decision-making in relations with Russia and the EU in February 2014 – February 2015

Annexation of Crimea	Insurgency and war in Donbas	Peace Agreements
Low awareness of resources ❖ Awareness of Ukraine's weaker position in Crimea ➢ In military resources ➢ Crimeans' support for Russia (triggered by possible cancellation of the language law and Russian propaganda) ❖ Lack of the new leaders' 'political will' to fight for Crimea ❖ Misjudgment of the EU's ability to constrain Russia ❖ Russia's advantage on time as a resource Impact: **Medium**	**Medium awareness of resources** ❖ Improvement of Ukraine's resources: ➢ The new President in May - improvement of foreign policy (counter attack in Donbas) ➢ Development of Ukrainian military (volunteers' help) ➢ Deterioration of Ukraine's capacity due to its elites' corruption ❖ Inattention to the role of Donbas elites and residents ❖ Improvement of awareness of Russia's readiness to use any resources ❖ Lack of full understanding of the EU's ability to use its resources Impact: **High**	**Good awareness of resources** ❖ Ilovaisk battle – 'cold shower' ➢ Russia ready for any use of resources ➢ the EU not ready to give more support ❖ Development of the EU's foreign policy, but still limited financial and diplomatic support Impact: **Low**

Broader implications

The role of the US in the armed conflict

There are a number of themes not addressed directly in this research, which can be developed in further studies. Perhaps the most crucial is the role of the USA in these events. Several respondents highlighted the US involvement in the war in Ukraine (Int-30 2021; Int-34 2021). As I explained in the introduction, I did not intend to downplay the US role, but aimed to provide a more nuanced discussion of the perceptions, decisions, and interactions of decision-makers from the three core actors in Europe. However, here I would like to highlight certain findings regarding the US. Firstly, my data suggest that policy-makers in Russia apparently perceived Ukraine and the EU to be dependent on the US and consequently saw the US as a core decision-maker in the armed conflict in Ukraine. In this way, Putin apparently preferred to discuss the situation in Ukraine with the US and viewed this war in terms of confrontation between the US and Russia (and he managed to convince his voters to agree with this view). Russia's perception of the US as the main decision-maker on Ukraine could possibly have hindered the prospect of finding a solution to the conflict by Ukraine, Russia, and the EU. There were also discussions amongst those in the EU and Ukraine about whether it would be better to have the US involved in the peace negotiations (Int-1 2020; Int-31 2021; Int-36 2021). Secondly, the US was introducing sanctions against Russia in tandem with the EU and was coordinating support for Ukraine together with the EU (Int-34 2021; Int-37 2021). Thirdly, in later periods (even before 2022), the US did provide Ukraine with more substantial help, such as sending Javelin portable anti-tank missiles. For this reason, help from the US was sometimes perceived in Ukraine to be greater than that of the EU (Int-31 2021). And thinking about 2022 Russian invasion of Ukraine, the US originally had intelligence about Russia's imminent attack and the US sent the most substantial military and financial help to Ukraine. Even though the role of the US seems large in 2022, the country was less of a player in 2014 and somehow let the EU to deal with the war in Ukraine. Yet the role of the US in the war in Ukraine is important and could be further explored. In particular, this research highlighted the need for further analysis of the US influence in Europe, EU-NATO interconnections and US-Russia relations.

The EU as a foreign policy actor

Another interesting theme is the EU's foreign actorness, which leads to diverse (mis)perceptions among its foreign interlocutors. Firstly, one of my findings was that Ukrainian decision-makers often viewed the EU's foreign policy as that of a single country (Int-20 2020; Int-30 2021). This was at odds with the EU's status as a partnership of different countries, which needs to achieve consensus for all major decisions and which consequently means slow and complicated decision-making. Secondly, contrary to the perceptions of certain Ukrainian policy-makers, the EU as an organisation could not support Ukraine militarily, nor offer it a membership perspective in 2014 – 2015, and it needed every member state's approval for the introduction of sanctions. However, the rapidly unfolding conflict required fast reactions and the EU's policy-makers were only able to express their concerns verbally, which led to disappointment in Ukraine. EU respondents also confirmed that the EU was not well-prepared to react to this armed conflict (Int-21 2020; Int-31 2021; Int-38 2021). On the other hand, European politicians tended to perceive Ukrainians' desire to come closer to the EU as a move towards building democratic institutions, transparency and the rule of law in Ukraine, but not of achieving EU-Ukraine political integration (Int-31 2021; Int-38 2021). However, the conflict in Ukraine did result in the EU developing its foreign policy mechanisms substantially. Many tools (like the creation of the Support Group for Ukraine at the European Commission, or unprecedented financial and consultancy help and extensive sanctions against Russia) were introduced for the first time in the EU's history (Int-2 2020; Int-12 2020; Int-37 2021).

The EU-Ukraine Association Agreement was also perceived differently in the EU and Russia. To the EU it was a development of economic relations between two independent entities; to Russia it constituted 'the abduction' of Ukraine from its traditional ties with Russia (Int-17 2020; Int-34 2021; Int-35 2021). In addition, my respondents also pointed to the inability of the EU to deal with countries that did not respect the signed agreements and international law (Int-27 2020; Int-33 2021; Int-36 2021). Comparing the approaches of the EU and Russia in Ukraine, a senior EU official stated: "The clash between external protection in the authoritarian system and the external protection of democratic market economies could not be stronger" (Int-35 2021). Additionally, a military expert pointed out that Russia took some of the EU's pronouncements (e.g., about the development of its foreign security tools) at 'face value' and felt threatened, while the EU's pronouncements often ran counter to reality (Int-30 2021). In 2022, the EU and its member-states were much faster than in 2014 in their reactions to the Russian aggression (will be explained in epilogue), but the EU's understanding of Russia and Putin was still limited. Clearly there is justification for further examination of the EU's foreign communication, the EU's perceived (both by domestic and foreign actors) and real foreign policy actorness both in the case of Ukraine and in other regions.

The role of Russia in Europe

Russia was one of the main actors in this war and was often the actor making 'the first move' in EU-Ukraine-Russia interactions. The armed conflict in Ukraine was seen as Russia's attempt to gain back the place it considered itself to deserve in the world. Thus, with scholars noting the impossibility of Russia being a regional power without control over Ukraine, Ukraine's desire to integrate with the EU instead of having a partnership with Russia could have been a valid reason for Russia's annexation of Crimea and support for pro-Russian insurgents in Donbas. Respondents confirmed that Russia could not accept losing influence over Ukraine (Int-35 2021; Int-36 2021; Int-37 2021). On the other hand, several interviewees mentioned that the EU's crucial economic business with Russia did not allow it to be tougher with Russia even after the latter's unlawful actions in Ukraine (Int-6 2020; Int-20 2020; Int-30 2021; Int-31 2021; Int-36 2021). This makes it clear that Russia was an important economic player in Europe, and this gave it more freedom of action, which was still very visible in 2022. In addition to fighting to maintain Russia's influence in the world, several respondents mentioned that Putin's desire to stay in power also inclined him to deliver 'successes' in foreign policy to Russians, instead of focussing on domestic developments (Int-17 2020; Int-26 2020; Int-29 2021; Int-31 2021). 2022 Putin's attack on Ukraine was claimed to be his last chance to get back Russia's control over Ukraine. Putin's ability to get support from ordinary Russians for such obvious international crime is remarkable. There was certainly underestimation of this in the West. Thus, Russia's foreign policy, its place in the world (especially in Europe) under Putin and Putin's authoritarian rule are scholarly interesting and relevant themes for further academic research.

Lessons for Ukraine's foreign policy

In my analysis of Ukrainian decision-makers' foreign moves, I found out that a degree of incompetence, an unwillingness to take responsibility, and corruption, all had an adverse effect on the achievement of a more beneficial outcome for the country and its people. According to a foreign journalist who worked in Ukraine for many years, Ukrainian decision-makers experienced "a lack of perspective, a lack of understanding of how geopolitics works", and so did not pay attention to the interests of other actors and consequently failed to achieve those of Ukraine (Int-15 2020). Another expert also mentioned a lack of professionalism and "a shortage of a common sense" amongst many Ukrainian decision-makers (Int-30 2021), whilst an EU senior official highlighted their naïve view that 'the world would change' if a new law was adopted in parliament (Int-33 2021). In addition, an advisor to a senior decision-maker in Ukraine noted that many officials at the central and regional levels were hiding or taking sick leave when the conflict was unfolding, in order to escape the decision-making (Int-7

2020). These issues likely led to a deterioration in Ukrainian decision-makers' capabilities in the country's foreign relations.

My analysis suggests different possible ways of action for Ukraine in this armed conflict in 2014-2015. For instance, with better understanding of their interlocutors, greater awareness of the EU's and Russia's preferences, payoffs and resources, and improved anticipation of trust, Ukrainian decision-makers could have avoided creating the optimal conditions for Russia to annex Crimea and to start the war in Donbas. On the one hand, consultations with Russia on the EU-Ukraine Association Agreement could have taken place in the early stages. This might have resulted in the feasibility of finding a win-win economic option for the EU, Ukraine, and Russia, as well as appeasing supporters of the maintenance of Ukraine-Russia ties inside Ukraine. On the other hand, it has to be acknowledged that the consultations that did take place with Russia on the Agreement before 2014 and then in 2015 confirmed that any close EU-Ukraine Agreement was unacceptable to Russia (Int-35 2021; Int-37 2021). Additionally, although Euromaidan used anti-Russian statements[79], the new leaders could have saved Crimea and Donbas through direct talks with Putin, residents and local elites in Crimea and Donbas, and applied themselves to the search for a compromise. The new Ukrainian decision-makers' discussions about the cancellation of the language law were seen as a mistake by many experts and this mistake both scared some residents of Donbas and Crimea and helped Russia to use this in its propaganda. It is also very important to highlight the fact that a number of EU, Ukrainian and Russian policy-makers pointed to the substantial influence of corruption amongst Ukrainian high officials concerning the country's possibility of reaching a more beneficial outcome in this war (Int-17 2020; Int-22 2020; Int-24 2020; Int-31 2021; Int-38 2021). The game theory-inspired analytical framework allowed me to reveal the decision-making process of Ukrainian leaders, and to highlight

---

79 According to an independent foreign journalist in Ukraine, "it was anti-governmental, anti-corruption protest, [but] it became anti-Russian protest after a while. That became a dominating narrative." (Int-15 2020).

certain issues within it. I would conclude that due to its geostrategic position, difficult past, and weak resources (military, economic and political), Ukraine cannot allow itself to break ties with some of its crucially important neighbours, nor trust too much that others will save it. Ukraine would be better off by developing its domestic strength and creating a more professional, wiser, and strategic foreign policy. In my further discussion in epilogue, I will show how Ukrainian leaders were able or not able to learn from past experiences and mistakes and how they dealt with the biggest challenge to Ukraine's statehood — Russian full-scale invasion in Ukraine, which started on 24th February 2022.

Epilogue: Russia's full-scale invasion in 2022

On 24th February 2022, Ukrainians in different cities around the country woke up to the sounds of bombing and air raid sirens. Something unbelievable was happening in the middle of Europe — it was the first time since the Second World War that one country decided to invade another one by marching its army towards a foreign capital and bombing civilian infrastructure in peaceful cities. Whilst these events are unprecedented and envisage the biggest change since the Minsk II Agreements, I decided to discuss them in the epilogue of this book, which has primarily concentrated on the first year of the Russian-Ukrainian war (February 2014 – February 2015). To support my analysis, I used media outlets, analytical pieces, official governmental communication, and decision-makers' interviews in the media. In what follows, I first describe events that preceded the invasion, then look at EU-Ukraine-Russia relations in this context and concentrate on foreign policy decision-making of Ukraine's current leadership.

From the previous discussion we already know how misperceptions in foreign policy can result in worse outcomes and conflicts. In accordance with Russia's worldview, both in 2014 and in 2022 it was the West with Ukraine that provoked Russia into its aggression against Ukraine. Indeed, before the expected signature of the EU-Ukraine Association Agreement in November 2013, Russia made it clear that closer EU-Ukraine ties were unacceptable. Russian trade wars against Ukraine and political pressure on Ukraine's President Viktor Yanukovych convinced him to freeze the preparations for the signature of the agreement. This decision angered a significant number of Ukrainians, who started the Euromaidan protests, that resulted in Yanukovych's removal and new pro-EU forces taking power in Kyiv. Russia refused to accept this (in particular the fact that Ukraine and the EU did not follow the 21st February agreement with Yanukovych) and Putin used the moment of instability in Ukraine, annexed Crimea and started the war in Donbas. Yet later in 2014, Ukraine did sign the Association Agreement with the EU. Thus, Russian aggression against

Ukraine did not stop Ukraine from developing relations with the EU.

Despite Russia's protest against EU-Ukraine integration, in Putin's Russia it was NATO that was always seen as far bigger threat than the EU. The current Russian leadership has claimed that NATO broke its promise of the 1990's not to expand after accepting Eastern Germany, though this promise is debatable (Wiegrefe 2022). The annexation of Crimea is also sometimes justified in Russia by the fear of NATO troops arriving at a strategically important peninsula, where the Russian Black Sea Fleet is based. During seven years of Russian occupation of Crimea and the war in Donbas, there was no substantial change in Ukraine-NATO relations. Yet, in 2021, Putin asked for new security arrangements in Europe and the guarantee that Ukraine would not join NATO. Complicated discussions between NATO members and Russia did not come to any acceptable solution. The NATO threat was used again by Russia as a pretext for starting a full-scale invasion against Ukraine in 2022. Russia would prefer Ukraine either to align with Russia or to stay neutral.

Let us briefly recall the history of Ukraine's 'neutrality'. In 1993, Ukraine's Military Doctrine proclaimed the country's non-aligned and non-nuclear statuses (Verkhovna Rada of Ukraine 1993), which meant refusal of Ukraine's joining any military blocks of states. However, Ukraine's 2004 Military Doctrine did not mention the country's desire to be non-aligned, and stated Ukraine's aim to deepen cooperation with the EU and NATO (President of Ukraine 2004). The next year, in his Presidential Decree, Yushchenko named entering NATO to be Ukraine's final goal (President of Ukraine 2005). This was changed again, when in President Yanukovych's 2012 Decree, NATO and EU aspirations were avoided and non-aligned status was included (President of Ukraine 2012). It is worth noting, that after Russia started the war against Ukraine in 2014, Ukrainians' support for NATO membership increased from 18% to 47.8% (Ukrainians' attitude to NATO membership). In the beginning of 2019, as an attempt to show some achievements in Ukraine's foreign policy before the elections, President Poroshenko proposed a Constitutional change which was subsequently incorporated after a vote in Parliament. The Constitution of Ukraine (which proclaimed Ukraine's non-aligned status) was accordingly amended so that it proclaimed Ukraine's membership in both the EU and NATO to be a strategic course of the country (Verkhovna Rada of Ukraine 2019). Since then, any public figure's words about Ukraine's neutrality were going against the country's constitution and thus subject to criticism.

Yet Poroshenko's change of Ukraine's constitution did not sustain him re-election. In spring 2019, a former comedy actor Volodymyr Zelensky won 75% of Ukrainians' votes (being the majority winner in almost every electoral area in contrast to East/West voting divides in previous elections) and became the next President. His victory could be explained by Ukrainian society's fatigue from old, corrupted elites and trust in Zelensky's promises both to end corruption and the war in Donbas. Just a few months later, the Normandy meeting brought Zelensky, Putin, Merkel, and Macron together at the negotiating table. Although supporters of the former president of Ukraine, Poroshenko, protested in Kyiv against Zelensky's 'capitulation', the meeting seemed to be a step forward in moving the Minsk Agreements from stalemate (at least an exchange of prisoners was agreed) (Higgins 2019). Thus, in those first months of his presidency, Zelensky tried to balance between not giving up Ukraine's sovereignty and keeping his promise to end the war in Donbas.

Ukraine-Russia relations started to deteriorate in March 2021, when Russia gathered an enormous amount of its troops near Ukraine's borders. This happened again in November 2021, and it was then when the US warned of a likely Russian invasion of Ukraine. In December 2021, the USA shared its intelligence about 175,000 Russian troops near Ukraine's border and the possible invasion in the beginning of the following year (Russia planning massive military offensive 2021). After Ukrainian leaders refused to believe in such a possibility, the USA shared certain parts of its intelligence with the public and named Russia's attack on Ukraine to be imminent (US intel predicted Russia's invasion plans 2022). In months and weeks leading to the catastrophe, Russia was open and persistent in its demands: guarantees that Ukraine would not enter NATO and limitations to NATO's presence in its Eastern European members (Roth 2021). However, up until 24th February, Russia denied that it would attack Ukraine (also in its media, e.g., Russia Today) and Russian officials lied to their Western counterparts about this (Harris et al. 2022; Kiely 2022). Apparently Western politicians, including Biden, told Putin that it was not likely that Ukraine would join NATO any time soon (Harris et al. 2022). However, neither could the Ukrainian President confirm that Ukraine would set aside its NATO aspirations, nor could NATO leaders close the door to Ukraine. Moreover, a few days before the invasion, speaking at Munich Security Conference, Zelensky suggested that Ukraine could obtain nuclear weapon once again (it gave up the third biggest nuclear arsenal in the world in 1994 in exchange for the US, UK and Russia's guarantees of Ukraine's sovereignty) (Independent 2022). Instead of satisfying Russia's demands, Zelensky got involved in diplomacy with Western countries and weeks before the invasion, Kyiv became one of the most visited capitals for foreign heads of states and ministers. It was during these few weeks before the invasion that Ukraine received tangible military support in the form of defensive equipment from several NATO member-states, e.g., US, Canada (Ministry of Defence of Ukraine 2022), UK (Mills 2022) and the Netherlands (Dutch agree to send sniper rifles to Ukraine 2022). The situation was developing dangerously.

On 21st February 2022, Russia recognised Donetsk and Luhansk People's Republics and openly entered them with Russia's Military Forces (Putin orders troops into eastern Ukraine 2022). On 22nd February 2022, Putin called the Minsk Agreements invalid and Russian Parliament allowed him to use Russian Military Forces in Ukraine (The Federation Council allowed Putin to use the Russian army abroad 2022). Russia started its full-scale invasion of Ukraine in the early morning of 24th February 2022. Below, I turn back to my game-theory inspired analytical framework and look at Ukraine's decision-making in relations with the EU and Russia during Russia's invasion of Ukraine in 2022.

Information: The same underestimation of Russia's commitment to fight

After eight years of war, the preferences of core actors did not experience major shifts. The EU still aimed at having stability in Ukraine and economic cooperation with its neighbours, including Russia. Russia wanted to get back its control over Ukraine. Ukraine preferred both to develop its integration with the West and to restore its territorial integrity. Although sensing everyone's preferences better than in 2014, Ukrainian decision-makers failed to prepare the country for the Russian invasion in 2022. Further, I will explain these preferences and the understanding about them by Ukrainian decision-makers.

The year of 2022 showed Putin's Russia follow its commitment to get back control over Ukraine. According to the CIA director (a former US ambassador to Russia), Putin was "fixated on Ukraine and control over the country was synonymous with Putin's concept of Russian identity and authority" (Harris et al. 2022). Putin explained his ideas clearly in his July 2021 essay (President of Russia 2021). Misinterpreting history, he claimed Ukrainians and Russians to be one nation and through the whole essay one could feel his grief over Ukraine's independence, since the country 'was supposed' to be part of Russia and to become Russia's borderland (President of Russia 2021). Although this essay together with Putin's speeches and actions displayed Russia's preferences clearly, Ukrainian leaders still could not take the threat of Russia's full-scale invasion of Ukraine seriously. Both Ukrainian and EU top officials did not comprehend Russia's commitment to follow its preference (the same happened in 2014) and rejected the US intelligence about the imminence of Russia's attack on Ukraine (Harris et al. 2022). On the other hand, Putin's personal preference — to stay in power — was also unchanged. Similarly to the annexation of Crimea, Putin's attack on Ukraine in 2022 increased his approval rating at home. Starting from November 2021 to March 2022 Putin's approval rating grew from 63% to 83%, and it fell to 77% only after the partial mobilisation in September (Levada Center 2022). Thus, we can observe that Putin's calculations were right once again — his attack on Ukraine increased his support in Russia and so far, he was able to achieve his core preference. Putin's strategy of following his own goal by convincing Russians (via the state propaganda machine) that he was satisfying their preference for "superpower Russia 'returning' Ukraine" was not considered well enough by Ukrainian decision-makers both in 2014 and 2022.

Let us now study Ukraine's own preferences. Months before the Russian invasion, Ukraine did not give up its NATO-facing perspective and was 'moving' closer to the EU. Such a Ukrainian foreign policy was unacceptable for Putin's Russia. The 'threat' of Ukraine joining NATO was used by Putin as one of his justifications for the start of the invasion in 2022. After Russia attacked Ukraine in February 2022, Zelensky submitted an official application for EU membership (Haltiwanger and Musumeci 2022). And in a few months the EU responded. In June 2022, Ukraine became a candidate for EU membership — something fought for by Ukrainian leaders for almost 30 years (Polityuk and Hnidyi 2022). Although this would not immediately make Ukraine an EU member and, for instance, Turkey or Bosnia and Herzegovina have had to wait in the queue for years, an EU candidate country status is a substantial symbolic step for Ukraine. In autumn the same year, Zelensky also submitted an application for NATO membership (Kramer and Bilefsky 2022), which, however, did not result in any status for Ukraine. As for Ukraine's internal preference, it stayed the same — the restoration of its borders of 1991. Victories of Ukrainian Armed forces in summer and autumn 2022 gave hope that this preference would be realised (which will be further explained during the discussion of payoffs). The reader may remember how I explained that keeping certain cooperation with Russia was still important for Ukraine even after the start of the war in Donbas in 2014. On the day of Russia's invasion of Ukraine in 2022, Ukraine finally broke diplomatic relations with Russia (Zelensky 2022). Yet there are allegations that some of Zelensky's close allies act in Russia's interests (Skorkin 2022, Spartz 2022). With not enough data to prove or reject this, we should keep in mind how the private interests of core Ukrainian decision-makers has been always influencing the direction of the country.

Turning to the EU, its preferences for stability and economic cooperation with its neighbours also persisted. Yet the EU did act somehow different to 2014. When the situation was deteriorating at the end of 2021 – beginning of 2022, EU leaders tried to prevent the escalation. When Russia's full-scale invasion started, the EU's response was much stronger than in 2014 (as will be explained below). Yet the EU's strong support for Ukraine was always an outcome of complicated internal discussions. A few member-states were unwilling to provide Ukraine with weaponry and to introduce harder sanctions against Russia (e.g., Hungary); some member-states received certain exemptions from anti-Russian sanctions (e.g., the trade in diamonds in Belgium). We still see how strong the EU preference for economic cooperation with Russia is. In the same way as Poroshenko's diplomacy was somehow successful in convincing the EU to provide stronger support for Ukraine, Zelensky's famous speeches at foreign parliaments also helped to achieve more support for Ukraine. In 2022, Ukrainian leaders seemed to understand better the EU's ties with Russia and tried to break them. What would be the next level, however, would be to offer the EU alternatives to cooperation with Russia. These could be found either in closer relations with Ukraine or with other countries. By offering the EU beneficial economic deals that it could substitute for cooperation with Russia, Ukraine could satisfy the EU's preference, at the same time following its own — to break EU-Russia ties.

Trust: Disbelief in Russia's brutality

After eight years of war with Russia, ordinary Ukrainians and Ukrainian policy-makers had learned that in most cases Russia cannot be trusted, and its actions are hard to predict. Ukrainians were aware that they could expect anything from their eastern neighbour. However, the possibility of a full-scale invasion with bombing of peaceful cities and the ruthless murder of thousands of civilians still was out of people's minds. Below, I will look at the role that trust in the EU's and Russia's strategies played in Ukrainian leaders' decision-making in 2022.

First, it is important to highlight that the Ukrainian leadership seemed not to believe in Russia's aggressive plans similarly as they did not believe in them in 2014. If Ukrainian leaders trusted in the possibility of such a relentless Russian war against Ukraine, they could have prepared the country better. Instead, Zelensky was trying to calm the population down and was rejecting Western intelligence about Russia's plans to invade Ukraine. When the invasion started, cities were bombed, and people were not evacuated in time, Zelensky and his team became a target of criticism. For instance, General Serhii Kryvonos mentioned concrete examples of how the Ukrainian leadership could have been more prepared for the war (Interview with General Serhii Kryvonos 2022). However, in his big interview to Washington Post, Zelensky said that he did not want people rapidly fleeing Ukraine in large numbers and the country's economy collapsing and that is why he did not warn Ukrainians beforehand (Khurshudyan 2022). It is hard to estimate if Zelensky and his team did not believe that the Russian full-scale invasion was imminent, or if the show of this distrust publicly was their actual tactic of ruling the country.

When the invasion started, there was the total destruction of trust in Russia both in Ukraine and in many countries around the world. Yet there was no expectation of the war crimes that Russians were willing to commit in Ukraine. Terrifying images of raped, tortured and killed civilians, mass graves in the de-occupied cities of Bucha, Irpin or Izium; the bombing of trade centres and a maternity hospital — all shocked Ukrainians and the world. Even with trust in Russia fully destroyed, it is hard to believe that humans could do such things. After Russia's fake referendums in occupied Donetsk, Luhansk, Kherson, and Zaporizhzhia regions of Ukraine and inclusion of them together with Donetsk and Luhansk regions into Russia, President Putin said he would respond to attacks on Russian territory with all means necessary. This led to numerous discussions about the possibility of Russia using tactical nuclear weapons in Ukraine. Does the Ukrainian leadership believe Putin's nuclear threats? Again, the

US takes these threats seriously and its leaders apparently warned Putin of destructive consequences for Russia (US would destroy Russia's troops 2022). Since Ukraine continues its counter-offensive in the South and Zelensky officially rejected any future negotiations with Putin (Zelensky rules out negotiations with Putin 2022), the Ukrainian leadership seems not to trust in the possibility of nuclear attack or it does not see this as a disaster. The situation is reminiscent of a game of chicken: Ukraine started a counter-offensive in the South, Russia formally annexed the occupied territory and threatened to respond with nuclear weapons, which does not stop Ukraine from liberating further territories from Russian occupation. Now, it is either side surrender, or a bigger catastrophe unfolds.

Payoffs: Destroyed *status quo*

Now switching to payoffs, I have also discovered certain similarities with the events of 2014-2015. Both in 2014 and in 2022 we can see the quick change of Russia's payoffs. Putin's goal to get Kyiv in three days changed to concentration on Donbas, which transformed into the tactic of conducting referendums and formal annexation of the occupied regions in the South and East of Ukraine. Ukraine was trying to adapt to Russia's changing tactics and, in some cases, succeeded. In turn, similarly to 2014, the EU's payoffs in 2022 were hard to define (due to diverse interests within the Union and comparatively slow decision-making process). However, in contrast to 2014, the EU's goals in 2022 were much more in line with Ukraine's, and Ukrainian leaders could understand them better. Let us look at these peculiarities in payoffs structure in more detail.

Were Ukrainian leaders able to predict the Russia's payoff of starting a full-scale invasion of Ukraine? Probably not. Months before the war, the US intelligence had clear signs that Putin was planning to conquer almost the whole of Ukraine the following winter (Harris et al. 2022). Specialists on Russia and Putin argued that it was the last chance for aging Putin to try to achieve his preference—to get Ukraine back under Russia's control—due to the US unwillingness to get involved in new wars after withdrawal from Afghanistan, Europe being weakened by the pandemic, Brexit and the new chancellor in Germany (Harris et al. 2022). Apparently these clear details from the US intelligence were provided to Zelensky in November 2021, but he did not take them seriously (Harris et al. 2022). Thus, this Russia's goal was most likely missed by Ukrainian leaders.

In my above discussion, I argued how Minsk II Agreements resulted in equilibrium and everyone's acceptance of each other's payoffs. In February 2022, Russia broke this *status quo* and attacked Ukraine. Ukraine's most urgent goal was to protect its territory in the most effective way possible. Interestingly, by the end of summer, after some victories of the Ukrainian Armed Forces, Ukrainian leaders saw once again the payoff of 2014 — a full restoration of Ukraine's territorial integrity. Zelensky named full de-occupation of Ukraine as the final goal for the country. There were even a number of Ukrainian Army attacks on Crimea in August, which Commander-in-Chief of the Armed Forces of Ukraine admitted to (Zaluzhnyi and Zabrodskyi 2022). Therefore, the goal of liberating Crimea was back on the table (after it waned in spring-summer 2014). The changed *status quo* offered both challenges and opportunities for Ukraine.

Since the EU's equilibrium position — stability in Ukraine — was destroyed, the EU aimed to restore peace in Ukraine. Through hard discussions between all 27 members, trying to follow both its preferences — for stability near its borders and economic cooperation with both Ukraine and Russia, the EU was developing measures to restrain Russia and to support Ukraine. Since Russia's actions in 2022 were so much more dangerous for peace and stability in Europe, the EU's preference for cooperation with Russia declined (at least for majority of EU member-states). This change of the EU's tactics met with the approval of Ukrainian leaders.

Resources: International anti-Russian coalition

Compared to the start of the war in 2014, there was a substantial change of all actors' resources and Ukrainian policy-makers' better awareness about this during the Russian invasion in 2022. Since Russia used almost all its military power and started a full-scale invasion of Ukraine, the EU and Ukraine had to give an appropriate answer. The whole Ukrainian nation mobilised against Russian aggression and the EU provided Ukraine with more substantial support. Let us look at everyone's resources in more detail.

Western countries provided Ukraine with far greater support in 2022 than they did in 2014. Already before the Russian invasion, the West began to strengthen Ukraine. After the publication of Putin's essay in July 2021, the US decided to send defence weaponry amounting to $60 million to Ukraine, which was increased to $200 million in December 2021 (Harris et al. 2022). In addition, after years of training by Western allies, Ukrainian military was in far better condition than it was in 2014 (Harris et al. 2022). When Russia's invasion started on 24th February, the EU and its member-states individually responded much stronger than in 2014-2015. For instance, in May 2022 the EU decided to ban 90% of Russian oil import until the end of 2022, but did not touch import of its gas, which was predicted to give Russia $80 billion in 2022 (EU sanctions includes a ban on 90% of Russian oil 2022). On 6th April, the US Congress accepted the law on Ukraine's land-lease (Congress 2022). On 26th April, the first Rammstein meeting of heads of defense departments and chiefs of staff of more than 40 countries was held in Germany to coordinate armed aid to Ukraine (Brzozowski 2022). During the meeting in July, British and American officials, apart from material help, provided Ukrainian leaders with consultancy regarding the development of military strategy to confront Russia and to liberate Ukraine's territories (Yaffa 2022). However, the higher prices for energy made the EU's payments for oil and gas to Russia even bigger, which dissatisfied Ukrainians in 2022. A year since the start of Russia's full-scale invasion of Ukraine, the EU adopted its tenth package of sanctions against Russia (European Commission 2023). Sending Western Leopard tanks to Ukraine in February 2023 marked a crucial turning point in support for Ukraine (Rankin and Borger 2023). The possibility of sending Western fighter jets to Ukraine is ever increasing (Garver 2023). Despite discussions, Russian oligarchs' assets were not confiscated in the West, and it is doubtful that they will be confiscated, since this is legally hard to do in a democracy. Although requested by Ukrainians, NATO did not close Ukrainian sky to protect civilians from Russian missiles. Thus, despite decisive and growing Western help for Ukraine, there are still more options for the West to stop Russia.

Let us now look at the usage of Ukraine's resources. According to President Zelensky, Ukraine could not prepare better for the invasion (despite knowing about this possibility months in advance), because the country did not have the needed weaponry (Harris et al. 2022). Zelensky's security advisor also mentioned that they were somehow preparing, but did not reveal everything to the public, so as to avoid panic (Yaffa 2022). Moreover, the commander-in-Chief of the Ukrainian Armed Forces, Valery Zaluzhnyi allegedly did not share his plans on Ukraine's defence either with US officials or even with Zelensky (Yaffa 2022). According to New Yorker, Zaluzhnyi's idea was to prevent the capture of Kyiv at all costs, and in other areas to allow Russian troops to run ahead of their logistics and supply lines, to cede part of the territory of Ukraine for a while in order to further destroy the parts of the Russian Armed Forces that were widely scattered along the front line (Yaffa 2022). Apparently he did not want to share his preparations with the President, fearing an order to stop the preparation (Yaffa 2022). This shows certain disagreements within Ukrainian higher officials and limited preparation for possible Russian aggression.

Yet there is certain critique of the above-mentioned approach of Ukrainian leaders. According to Ukrainian General Serhyi Kryvonos, there were many ways in which the country could have prepared for the war, for instance, by making strongholds (one could be created in seven days by a rota of soldiers and would have been effective in stopping Russians), producing more ammunition at the plant "Artem", missiles at the plan "Luch" and not taking 50 billion UAN from the country's military budget (Interview with General Serhii Kryvonos 2022). If such actions were taken when information reached Ukrainian decision-makers in

November 2021, this possibly would have saved many lives (Interview with General Serhii Kryvonos 2022). However, Zelensky was afraid that Ukrainians would panic, leave the country and withdraw money from banks (Harris et al. 2022). Thus, both in 2014 and in 2022 Ukraine did not use its resources in full. The influence of good/bad decisions of Ukrainian leaders on Ukraine's capabilities to protect itself from Russia in 2022 could become a valuable theme for future academic research. At the moment of this book going to press in March 2023, it is not yet clear how this Russian-Ukrainian war will end.

Through this book, we have seen how misperceptions in foreign policies may bring worse outcomes for all participants. We have also discovered that Ukraine, although being in a weaker position than the EU and Russia, was able to influence international relations. Unfortunately, this influence was not only a positive one due to certain unprofessionalism and corruption of Ukrainian decision-makers. However, the possibility of such a country like Ukraine to impact its foreign relations rejects realist arguments about the world of power. This gives hope to each country, and in our case Ukraine, that building strategic foreign policy, creating a functional democracy, and fighting corruption at home will result in more beneficial outcomes in foreign policy. The game theory-inspired analytical framework that I have developed in this book has served as a magnifying glass that helps us to clearly see the decision-making process of EU, Russian and in particular Ukrainian leaders. The framework has not only revealed and explained the facts, but also revealed the misperceptions that leaders experience and the mistakes they make in their foreign policy steps during war time. My approach to foreign policy analysis offers a comprehensive and understandable tool to uncover historical events in international relations and to check national leaders' rationality in dealing with these events. It also hints at ways to improve the foreign policy decision-making of one's country. I hope that this book provided readers with relevant facts and analysis of EU-Ukraine-Russia relations and Ukraine's foreign policy. I hope that knowledge that you gained and your reflections will help in research and political activities aimed at building secure, prosperous, and united Europe with Ukraine being an equal part of it.

Annex 1. Interview guide

Now let's begin our interview. I am beginning to record — should you want me to stop the recording at any time, please do let me know.

1) Details about the respondent
   a. IF NOT ANONYMOUS: Can you please state your, your position, and affiliation for the record?
   b. IF ANONYMOUS: Can you please state your position, and affiliation as you would like me to report, when I quote you anonymously?
2) SKIP ONLY IF THE PERSON IS PRESSED FOR TIME (Do not ask if the person is famous as the question may offend him/her): In one or two sentences, could you please very briefly describe your role/involvement in Ukrainian/EU/Russian politics/policy making during the first year of the conflict in Ukraine?
   a. POTENTIALLY ASK: Is there anything else you think I should know about your past experience?

I. INFORMATION

Thank you that is really interesting. Now let us talk about how policy decisions are made...

3) In your opinion, what are important types of information for policy-makers when making crucial decisions in relation to international politics/policy?
   ONLY ASK THE BELOW AS PROMPTS IF YOU DECIDED IT IS USEFUL & NOT TIME CONSUMING:
   a. official documents,
   b. public statements of core policy-makers,
   c. communication with their embassies,
   d. communication with interlocutors,
   e. intelligence reports.
4) And now thinking back to the first year of the conflict in Ukraine (in Ukrainian version use "Ukrainian-Russian war" and not "the conflict in Ukraine" if it is noticed that interviewees are very sensitive to this wording), were these sources that you just listed, present and available to you (to Ukrainian policy-makers) when making decisions?
   a. IF NO, what was not available?

b. IF YES, in your opinion—and please reflect on your specific role — what was the most important source for your work/taking decisions?
5) Based on these sources of information, were you able to identify Ukraine's/Russia's/EU's preferences [ask every interviewee about everyone's preferences] for outcomes? (What did you think Ukraine/Russia/EU preferred (liked) most to happen?)
   a. IF YES: What were these (follow up with …and for the short term /…and for the long term)?
   b. POTENTIAL FOLLOW UP: Were you also taking into account the personal preferences (not those of their countries) of individual policy-makers?
   c. POTENTIAL PROMPS:
      i. staying in power
      ii. self-enrichment?
   SKIP IF THE PERSON IS PRESSED FOR TIME: When making your decisions about relations with EU/Ukraine/Russia [adjust as appropriate], were you taking into account its internal political situation?
   a. POTENTIAL PROMPS:
      i. political changes (elections, public dissatisfaction)
      ii. internal issues (like enlargement fatigue in EU)
6) Was there any information that revealed itself in later stages of the conflict that was not available to you when making initial decisions?
   a. IF YES, POTENTIAL FOLLOW UP: How would it have altered your decision making?

II. TRUST

Thank you. Now, let's switch gears and talk a little bit about the role of trust in the conflict in Ukraine [as above, use where appropriate "Ukrainian-Russian war"].

7) Thinking back to the first year of the conflict (February 2014 – February 2015), how would you describe the level of trust towards the EU/Russia/Ukraine (and here I mean how much could you trust that they would do what they said they would or trust in the predictability of their actions)?
   a. POTENTIAL FOLLOW UP: Did this assessment change over time?
   b. Was there any particular interlocutor on the EU/Russian/Ukrainian side that you could turn to?

ANNEX 1

      i. IF YES, POTENTIAL FOLLOW UP: Who were they?
      ii. IF YES, POTENTIAL FOLLOW UP: How long did you know them previously?
      iii. IF YES, POTENTIAL FOLLOW UP: Did you feel you could trust them, or did you have your hesitations?

8) Did you ever suspect that your EU/Russian/Ukrainian interlocutors were purposefully trying to mislead you?
    a. IF YES, POTENTIAL FOLLOW UP: Can you tell me more about this?
    b. POTENTIAL FOLLOW UP: And what about not being able to trust certain individuals, sources, institutions?
    c. IF YES, POTENTIAL FOLLOW UP: How did you know that these could not be trusted?
    d. IF YES, POTENTIAL FOLLOW UP: Did some turn out to be in hindsight trustworthy?
9) Thinking of it now, do you see any common interests, which were not reached due to mutual mistrust in EU-Ukraine-Russia relations?

III. PAYOFFS

And now let's talk about the goals of the key protagonists in the conflict.

10) If you can recall, as the conflict was beginning (February-March 2014), what were different possible outcomes/payoffs (development of events) for EU, Ukraine and Russia? (Here I mean … in different scenarios what Ukraine, Russia, EU would get out of this?)
11) How did you and your colleagues at institution/organization/ministry X understand the preferred outcome for Ukraine? (What did Ukraine want/hoped to get out of this particular incident/phase?)
    a. POTENTIAL FOLLOW UP: Did your assessment of what was the preferred outcome for Ukraine change as the conflict unfolded?
    b. IF YES, POTENTIAL FOLLOW UP: Can you remember key events when your thinking/assessment changed during the first year of the conflict?
12) In your opinion, did Ukraine's preferred outcome contradict or coincide with the aims of other actors (EU and Russia) during the first year?
    a. Did your assessment of what was the preferred outcome for the EU and/or Russia change as the first year of the conflict in Ukraine unfolded?

b. IF YES, POTENTIAL FOLLOW UP: Can you remember the key events leading to this change?
   c. POTENTIAL FOLLOW UP ONLY IF NOT PRESSED FOR TIME: Do you think your interlocutors in Ukraine/Russia/EU also recognized this? Please explain how you know this [or] how you came to know this?
13) And now, thinking back to the initial months of the conflict [March - May 2014], how did you and your colleagues understand the most likely outcome in the conflict?
   a. And how about midway through summer 2014, did your assessment of the most likely outcome change?
      i. POTENTIAL FOLLOW UP: How so? Why? Why not?
   b. And how about at the end of 2014 and leading up to Minsk II, did your assessment of the most likely outcome change?
      i. POTENTIAL FOLLOW UP: How so? Why? Why not?

IV. RESOURCES

Now, let's speak about the tools at your disposal to meet your objectives.

14) In your opinion, what are the most important factors (resources) that shaped the outcome/development of the conflict for all participants (EU, Ukraine, Russia) involved?
   ONLY ASK THE BELOW AS PROMPTS IF YOU DECIDED IT IS USEFUL & NOT TIME CONSUMING
   a. political power
      i. such as: influence over other countries, membership in integration organisations and their bodies (EU, NATO, UN Security Council, CIS)
   b. economic power
      i. such as: GDP, export/import diversification, possession of natural (energy resources) and human resources (educated professionals)
   c. military power
      i. such as: the strength of Army (in numbers, expertise and technological advancement), possession of nuclear weapons
15) Thinking back to the first year of the conflict only, in your opinion, and to the best of your knowledge, did Ukraine/Russia/EU possess some of these resources and not others? Please explain which ones.

a. How about the resources of the other parties—did you take into account which resources were available to the EU/Russian/Ukraine [as appropriate] when you were making strategic decisions in relation to the conflict?
b. Do you think other Ukrainian/Russian/EU [adjust as appropriate] policy-makers took into account which resources were available to each party when making their decisions in regard to the conflict?
16) ASK ONLY IF NOT ALREADY ANSWERED ABOVE IN SOME WAY AND IF THERE IS TIME: From your perspective, do you believe that Ukrainian policy makers understood the extent to which Russia was ready to employ the resources we already mentioned to reach their aims?
a. How about the extent to which the EU was ready/or not ready to employ the resources we already mentioned to reach their aims?
17) ASK ONLY IF NOT ALREADY ANSWERED ABOVE IN SOME WAY AND IF THERE IS TIME: Thinking back to the first year of the conflict **only**, do you think that the resources available to different actors changed as the conflict unfolded?
18) ONLY ASK IF THERE IS TIME TO SPARE: At any point in time throughout the first year of conflict, did you feel your interlocutors in Ukraine/Russian/The EU [adjust as appropriate] sought to reveal or conceal resources in order to change or strengthen their bargaining powers?
19) Is there anything that I missed that you think is important for me to know?
a. IF YES: what is it?

Annex 2. Changes in Ukrainian leaders' decision-making in relations with Russia and the EU in Feb 2014 - Feb 2015

	Annexation of Crimea (22nd Feb - 25th March 2014)	Insurgency and war in Donbas (26th March - 4th Sept 2014)	Peace Agreements (5th Sept 2014 - 12th Feb 2015)
Information	**Weak institutional/state informational environment**	**Minimal improvement of institutional informational capacity**	**Improvement of institutional informational capacity / new communication channels**
	❖ Post-Euromaidan change in power structures ➢ Crimea power vacuum (confusion about the legality of the new power in Kyiv) ➢ Broken information channels, specifically at the informal level ➢ Flawed procession of information ❖ Russian intelligence structures ➢ Russian intelligence/security infiltration in all state institutions ➢ Russian disinformation in Crimea ❖ Weak understanding of preferences ➢ the EU's ones: no wars + economic cooperation with neighbours ➢ Russia's ones: Putin's preference to stay in power + control of Ukraine Impact on decision-making: **High**	❖ Poor analysis of the available information ➢ Underestimation of separatist tendencies in Donbas (since 2004 + reactivation during Euromaidan) ➢ Power vacuum in Donbas + missed preferences of local elites ➢ Inability to decode Putin's preferences, but understanding of Russia's geo-strategic goals ➢ Incomplete awareness of the EU's preferences (no wars and economic importance of Russia for the EU) ❖ Improved information background ➢ New President, but rapid change of decision-makers and information transfer ➢ Imposing ban on Russian State TV Impact on decision-making: **Medium**	❖ Personal experience of policy makers through interaction ❖ Better understanding of the EU's preference (cooperation, but no membership + business with Russia) ❖ Improved understanding of Russia's commitment to prevent Ukraine's integration into the EU and NATO Impact on decision-making: **Medium**

Ukraine Vis-à-Vis Russia and the EU

	Position of trust based on internal law and agreements	Trust position updating following escalation of conflict	Trust position shifted to no or low trust
Trust	❖ International laws ➤ Trust in legal power of Budapest Memorandum and friendship treaties with Russia ❖ Russia's bluffing and threats ➤ Consequent confused and delayed actions of the EU and Ukraine ❖ EU discourse of peace in Europe ➤ Trust in the EU to preserve Ukraine's territorial integrity Impact on decision-making: **High**	❖ Distrust in Russia's threats (March-May) ❖ Decrease of trust between Ukrainian government and the local population in Donbas ❖ Russian hardware and personnel cross boarder/fighting breaks out ➤ Decrease of trust towards Russia and the EU – Ukraine's fighting back in Donbas ➤ Downing MH17 (core critical juncture for the EU) ❖ Russia's mistrust in the EU and Ukrainian interlocutors – hardship in reaching any compromise Impact on decision-making: **Medium**	❖ Peace agreements, but no peace ➤ No trust in Russia's words ➤ Further decrease of trust in the EU's willingness to support Ukraine ➤ Mutual bluffing during Minsk negotiations ❖ Minsk Agreements - poorly designed, but accepted by all actors – deadlock in implementation Impact on decision-making: **Low**

ANNEX 2

	"Eyes wide shut" miscalculation of first + second order payoffs for the EU/Russia	Recalibration of perception of payoffs structure	"Eyes wide open" understanding and acceptance of Russia/EU payoffs

Payoffs	❖ Flawed perceptions of Russian payoffs
	    ➢ Perceived: threat Ukraine, possibly annex Crimea or start an all-out war;
	    ➢ Russia's 'true' payoff:
	        ■ 1st order: respect for 21st Feb Agreement
	        ■ 2nd order: reassert regional control through annexation of Crimea
	        ■ 3rd: to increase Putin's domestic support
	❖ Flawed perceptions of the EU payoffs
	    ➢ Perceived: saving Crimea, integration with Ukraine
	    ➢ The EU's 'true' payoff
	        ■ 1st order: avoiding an all-out war
	        ■ 2nd order: economic cooperation (AA)
	❖ Ukraine's perceived payoffs: EU integration; preservation of territory
	
	Impact on decision-making: **Medium**
		❖ Recalibration of perception of the payoffs structure post-annexation
		    ➢ Crimean question 'pushed to the background';
		    ➢ Concentration on regaining Donbas;
		    ➢ Poor analysis of Kremlin tactic decision-making/strategy
		    ➢ Understanding Russia would not give up on Donbas
		■ plan Novorossiya tested and paused (due to weak local support for Russia)
		❖ Not full awareness of the EU's payoffs: to stop the war - sanctions (after MH17), but no military help
		❖ Regaining Donbas up until end August - Russia changed payoffs via entrance of its military
		
		Impact on decision-making: **Medium**
			❖ "Eyes wide open" – a frozen conflict instead of "hot" is a 2nd order payoff for the EU and Russia (reached preferences: Russia's – to control Ukraine; the EU's – to stop the war)
			❖ No longer about protecting territorial integrity pre-2014 borders, but prevention of further territorial loss
			❖ Compromise for "peace"
			
			Impact on decision-making: **High** (acceptance of new *status quo* after Minsk II)

UKRAINE VIS-À-VIS RUSSIA AND THE EU

	Low resources – and unmatched with a strong opponent	Low-medium resource context - but still unmatched with a strong and resolute opponent	Medium resource context - better awareness about opponents and own military experience
Resources	❖ Awareness of Ukraine's weaker position in Crimea ➢ Military resources ➢ Crimeans' support for Russia (triggered by possible cancellation of the language law and Russian propaganda) ❖ Lack of the new leaders' 'political will' to fight for Crimea ❖ Misjudgement on the EU's will and ability to stop Russia from the annexation ❖ Russia's advantage on time Impact on decision-making: **Medium**	❖ Improvement of Ukraine's resources: ➢ The new President in May - improvement of foreign policy and contra attack in Donbas ➢ Development of Ukrainian military (volunteers' help) ➢ Deterioration of Ukraine's capacity due to its elites' corruption ❖ Inattention to the role of Donbas elites and residents ❖ Gradual improvement of awareness of Russia's readiness to use any resources ❖ Not full understanding of the EU's willingness and ability to use its resources (weak knowledge of the EU as a foreign policy actor) Impact on decision-making: **High**	❖ Ilovaisk battle "cold shower": ➢ Russia ready for any usage of resources ➢ the EU not ready to support more ❖ Minsk I - either a betrayal or an opportunity to build military and to fight back ❖ Development of the EU's response, but limited support (No EU in peace negotiations, but Germany and France during Minsk II) Impact on decision-making: **Low**

List of interviews

Int-1. Verygina, Iryna. 2020. 'Governor of Luhansk region in May 2014 - September 2014, Kyiv, 18 February 2020'.

Int-2. Unnamed. 2020. 'EU Official, Kyiv, 18 February 2020'.

Int-3. Chudovskiy, Ihor. 2020. 'Lawyer and civil activist from Luhansk, Kyiv, 27 February 2020'.

Int-4. Ogrysko, Volodymyr. 2020. 'Minister of Foreign Affairs of Ukraine in 2007-2009, Director of Centre for Russian Studies, Kyiv, 28 February 2020'.

Int-5. Chubarov, Refat. 2020. 'Chairman of the Mejlis of the Crimean Tatar People from 2013, former MP and leader of Crimean Tatars in the world, Kyiv, 02 March 2020'.

Int-6. Chyigoz, Ahtem. 2020. 'Deputy Head of the Mejlis of the Crimean Tatar People, present MP, former political prisoner in Crimea, Kyiv, 02 March 2020'.

Int-7. Unnamed. 2020. 'Advisor to one of the highest decision-makers in Ukraine in 2014-2019, Kyiv, 03 March 2020'.

Int-8. Burakovsky, Igor. 2020. 'Head of Board, Institute for Economic Research and Policy Consulting, 05 March 2020, Kyiv'.

Int-9. Shulipa, Yuriy. 2020. 'Director of the Institute of Russian Aggression Research, Russian Social Activist, Kyiv, 05 March 2020'.

Int-10. Lytvyn, Mykola. 2020. 'Chief of the State Border Guard Service of Ukraine since 2003 to 2014, Kyiv, 06 March 2020'.

Int-11. Teteruk, Andrii. 2020. 'Commander of the Myrotvorets volunteer battalion, Member of Ukrainian Parliament in 2014-2019, 06 March 2020, Kyiv'.

Int-12. Unnamed. 2020. 'EU Official, Brussels, 10 March 2020'.

Int-13. Freudenstein, Roland. 2020. 'Policy Director, Martens Centre, Brussels, 12 March 2020'.

Int-14. Unnamed. 2020. 'Ambassador of One of the Baltic States to Ukraine in 2012-2016, 20 March 2020, Skype'.

Int-15. Waller, Nicholas. 2020. 'Chief Redactor of New Europe, Independent Foreign Journalist in Ukraine, 01 April 2020, Skype'.

Int-16 Kozlovsky, Oleg. 2020. 'Researcher at Amnesty International Eastern Europe & Central Asia in Moscow, Social Activist, 01 May 2020, Zoom'.

Int-17. Ponomarev, Ilya. 2020. 'Russian politician and businessman, former member of the State Duma of Russia, 05 May 2020, Zoom'.

Int-18. Dobrokhotov, Roman. 2020. 'Moscow-Based Journalist and Civil Activist, Editor-in-Chief of Investigative Online Newspaper the Insider, 08 May 2020, Zoom'.

Int-19. Unnamed. 2020. 'Official Russian journalist, Zoom, 27 May 2020'.

Int-20. Jozwiak, Rikard. 2020. 'Brussels Correspondent for Radio Free Europe, 18 August 2020, Zoom'.

Int-21. Füle, Štefan. 2020. 'The European Commissioner for Enlargement and European Neighbourhood Policy in 2010-2014, Zoom, 10 September 2020'.

Int-22. Semenchenko, Semen. 2020. 'Founder of Donbass voluntary battalion, MP in 2014-2019, 29 September 2020, Zoom'.

Int-23. Ušackas, Vygaudas. 2020. 'Minister of Foreign Affairs of Lithuania in 2008-2010, the European Union's Ambassador to Russia in 2013-2017, Zoom, 2 October 2020'.

Int-24. Soboliev, Yehor. 2020. 'Journalist, MP in 2014-2019, 16 October 2020, Zoom'.

Int-25. Kowal, Paweł. 2020. 'Polish Politician, Former MEP (Head of EU Delegation to Ukraine), Current MP, 02 November 2020, Zoom'.

Int-26. Gretskiy, Igor. 2020. 'Russian analyst and scholar, Associate Professor of the Department of International Relations in the Post-Soviet Space at St. Petersburg State University, 16 December 2020, Zoom'.

Int-27. Lubinets, Dmytro. 2020. 'Dmytro Lubinets, Ukrainian MP since 2014, 29 December 2020, Zoom'.

Int-28. Kolerov, Modest. 2021. 'Chief redactor of Russian information agencies Rux and Regnum, 27 January 2021, Zoom'.

Int-29. Volkov, Denis. 2021. 'Deputy Director at the Levada Center in Moscow, 05 February 2021, Zoom'.

Int-30. Grant, Glen. 2021. 'British Military Expert, National Security Expert at the Ukrainian Institute for Future, 18 February 2021, Zoom'.

Int-31. Unnamed. 2021. 'MEP in 2004-2019, Member of the Greens–European Free Alliance Group in the European Parliament, 26 February 2021, Zoom'.

Int-32. Unnamed. 2021. 'EU Official from the Support Group for Ukraine at the European Commission, 18 March 2021, Zoom'.

Int-33. Unnamed. 2021. 'Senior EU Official at the European Commission, 26 March 2021, Zoom'.

Int-34 Van Rompuy, Herman. 2021. 'Former Prime Minister of Belgium, President of the European Council in 2009 – 2014, 19 April 2021, Zoom'.

List of Interviews

Int-35 Unnamed. 2021. 'EU Official at the European Commission, 23 April 2021, Zoom'.

Int-36. Deshchytsia, Andrii. 2021. 'Acting Minister of Foreign Affairs of Ukraine in February-June 2014, Ukraine's Ambassador to Poland in 2014-2022, 13 May 2021, Zoom'.

Int-37. Unnamed. 2021. 'Senior EU Official, Involved in EU-Ukraine-Russia Economic Relations in 2014-2015, 17 May 2021, Zoom'.

Int-38. Unnamed. 2021. 'Member of the German Parliament in 1994-2017, 02 Jane 2021, Zoom'.

Bibliography

5 Channel. 2014. *Occupation of Crimea: The View from Insifr*. https://www.youtube.com/watch?v=wdI3rzWrV9g (August 8, 2021).

98/149/EC, ECSC, Euratom: Council and Commission Decision of 26 January 1998 on the Conclusion of the Partnership and Cooperation Agreement between the European Communities and Their Member States, of the One Part, and Ukraine, of the Other Part. 1998. 049 OJ L (CONSIL, COM) http://data.europa.eu/eli/dec/1998/149/oj/eng (November 14, 2021).

'2014 Parliamentary elections: expert assessments'. 2014. *Ilko Kucheriv Democratic Initiatives Foundation*. https://dif.org.ua/article/parlamentski-vibori-2014-otsinki-ekspertiv (February 6, 2021).

'A Few Points about Ukrainians' Value Orientations'. 2013. *Rating Group*. http://ratinggroup.ua/research/ukraine/neskolko_tezisov_o_cennostnyh_orientirah_ukraincev.html (November 19, 2019).

'After the negotiations, the "guest performer" Tsarev tried to rescue Kuchma and Shufrich from the angry crowd'. 2014. *TCH.ua*. https://tsn.ua/ru/politika/posle-peregovorov-gastroler-carev-vzyalsya-s pasat-kuchmu-i-shufricha-ot-razyarennoy-tolpy-373176.html (February 10, 2021).

'Agreement on the Settlement of Crisis in Ukraine'. 2014. *The Guardian*. https://www.theguardian.com/world/2014/feb/21/agreement-on-the-settlement-of-crisis-in-ukraine-full-text (October 31, 2019).

Alcaro, Riccardo. 2015. *West-Russia Relations in Light of the Ukraine Crisis*. Istituto Affari Internazionali.

Alexseev, Mikhail. 2016. 'The Tale of Three Legitimacies: The Shifting Tone and Enduring Substance of Moscow's Ukraine Policy'. *PonarsEuarasia - Policy Memos*. http://www.ponarseurasia.org/memo/tale-three-legitimacies-shifting-tone-and-enduring-substance-moscows-ukraine-policy (October 28, 2019).

Allison, Graham. 1971. *Essence of Decision: Explaining the Cuban Missile Crisis*.

Allison, Roy. 2014. 'Russian "Deniable" Intervention in Ukraine: How and Why Russia Broke the Rules'. *International Affairs* 90(6): 1255–97.

'Almost half of Ukrainians - for signing an association agreement with the EU - a study by GfK Ukraine'. 2013. *Interfax*. https://ua.interfax.com.ua/news/general/174482.html (July 29, 2021).

Approval of President Putin's activity. 2022. *Levada Center*. https://www.levada.ru/indikatory/ (October 9, 2022).

Åtland, Kristian. 2016. 'North European Security after the Ukraine Conflict'. *Defense & Security Analysis* 32(2): 163–76.

Averre, Derek. 2016. 'The Ukraine Conflict: Russia's Challenge to European Security Governance'. *Europe-Asia Studies* 68(4): 699–725.

Averre, Derek, and Kataryna Wolczuk. 2016. 'Introduction: The Ukraine Crisis and Post-Post-Cold War Europe'. *Europe-Asia Studies* 68(4): 551–55.

Axelrod, Robert. 1985. *The Evolution of Cooperation*. Reprint edition. New York, NY: Basic Books.

'Azarov: Ukraine is very cautious about relations with the Customs Union'. 2012. *Terminal*. http://oilreview.kiev.ua/2012/08/03/azarov-ukraina-ochen-ostorozhno-otnositsya-kotnosheniyam-stamozhennym-soyuzom/ (June 1, 2020).

Bachmann, Reinhard. 2001. 'Trust, Power and Control in Trans-Organization Relations'. *Organization Studies* 22(2): 337–65.

Baker, Peter. 2014. 'Pressure Rising as Obama Works to Rein In Russia (Published 2014)'. *The New York Times*. https://www.nytimes.com/2014/03/03/world/europe/pressure-rising-as-obama-works-to-rein-in-russia.html (October 24, 2020).

Balmaceda, Margarita Mercedes. 1998. 'Gas, Oil and the Linkages between Domestic and Foreign Policies: The Case of Ukraine'. *Europe-Asia Studies* 50(2): 257–86.

Baranovskaya, Marina, and Mikhail Stepovik. 2011. 'Ukraine refused to join the Customs Union of Russia, Belarus and Kazakhstan'. *Deutsche Welle*. https://www.dw.com/ru/%D1%83%D0%BA%D1%80%D0%B0%D0%B8%D0%BD%D0%B0-%D0%BE%D1%82%D0%BA%D0%B0%D0%B7%D0%B0%D0%BB%D0%B0%D1%81%D1%8C-%D0%B2%D1%81%D1%82%D1%83%D0%BF%D0%B0%D1%82%D1%8C-%D0%B2-%D1%82%D0%B0%D0%BC%D0%BE%D0%B6%D0%B5%D0%BD%D0%BD%D1%8B%D0%B9-%D1%81%D0%BE%D1%8E%D0%B7-%D1%80%D0%BE%D1%81%D1%81%D0%B8%D0%B8-%D0%B1%D0%B5%D0%BB%D0%B0%D1%80%D1%83%D1%81%D0%B8-%D0%B8-%D0%BA%D0%B0%D0%B7%D0%B0%D1%85%D1%81%D1%82%D0%B0%D0%BD%D0%B0/a-15024273 (June 1, 2020).

Barkley, Andrew. 2016. *The Economics of Food and Agricultural Markets*. New Prairie Press.

Barnett, Michael, and Raymond Duvall. 2005. 'Power in International Politics'. *International Organization* 59(1): 39–75.

Beitz, Charles R. 1975. 'Justice and International Relations'. *Philosophy & Public Affairs* (4): 360–89.

Bibliography

Bennett, Peter G. 1995. 'Modelling Decisions in International Relations: Game Theory and Beyond'. *Mershon International Studies Review* 39(1): 19–52.

BIHUS info. 2021a. *Medvedchuk's Recordings 2: Who Helped Putin's Friend Get the Pipe /// OM №351(2021.05.24)*. https://www.youtube.com/watch?v=qoWeJPiF5us (June 29, 2021).

— — —. 2021b. *Medvedchuk's Recordings: Relations with Poroshenko, Putin, and Militants (Part1)/OM 350 (2021.05.17)*. https://www.youtube.com/watch?v=VZJG_RKktBQ (June 29, 2021).

— — —. 2021c. *Occupied Coal for Our Money: Medvedchuk's Recordings 3 /// Our Money №352 (2021.05.31)*. https://www.youtube.com/watch?v=WCHlr2-AzSw (June 29, 2021).

Birchfield, Vicki L., and Alasdair R. Young, eds. 2018. *Triangular Diplomacy among the United States, the European Union, and the Russian Federation*. Cham: Springer International Publishing.

Booth, Ken, and Nicholas J. Wheeler. 2008. *The Security Dilemma: Fear, Cooperation and Trust in World Politics*. 2007th edition. Basingstoke England; New York: Palgrave.

Bossuyt, Fabienne, and Dmytro Panchuk. 2017. 'The Participation of CEECs in EU Twinning Projects: Offering Specific Added Value for EU Transgovernmental Cooperation in the Eastern Neighbourhood?' *East European Politics & Societies and Cultures* 31(2): 334–59.

Brams, Steven J. 1985. *Superpower Games: Applying Game Theory to Superpower Conflict*. First Thus Edition. New Haven: Yale University Press.

Bretherton, Charlotte, and John Vogler. 2005. *The European Union as a Global Actor*. 2nd ed. London: Routledge.

'Briefing at the Ministry of Foreign Affairs'. 2014. https://mfa.gov.ua/news/1197-brifing-v-mzs (August 4, 2021).

Brzozowski, Alexandra. 2022. "Ramstein Meeting Gives Birth to Global 'contact Group' to Support Ukraine." www.euractiv.com. https://www.euractiv.com/section/defence-and-security/news/ramstein-meeting-gives-birth-to-global-contact-group-to-support-ukraine/ (October 11, 2022).

Burlyuk, Olga. 2014. 'A Thorny Path to the Spotlight: The Rule of Law Component in EU External Policies and EU–Ukraine Relations'. *The European Journal of Law Reform* (16): 133–53.

— — —. 2015. 'Variation in EU External Policies as a Virtue: EU Rule of Law Promotion in the Neighbourhood: Variation in EU External Policies as a Virtue'. *JCMS: Journal of Common Market Studies* 53(3): 509–23.

---. 2017. 'Same End, Different Means: The Evolution of Poland's Support for Ukraine at the European Level'. *East European Politics and Societies* 31(2): 311–33.

Burlyuk, Olga, and Natalia Shapovalova. 2017. '"Veni, Vidi, ... Vici?" EU Performance and Two Faces of Conditionality towards Ukraine'. *East European Politics* 33(1): 36–55.

Butusov, Yurii. 2016. 'Arsen Avakov: "On April 8, Ukraine won its first victory. We broke the back of the" Russian spring "and saved Kharkov from the" KhNR "and the war"'. *Censor.net*. https://censor.net/ru/resonance/386797/arsen_avakov_8_aprelya_ukraina_oderjala_pervuyu_pobedu_my_slomali_hrebet_russkoyi_vesne_i_spasli_harkov (September 25, 2020).

Canadian Institute of Ukrainian Studies. 2001. 'Internet Encyclopedia of Ukraine'. http://www.encyclopediaofukraine.com/default.asp (May 25, 2020).

Central Electoral Committee of Ukraine. 2010. *Results of voting in Ukraine*. https://cvk.gov.ua/pls/vp2010/wp300f0d8.html?PT001F01=700 (May 29, 2020).

Charap, Samuel, and Timothy J. Colton. 2017. *Everyone Loses: The Ukraine Crisis and the Ruinous Contest for Post-Soviet Eurasia*. The International Institute for Strategic Studies.

Clark, David H., Timothy Nordstrom, and William Reed. 2008. 'Substitution Is in the Variance: Resources and Foreign Policy Choice'. *American Journal of Political Science* 52(4): 763–73.

Clausewitz, Carl von, Michael Howard, and Peter Paret. 1976. *On War*. Princeton, N.J: Princeton University Press.

Coleman, James S. 1990. 'Rational Organization'. *Rationality and Society* 2(1): 94–105.

Congress. 2022. Text - S.3522 - *117th Congress (2021-2022): Ukraine Democracy Defense Lend-Lease Act of 2022*. http://www.congress.gov/ (October 11, 2022).

Constitutional Court of Ukraine. 2014. *Decision of Constitutional Court of Ukraine from 14.03.2014 № 2-rp/2014*. https://zakon.rada.gov.ua/go/v002p710-14 (June 26, 2019).

Council of the European Union. 2014. 'Extraordinary Meeting of EU Heads of State or Government on Ukraine, 6 March 2014'. https://www.consilium.europa.eu/en/meetings/european-council/2014/03/06/ (January 22, 2021).

D'Anieri, Paul. 2019. *Ukraine and Russia: From Civilized Divorce to Uncivil War*. Cambridge, United Kingdom; New York, NY, USA: Cambridge University Press.

Dannreuther, Roland. 2013. 'Geopolitics and International Relations of Resources'. In *Global Resources*, London, 79–97.

Davis, Christopher Mark. 2016. 'The Ukraine Conflict, Economic-Military Power Balances and Economic Sanctions'. *Post-Communist Economies* 28(2): 167–98.

De Mesquita, Bruce Bueno. 2006. 'Game Theory, Political Economy, and the Evolving Study of War and Peace'. *American Political Science Review* 100(04): 637–42.

Dean, James. 2000. 'Ukraine: Europe's Forgotten Economy'. *Challenge* 43(6): 93–108.

Delcour, Laure. 2010. 'The European Union, a Security Provider in the Eastern Neighbourhood?' *European Security* 19(4): 535–49.

Delegation of the European Union to Ukraine. 2016. 'Chronology of Bilateral Relations'. *European Union - EEAS (European External Action Service)*. http://eeas.europa.eu/archives/delegations/ukraine/eu_ukraine/chronology/index_en.htm (January 5, 2020).

Devetak, Richard, Jim George, and Sarah Percy, eds. 2017. *An Introduction to International Relations*. 3 Edition. Cambridge, United Kingdom; New York: Cambridge University Press.

DIF, and KIIS. 2005. *Thoughts and views of the population of Ukraine*. Ilko Kucheriv Democratic Initiatives Foundation. https://dif.org.ua/article/dumki-i-poglyadi-naselennya-ukraini-lyutiy-2005-roku (May 29, 2020).

Dragneva, Rilka, and Kataryna Wolczuk. 2014. 'The EU-Ukraine Association Agreement and the Challenges of Inter-Regionalism'. *Review of Central and East European Law*: 33.

———. 2016. 'Between Dependence and Integration: Ukraine's Relations with Russia'. *Europe-Asia Studies* 68(4): 678–98.

Dragneva-Lewers, Rilka, and Kataryna Wolczuk. 2015. *Ukraine between the EU and Russia: The Integration Challenge*. Houndmills, Basingstoke, Hampshire; New York, NY: Palgrave Macmillan.

Dubinsky, Dasha, and Peter Rutland. 2019. 'Russia's Legal Position on the Annexation of Crimea'. *Journal of Soviet and Post-Soviet Politics and Society* 5(1): 45–81.

"Dutch Agree to Send 100 Sniper Rifles and and Protective Gear to Ukraine." 2022. DutchNews.nl. https://www.dutchnews.nl/news/2022/02/dutch-agree-to-send-100-sniper-rifles-and-and-protective-gear-to-ukraine/ (October 10, 2022).

Encyclopedia of Ukrainian history. 2020. 'Referendum of the First December 2014'. http://resource.history.org.ua/cgi-bin/eiu/history.exe?&I21DBN=EIU&P21DBN=EIU&S21STN=1&S21REF=10&S21FMT=eiu_all&C21COM=S&S21CNR=20&S21P01=0&S21P02=0&S21P03=TRN=&S21COLORTERMS=0&S21STR=Referendum (May 25, 2020).

Ericson, Richard E., and Lester A. Zeager. 2015. 'Ukraine Crisis 2014: A Study of Russian-Western Strategic Interaction'. *Peace Economics, Peace Science and Public Policy* 21(2).

"EU Agrees 10th Package of Sanctions against Russia." 2023. *European Commission*. https://ec.europa.eu/commission/presscorner/detail/en/ip_23_1185 (February 26, 2023).

Eurasian Economic Commission. 2009. 'Agreement on the Customs Code of the Customs Union'. http://www.tsouz.ru/Docs/Pages/mgs4proekt.aspx (June 1, 2020).

Eurasian Economic Community. 2000. 'History - Eurasian Economic Community'. http://www.evrazes.com/ (May 31, 2020).

European Commission. 2005. 'EU/Russia: The Four "Common Spaces"'. *European Commission*. https://ec.europa.eu/commission/presscorner/detail/en/MEMO_05_103 (May 31, 2020).

European Council. 2007. *Press Release, 2776th Council Meeting, General Affairs and External Relations.*

European External Action Service. 2016. 'Eastern Partnership'. *EEAS - European External Action Service - European Commission*. https://eeas.europa.eu/diplomatic-network/eastern-partnership/419/eastern-partnership_en (May 31, 2020).

European Integration of Ukraine: Experience of Neighbours and Perspectives. 2014. Kyiv: Ilko Kucheriv Democratic Initiatives Foundation.

European Parliament. 2005. (European Parliament) *European Parliament Resolution on the Results of the Ukraine Elections*. http://www.europarl.europa.eu/sides/getDoc.do?pubRef=-//EP//TEXT+TA+P6-TA-2005-0009+0+DOC+XML+V0//EN (November 25, 2019).

———. 2013. 'Pressure Exerted by Russia on Eastern Partnership Countries (in the Context of the Upcoming Eastern Partnership Summit in Vilnius) - P7_TA (2013)0383'. http://www.europarl.europa.eu/sides/getDoc.do?pubRef=-//EP//TEXT+TA+P7-TA-2013-0383+0+DOC+XML+V0//EN (December 7, 2018).

'EU-Ukraine Relations - Factsheet'. 2021. *EEAS - European External Action Service - European Commission*. https://eeas.europa.eu/headquarters/headquarters-homepage/4081/eu-ukraine-relations-factsheet_en (February 11, 2021).

Fearon, James D. 1995. 'Rationalist Explanations for War'. *International Organization* 49(3): 379–414.

———. 2005. 'Primary Commodity Exports and Civil War'. *The Journal of Conflict Resolution* 49(4): 483–507.

Fedorovyh, Andrey. 2007. Partitioning of the Black Sea Fleet in facts and numbers'. http://fondiv.ru/articles/3/193/ (November 10, 2019).

Firsov, Yegor. 2017. *Kleptocracy. The film banned.* Youtube. https://www.youtube.com/watch?v=vaaAaN-ckQE (August 9, 2020).

Fix, Liana. 2018. 'The Different "Shades" of German Power: Germany and EU Foreign Policy during the Ukraine Conflict'. *German Politics* 27: 1–18.

Flores, Cardenete, Manuel Alejandro, and Cristobal Campoamor. 2016. 'The EU-Ukraine Free Trade Agreement and Russia's Retaliation: A Negative Side of Free Trade Agreements?' *EcoMod 2016 Conference*: 16.

'Foreign and Security Policy'. 2022. *European Union*. https://european-union.europa.eu/priorities-and-actions/actions-topic/foreign-and-security-policy_en (April 25, 2022).

Freedman, Lawrence. 2014. 'Ukraine and the Art of Limited War'. *Survival* 56(6): 7–38.

Freyburg, Tina et al. 2011. 'Democracy Promotion through Functional Cooperation? The Case of the European Neighbourhood Policy'. *Democratization* 18(4): 1026–54.

Friedman, George. 2013. 'Ukraine: On the Edge of Empires'. *Stratfor*. https://worldview.stratfor.com/article/ukraine-edge-empires (December 12, 2020).

———. 2014. 'Why Is Ukraine so Important?' *Stratfor*. www.reddit.com/r/Stratfor/comments/jxk599/posg/ (December 12, 2020).

Galeotti, Mark. 2015. '"Hybrid War" and "Little Green Men": How It Works, and How It Doesn't'. In *Ukraine and Russia: People, Politics, Propaganda and Perspectives*, eds. Agnieszka Pikulicka-Wilczewska and Richard Sakwa. E-International Relations. https://www.e-ir.info/2015/04/16/hybrid-war-and-little-green-men-how-it-works-and-how-it-doesnt/ (September 30, 2020).

Garver, Rob. 2023. "Political Momentum Grows for Sending F-16 Jets to Ukraine." *Voa News*. https://www.voanews.com/a/political-momentum-grows-for-sending-f-16-jets-to-ukraine/6973498.html (February 26, 2023).

Gates, Scott, and Brian D. Humes. 1997. *Games, Information, and Politics: Applying Game Theoretic Models to Political Science*. University of Michigan Press.

Gehring, Thomas, Kevin Urbanski, and Sebastian Oberthür. 2017. 'The European Union as an Inadvertent Great Power: EU Actorness and the Ukraine Crisis'. *JCMS: Journal of Common Market Studies* 55(4): 727–43.

'Geneva Statement on Ukraine'. 2014. //2009-2017.state.gov/r/pa/prs/ps/2014/04/224957.htm (September 26, 2020).

Giuliano, Elise. 2018. 'Who Supported Separatism in Donbas? Ethnicity and Popular Opinion at the Start of the Ukraine Crisis'. *Post-Soviet Affairs* 34(2–3): 158–78.

"Glazyev tapes." 2018. *Censor.net.* https://censor.net/ua/resonance/3048811/vony_vidmobilizuyut_na_zahidniyi_ukrayini_vidmorozkiv_ozbroyat_yih_tse_stanovyt_seryioznu_zagrozu_plivky (August 17, 2022).

Gordon, Dmitriy. 2020. *Nataliya Poklonskaya.* https://www.youtube.com/watch?time_continue=7725&v=Tj7zEHRX0I8&feature=emb_logo (May 14, 2020).

Gordon, Michael R. 2014. 'Russia Moves Artillery Units into Ukraine, NATO Says'. *The New York Times.* https://www.nytimes.com/2014/08/23/world/europe/russia-moves-artillery-units-into-ukraine-nato-says.html (September 26, 2020).

Gretskiy, Igor. 2013. 'Ukraine's Foreign Policy under Yushchenko'. *The Polish Quarterly of International Affairs; Warsaw* 22(4): 7–II.

Gretskiy, Igor, Evgeny Treshchenkov, and Konstantin Golubev. 2014. 'Russia's Perceptions and Misperceptions of the EU Eastern Partnership'. *Communist and Post-Communist Studies* 47(3): 375–83.

Gromadzki, Grzegorz et al. 2004. 'Ukraine and the EU after the Orange Revolution'. *The Batory Foundation*: 6.

Guy-Nizhnik, P.P. 2017. 'Ukrainian-Russian interstate relations of the presidency V. Yushchenko (2004–2010): a look from the recent past'. *Gilea. Scientific Bulletin. Collection of scientific works* 126(11): 448–56.

Guzman, Andrew. 2008. *How International Law Works: A Rational Choice Theory.* New York: Oxford University Press.

Hale, Henry E., Oxana Shevel, and Olga Onuch. 2018. 'Believing Facts in the Fog of War: Identity, Media and Hot Cognition in Ukraine's 2014 Odesa Tragedy'. *Geopolitics* 23(4): 851–81.

Haltiwanger, John, and Natalie Musumeci. 2022. "Zelensky Says He Has Officially Applied to Make Ukraine a Member of the European Union." Business Insider. https://www.businessinsider.com/zelensky-officially-applied-for-ukraine-to-join-european-union-2022-2 (October 25, 2022).

Harris, Shane et al. 2022. "Road to War: U.S. Struggled to Convince Allies, and Zelensky, of Risk of Invasion." *Washington Post*. https://www.washingtonpost.com/national-security/interactive/2022/ukraine-road-to-war/ (October 9, 2022).

Hart, Jeffrey. 1976. 'Three Approaches to the Measurement of Power in International Relations'. *International Organization* (2): 289–305.

Haukkala, Hiski. 2015. 'From Cooperative to Contested Europe? The Conflict in Ukraine as a Culmination of a Long-Term Crisis in EU–Russia Relations'. *Journal of Contemporary European Studies* 23(1): 25–40.

———. 2016. 'A Perfect Storm; Or What Went Wrong and What Went Right for the EU in Ukraine'. *Europe-Asia Studies* 68(4): 653–64.

———. 2018. '"Crowdfunded Diplomacy"? The EU's Role in the Triangular Diplomacy Over the Ukraine Crisis'. In *Triangular Diplomacy among the United States, the European Union, and the Russian Federation*, eds. Vicki L. Birchfield and Alasdair R. Young. Cham: Springer International Publishing, 77–94.

Higgins, Andrew. 2019. "In First Meeting With Putin, Zelensky Plays to a Draw Despite a Bad Hand." The New York Times. https://www.nytimes.com/2019/12/09/world/europe/putin-zelensky-paris-ukraine.html (October 5, 2022).

'High Relations'. 2013. *Lenta.ru*. https://lenta.ru/features/rosukr/friendship/ (November 11, 2019).

Hill, Christopher. 2002. *The Changing Politics of Foreign Policy*. Houndmills, Basingstoke, Hampshire; New York: Palgrave Macmillan.

Hipel, Keith W., and Niall M. Fraser. 1988. 'Using Game Theory to Model Political Uncertainty'. *Peace & Change* 13(s1): 118–31.

Hoffman, Aaron M. 2002. 'A Conceptualization of Trust in International Relations'. *European Journal of International Relations* 8(3): 375–401.

Holsti, K. J. 1964. 'The Concept of Power in the Study of International Relations'. *Background* 7(4): 179–94.

Horowitz, Michael. 2009. 'The Spread of Nuclear Weapons and International Conflict: Does Experience Matter?' *Journal of Conflict Resolution* 53(2): 234–57.

How Relations between Ukraine and Russia Should Look like? Public Opinion Polls' Results. 2014a. Kyiv International Institute of Sociology. http://www.kiis.com.ua/?lang=eng&cat=reports&id=236&page=1 (September 25, 2020).

"How Ukrainians' attitude to NATO membership was changing." 2022. Slovo i Dilo. https://www.slovoidilo.ua/2022/10/03/infografika/suspilstvo/yak-zminyuvalosya-stavlennya-ukrayinczivc-hlenstva-nato (October 25, 2022).

Hudson, Valerie M. 2020. *Foreign Policy Analysis: Classic and Contemporary Theory*. Third edition. Lanham, Maryland: Rowman & Littlefield Publishing Group.

Hutchings, Stephen, and Joanna Szostek. 2015. 'Dominant Narratives in Russian Political and Media Discourse during the Ukraine Crisis'. In *Ukraine and Russia: People, Politics, Propaganda and Perspectives*, eds. Agnieszka Pikulicka-Wilczewska and Richard Sakwa. E-International Relations Publishing. https://www.research.manchester.ac.uk/portal/en/publications/dominant-narratives-in-russian-political-and-media-discourse-during-the-ukraine-crisis(451fdbcd-1c9c-4f1b-9b67-25997ca64ca2)/export.html (October 1, 2020).

Ilko Kucheriv Democratic Initiatives Foundation. 2004. *Public opinion poll in Ukraine - April 2004*. https://dif.org.ua/article/gromadska-dumka-naselennya-ukraini-kviten-2004-roku (May 28, 2020).

'In Donetsk, pro-Russian Protesters Tore the Ukrainian Flag of Ukraine and Hung the Russian One'. 2014. *Portal Lviv*. https://web.archive.org/web/20140303022219/http://portal.lviv.ua/news/2014/03/01/150023.html (October 27, 2019).

Interview with General Serhii Kryvonos. 2022. https://www.youtube.com/watch?v=-TG38oYrKdA (October 9, 2022).

Ivakhnenko, Vladimir. 2009. 'EU postponed Association with Ukraine'. *Radio Svoboda*. https://www.svoboda.org/a/1895496.html (January 19, 2021).

Kapsamun, Ivan. 2014. 'Evgeny Marchuk: "Crimea can be returned"'. http://day.kyiv.ua/ru/article/tema-dnya-podrobnosti/evgeniy-marchuk-krym-mozhno-vernut (November 10, 2019).

Katchanovski, Ivan. 2015. 'Crimea: People and Territory before and after Annexation'. In *Ukraine and Russia: People, Politics, Propaganda and Perspectives*, ed. Agnieszka Pikulicka-Wilczewska. E-International Relations. https://www.e-ir.info/2015/03/24/crimea-people-and-territory-before-and-after-annexation/ (September 5, 2020).

———. 2017. 'The Separatist War in Donbas: A Violent Break-Up of Ukraine?' In *Ukraine in Crisis*, ed. Nicolai N. Petro. Routledge.

Keohane, Robert O. 1986. 'Reciprocity in International Relations'. *International Organization* 40(01): 1–27.

Khumalo, Njabulo Bruce, and Miniyothabo Baloyi. 2018. 'The Importance of Information in International Relations'. *Library Philosophy and Practice*: 15.

Khurshudyan, Isabelle. 2022. "An Interview with Ukrainian President Volodymyr Zelensky." Washington Post. https://www.washingtonpost.com/national-security/2022/08/16/zelensky-interview-transcript/ (October 25, 2022).

Kiely, Eugene. 2022. "Russian Rhetoric Ahead of Attack Against Ukraine: Deny, Deflect, Mislead." FactCheck.org. https://www.factcheck.org/2022/02/russian-rhetoric-ahead-of-attack-against-ukraine-deny-deflect-mislead/ (October 6, 2022).

Kissinger, Henry. 2014. 'Henry Kissinger: To Settle the Ukraine Crisis, Start at the End'. *Washington Post*. https://www.washingtonpost.com/opinions/henry-kissinger-to-settle-the-ukraine-crisis-start-at-the-end/2014/03/05/46dad868-a496-11e3-8466-d34c451760b9_story.html (May 14, 2019).

Kondrashov, Andrei. 2015. *Crimea. Way home. Documentary film by Andrei Kondrashov*. Rossiya 24. https://www.youtube.com/watch?v=t42-71RpRgI (October 27, 2019).

Korosteleva, Elena A. 2013. 'Evaluating the Role of Partnership in the European Neighbourhood Policy: The Eastern Neighbourhood'. *Eastern Journal of European Studies* (4): 11–36.

Kramer, Andrew E., and Dan Bilefsky. 2022. "Ukraine Submits an Application to Join NATO, with Big Hurdles Ahead." The New York Times. https://www.nytimes.com/2022/09/30/world/europe/ukraine-nato-zelensky.html (October 25, 2022).

'Kremlin denied reports of Putin's threats in conversation with Poroshenko'. 2014. *RBK*. https://www.rbc.ru/politics/27/11/2014/5476f34dcbb20f7509dd8c02 (February 19, 2021).

'Kuchma on Tuzla and after Tuzla'. 2003. *Ukrainska Pravda*. http://www.pravda.com.ua/news/2003/10/23/2996101/ (December 26, 2019).

Kudelia, Serhiy. 2014. 'Domestic Sources of the Donbas Insurgency'. *PonarsEuarasia - Policy Memos*. https://www.ponarseurasia.org/memo/domestic-sources-donbas-insurgency (February 24, 2021).

———. 2016. 'The Donbas Rift'. *Russian politics and law* 54(1): 5–27.

———. 2019. The Politics of Resilience and Transatlantic Order *Ukraine Crises and the Limits of Transatlantic Cooperation*. Routledge. https://www.taylorfrancis.com/chapters/ukraine-crises-limits-transatlantic-cooperation-sergiy-kudelia/e/10.4324/9780429028847-3 (March 22, 2021).

Kuzio, Taras. 2005a. 'From Kuchma to Yushchenko Ukraine's 2004 Presidential Elections and the Orange Revolution'. *Problems of Post-Communism* 52(2): 29–44.

———. 2005b. 'Neither East nor West: Ukraine's Security Policy Under Kuchma'. *Problems of Post-Communism* 52(5): 59–68.

———. 2005c. 'Russian Policy toward Ukraine during Elections'. *Demokratizatsiya: The Journal of Post-Soviet Democratization* 13: 491–517.

Kydd, Andrew. 2000. 'Trust, Reassurance, and Cooperation'. *International Organization* 54(2): 325–57.

Lacy, Dean, and Emerson M. S. Niou. 2004. 'A Theory of Economic Sanctions and Issue Linkage: The Roles of Preferences, Information, and Threats'. *Journal of Politics* 66(1): 25–42.

Larrabee, F. Stephen. 1994. 'Ukraine: Europe's Next Crisis?' *Arms Control Today* (July/August 1994): 7.

Larson, Deborah Welch. 1997. 'Trust and Missed Opportunities in International Relations'. *Political Psychology* 18(3): 701–34.

'Latest from the Special Monitoring Mission to Ukraine – Based on Information Received up until 20 April 2014, 20:00 (Kyiv Time)'. 2014. *OSCE*. https://www.osce.org/ukraine-smm/117881 (September 26, 2020).

'Lavrov Criticizes Absence of Negotiations Clause in Poroshenko Peace Plan'. 2014. *KyivPost*. https://www.kyivpost.com/article/content/ukraine-politics/lavrov-criticizes-absence-of-negotiations-clause-in-poroshenko-peace-plan-352848.html (September 26, 2020).

'Lavrov urged the ministers of Germany, Poland and France to put pressure on the Ukrainian opposition to implement the agreements of February 21'. 2014. *RBK Ukraiina*. https://www.rbc.ua/rus/news/lavrov-prizval-ministrov-frg-polshi-i-frantsii-nadavit-22022014174900 (June 4, 2020).

Lazareva, Alla. 2018. 'Hollande's Memoirs: "I Will Crush You!" Putin Shouted at Poroshenko'. *Tyzhden*. https://tyzhden.ua/World/218986 (February 11, 2021).

Le Billon, Philippe. 2001. 'The Political Ecology of War: Natural Resources and Armed Conflicts'. *Political Geography* 20(5): 561–84.

Leshoukov, Igor. 1998. *Beyond Satisfaction: Russia's Perspectives on European Integration. ZEI Discussion Papers: 1998, C 26.* Discussion Paper. http://aei.pitt.edu/335/ (May 16, 2019).

Levyk, Bogdan. 2014. 'The Black Sea Fleet of the Russian Federation in Russian-Ukrainian relations (post-Soviet period)'. *Shid* (3): 48–53.

Lieberman, Bernhardt. 1964. 'I-Trust: A Notion of Trust in Three-Person Games and International Affairs'. *Journal of Conflict Resolution* 8(3): 271–80.

Light, Margot, Stephen White, and John Löwenhardt. 2000. 'A Wider Europe: The View from Moscow and Kyiv'. *International Affairs* 76(1): 77–88.

Lightfoot, Simon, Balázs Szent-Iványi, and Kataryna Wolczuk. 2016. 'Mesmerized by Enlargement: The EU's Eastern Neighborhood Policy and New Member State Transition Experience'. *East European Politics and Societies* 30(3): 664–84.

Lindblom, Charles E. 1959. 'The Science of "Muddling Through"'. *Public Administration Review* (2): 79–88.

Luce, R. Duncan, and Ernest W. Adams. 1956. 'The Determination of Subjective Characteristic Functions in Games with Misperceived Payoff Functions'. *Econometrica* 24(2): 158–71.

Luhmann, Niklas. 1979. *Trust; And, Power: Two Works*. Wiley.

Lukyanov, Fyodor. 2016. 'Putin's Foreign Policy: The Quest to Restore Russia's Rightful Place'. *Foreign Affairs* 95(3). https://go-gale-com.manchester.idm.oclc.org/ps/i.do?p=AONE&sw=w&issn=00157120&v=2.1&it=r&id=GALE%7CA451952540&sid=googleScholar&linkaccess=abs (November 29, 2020).

Lynn, Erica. 2005. 'Analysis of the Dispute over Taiwan Using a Game Theory Approach'. *Defense & Security Analysis* 21(4): 413–18.

Lytvyn, Mykola. 2019. *The line of demarcation*. Kyiv: Zelenyi pes.

Maass, Anna-Sophie. 2019. 'The Actorness of the EU's State-Building in Ukraine - Before and after Crimea'. *Geopolitics*: 1–20.

Magnay, Diana, and Tim Lister. 2014. 'Air Attack on Pro-Russian Separatists in Luhansk Kills 8, Stuns City'. *CNN*. https://www.cnn.com/2014/06/03/world/europe/ukraine-luhansk-building-attack/index.html (August 26, 2020).

Magocsi, Paul Robert. 2014. *Ukraine: An Illustrated History*. ILL Edition. University of Toronto Press, Scholarly Publishing Division.

'Maidan online. The truce: Council voted for Zakharchenko's dismissal and Tymoshenko's release'. 2014. *Korrespondent.net*. https://ua.korrespondent.net/ukraine/politics/3307123-maidan-onlain-peremyria-rada-proholosuvala-za-vidstoronennia-zakharchenka-i-zvilnennia-tymoshenko (April 24, 2020).

Majeski, Stephen J., and Shane Fricks. 1995. 'Conflict And Cooperation in International Relations'. *The Journal of Conflict Resolution* 39(4): 622–45.

Malek, Martin. 2009. 'The "Western Vector" of the Foreign and Security Policy of Ukraine'. *The Journal of Slavic Military Studies* 22(4): 515–42.

Marples, David. 2016. 'Ethnic and Social Composition of Ukraine's Regions and Voting Patterns'. In *Ukraine and Russia: People, Politics, Propaganda and Perspectives*, ed. Pikulicka-Wilczewska. E-International Relations Publishing.

Martynov, A. Yu. 2005. 'Single Economic Space'. *Encyclopedia of the History of Ukrainr*. http://resource.history.org.ua/cgi-bin/eiu/history.exe?&I21DBN=EIU&P21DBN=EIU&S21STN=1&S21REF=10&S21FMT=eiu_all&C21COM=S&S21CNR=20&S21P01=0&S21P02=0&S21P03=TRN=&S21COLORTERMS=0&S21STR=EEP (May 30, 2020).

McDermott, Roger. 2015. 'Brothers Disunited: Russia's Use of Military Power in Ukraine'. *Foreign Military Studies Office Monographs*. https://www.academia.edu/11853815/Brothers_Disunited_Russia_s_Use_of_Military_Power_in_Ukraine (October 26, 2019).

Mearsheimer, John J. 1993. 'The Case for a Ukrainian Nuclear Deterrent'. *Foreign Affairs* 72(3): 50–66.

———. 2014. 'Why the Ukraine Crisis Is the West's Fault: The Liberal Delusions That Provoked Putin'. *Foreign Affairs* (5): 77–84.

Medvedev, Sergey. 2015. 'Where did "Krymnash" come from?' *Krym.Realii*. https://ru.krymr.com/a/27148420.html (April 26, 2020).

Meister, Stefan. 2019. 'Hedging and Wedging: Strategies to Contest Russia's Leadership in Post-Soviet Eurasia'. In *Regional Powers and Contested Leadership*, Palgrave Macmillan, Cham.

Merry, E. Wayne. 2015. 'The Origins of Russia's War in Ukraine'. In *Roots of Russia's War in Ukraine*, Washington, D.C: New York: Woodrow Wilson Center Press / Columbia University Press.

Mezentsev, Yaroslav. 2008. 'Cold war for Crimea'. *Tyzhden*. https://tyzhden.ua/Publication/3799 (November 10, 2019).

Michel, Torsten. 2013. 'Time to Get Emotional: Phronetic Reflections on the Concept of Trust in International Relations'. *European Journal of International Relations* 19(4): 869–90.

Miller, Christopher. 2014. 'Two Ukrainian Troops Killed in Battles with Insurgents on June 3; OSCE Says Luhansk Blast on June 2 Likely Caused by Airstrike (UPDATES, VIDEO) - Jun. 03, 2014'. *KyivPost*. https://www.kyivpost.com/article/content/ukraine-politics/heavy-fighting-in-eastern-ukraine-as-government-restarts-active-phase-of-anti-terror-operation-350453.html (September 27, 2020).

Mills, Claire. 2022. "Military Assistance to Ukraine 2014-2021." *House of Commons Library*. https://commonslibrary.parliament.uk/research-briefings/sn07135/ (October 10, 2022).

Milner, Helen V. 1997. *Interests, Institutions, and Information: Domestic Politics and International Relations*. Princeton University Press.

Ministry of Defence of Ukraine. 2022. 'Canada Delivered Weapons for the Armed Forces of Ukraine'. https://web.archive.org/web/20220220001140/https://www.mil.gov.ua/news/2022/02/19/kanada-dostavila-zbroyu-dlya-zbrojnih-sil-ukraini/ (October 9, 2022).

Ministry of Foreign Affairs of the Russian Federation. 2014. '*Comment by the Information and Press Department of the Russian Ministry of Foreign Affairs regarding the situation in Ukraine*'. https://www.mid.ru/kommentarii_predstavitelya/-/asset_publisher/MCZ7HQuMdqBY/content/id/71810?p_p_id=101_INSTANCE_MCZ7HQuMdqBY&_101_INSTANCE_MCZ7HQuMdqBY_languageId=en_GB (February 28, 2021).

Ministry of Justice of Ukraine. 2020. '*History of Ukraine's membership in the Commonwealth of Independent States*'. https://minjust.gov.ua/m/str_55 (May 29, 2020).

Mock, William. 1992. 'Game Theory, Signalling, and International Legal Relations'. *6 Geo. Wash. J. Int'l L. & Econ.* 33. https://repository.law.uic.edu/facpubs/236.

Moore, Will H. 1995. 'Action-Reaction or Rational Expectations?: Reciprocity and the Domestic-International Conflict Nexus during the "Rhodesia Problem"'. *Journal of Conflict Resolution* 39(1): 129–67.

Moravcsik, Andrew. 2010. 'Liberal Theories of International Relations: A Primer'. http://www.princeton.edu/~amoravcs/publications.html.

Moroney, Jennifer D.P. 2001. 'Frontier Dynamics and Ukraine's Ties to the West'. *Problems of Post-Communism* 48(2): 15–24.

Morrow, James D. 1986. 'A Spatial Model of International Conflict'. *American Political Science Review* 80(4): 21.

Morrow, James D. 2002. 'The Laws of War, Common Conjectures, and Legal Systems in International Politics'. *The Journal of Legal Studies* 31(S1): S41–60.

Moshes, Arkady. 2012. 'Russia's European Policy under Medvedev: How Sustainable Is a New Compromise?' *International Affairs* 88(1): 17–30.

Mroz, John Edwin, and Oleksandr Pavliuk. 1996. 'Ukraine: Europe's Linchpin'. *Foreign Affairs* 75(3): 52–62.

Mueller, Dennis C. 2003. *Public Choice III*. Cambridge: Cambridge University Press. https://www.cambridge.org/highereducation/books/public-choice-iii/32B490B6DAE290EC773E4F4ACB7BB451 (May 11, 2022).

Mukhametov, Ruslan Salikhovich. 2011. 'Russian-Ukrainian Relations and the Presidency of Yanukovych'. *News of the Ural Federal University. Series 1. Problems of education, science and culture* 95(4): 272–78.

Müller, Harald. 2004. 'Arguing, Bargaining and All That: Communicative Action, Rationalist Theory and the Logic of Appropriateness in International Relations'. *European Journal of International Relations* 10(3): 395–435.

Mylovanov, Tymofiy, Yuri Zhukov, and Yuriy Gorodnichenko. 2018. 'Review of the EU Policy for Ukraine: Rethinking Approaches to Conflict'. In *EU Global Strategy and Human Securit*, , 30–45.

'Myths about the EU-Ukraine Association Agreement - Setting the Facts Straight'. 2014. http://trade.ec.europa.eu/doclib/docs/2014/january/tradoc_152074.pdf.

National Security and Defense Council of Ukraine. 2014. 'Transcript of the NSDC meeting in connection with the beginning of Russian aggression in Crimea'. http://www.pravda.com.ua/articles/2016/02/22/7099911/ (March 28, 2020).

NATO. 2008. 'Bucharest Summit Declaration - Issued by the Heads of State and Government Participating in the Meeting of the North Atlantic Council in Bucharest on 3 April 2008'. http://www.nato.int/cps/en/natohq/official_texts_8443.htm (December 25, 2019).

'NATO is dissolved into packages of blocks'. 2008. *Kommersant*. https://www.kommersant.ru/doc/877224 (January 3, 2020).

Natorski, Michal, and Karolina Pomorska. 2017. 'Trust and Decision-Making in Times of Crisis: The EU's Response to the Events in Ukraine: Europe's Hybrid Foreign Policy'. *JCMS: Journal of Common Market Studies* 55(1): 54–70.

Nye, Joseph. 2005. *Understanding International Conflicts: An Introduction to Theory and History*. 5th ed. New York: Pearson Education.

Odushkin, Ostap. 2001. 'The Acceptance of Ukraine to the European Union: Integrating and Disintegrating Factors for the EU'. *Polish Sociological Review* (136): 365–78.

Olearchyk, Roman. 2013. 'Russia Accused of Triggering Trade War with Ukraine'. *The Financial Times*.

Onuch, Olga. 2014a. *Mapping Mass Mobilization: Understanding Revolutionary Moments in Argentina and Ukraine*. Basingstoke: Palgrave Macmillan.

———. 2014b. 'Who Were the Protesters?' *Journal of Democracy* 25(3): 44–51.

OSCE Special Monitoring Mission to Ukraine. 2014. *Spot Report by the OSCE Special Monitoring Mission to Ukraine (SMM), 7 September 2014: The Situation at Donetsk International Airport and Shchastya (Luhansk Region)*. https://www.osce.org/ukraine-smm/123267 (February 11, 2021).

Pahre, Robert, and Paul A. Papayoanou. 1997. 'Using Game Theory to Link Domestic and International Politics'. *Journal of Conflict Resolution* 41(1): 4–11.

Papadimitriou, Dimitris, Dorina Baltag, and Neculai-Cristian Surubaru. 2017. 'Assessing the Performance of the European Union in Central and Eastern Europe and in Its Neighbourhood'. *East European Politics* 33(1): 1–16.

'Part of the Russian troops was withdrawn from Ukraine'. 2014. *Deutsche Welle*. https://www.dw.com/uk/%D1%87%D0%B0%D1%81%D1%82%D0%B8%D0%BD%D1%83-%D1%80%D0%BE%D1%81%D1%96%D0%B9%D1%81%D1%8C%D0%BA%D0%B8%D1%85-%D0%B2%D1%96%D0%B9%D1%81%D1%8C%D0%BA-%D0%B2%D0%B8%D0%B2%D0%B5%D0%B4%D0%B5%D0%BD%D0%BE-%D0%B7-%D1%83%D0%BA%D1%80%D0%B0%D1%97%D0%BD%D0%B8/a-17912719 (February 19, 2021).

Pastore, Gunta. 2014. 'The EU-Ukraine Association Agreement Prior to the Vilnius Eastern Partnership Summit'. *Baltic Journal of European Studies* 4(2): 5–19.

"Petraeus: US Would Destroy Russia's Troops If Putin Uses Nuclear Weapons in Ukraine." 2022. *The guardian*. https://www.theguardian.com/world/2022/oct/02/us-russia-putin-ukraine-war-david-petraeus (October 25, 2022).

Petro, Nicolai N. 2015. 'Understanding the Other Ukraine: Identity and Allegiance in Russophone Ukraine'. In *Ukraine and Russia: People, Politics, Propaganda and Perspectives*, eds. Agnieszka Pikulicka-Wilczewska and Richard Sakwa. E-International Relations. http://www.e-ir.info/wp-content/uploads/2015/03/Ukraine-and-Russia-E-IR.pdf (November 19, 2019).

'Petro Poroshenko Presented His Peace Plan for Donbass'. 2014. *Podrobnosti*. https://podrobnosti.ua/981383-petr-poroshenko-predstavil-svoj-mirnyj-plan-po-donbassu.html (February 10, 2021).

Pew Research Center. 2014. *Despite Concerns about Governance, Ukrainians Want to Remain One Country*. https://web.archive.org/web/20140509001422/http://www.pewglobal.org/files/2014/05/Pew-Global-Attitudes-Ukraine-Russia-Report-FINAL-May-8-2014.pdf (September 25, 2020).

Pifer, Steven. 2009. 'Ukraine's Geopolitical Choice'. *Eurasian Geography and Economics* 50(4): 387–401.

Pogrebinskiy, Mikhail. 2015. 'Russians in Ukraine: Before and After Euromaidan'. *Ukraine and Russia: People, Politics, Propaganda and Perspectives*: 90–99.

Polityuk, Pavel, and Vitalii Hnidyi. 2022. "EU Grants Ukraine Candidate Status in 'historic Moment' | Reuters." Reuters. https://www.reuters.com/business/aerospace-defense/ukraine-becomes-eu-membership-candidate-battle-east-enters-fearsome-climax-2022-06-23/ (October 25, 2022).

Polukhina, Yulia. 2020. 'Inglorious hybrids. Strelkov, "Bes", "Abwehr": what they did in Donbass and what they say about each other now'. *Novayagazeta.ru*. https://novayagazeta.ru/articles/2020/07/17/86300-besslavnye-gibridy (September 27, 2020).

'Poroshenko and Putin shook hands in Minsk, announced the search for a way out of the crisis'. 2014. *Radio Svoboda*. https://www.radiosvoboda.org/a/26551148.html (September 6, 2021).

'Poroshenko: ATO should last not months, but hours'. 2014. *Ukrainska Pravda*. http://www.pravda.com.ua/news/2014/05/26/7026737/ (October 23, 2020).

'Poroshenko decided to hold peace talks in Minsk'. 2014. *Vesti*. https://vesti.ua/donbass/63285-poroshenko-reshil-provesti-trehstoronnie-peregovory-v-minske (February 10, 2021).

'Poroshenko did not hear Putin's phone threats about the offensive'. 2014. *Vesti*. https://vesti.ua/strana/79236-poroshenko-ne-uvidel-telefonnyh-ugroz-putina-o-nastuplenii (February 19, 2021).

'Poroshenko reached an agreement with Putin on a truce in Donbas by phone'. 2014. *Vesti*. https://vesti.ua/donbass/68052-poroshenko-i-putin-dogovorilis-o-postojannom-prekrawenii-ognja-na-donbasse (February 10, 2021).

'Poroshenko received an ultimatum from Putin through Zurabov'. 2014. *Vesti*. https://vesti.ua/donbass/79213-poroshenko-poluchil-ot-putina-ultimatum-cherez-zurabova (February 19, 2021).

'Poroshenko: Russia can "take" not only Kyiv, but any city, if it is not stopped'. 2014. *Ukrainska Pravda*. http://www.pravda.com.ua/news/2014/09/6/7036939/ (February 12, 2021).

'Poroshenko Unveils Peace Plan during Visit to Ukraine's Restive East'. 2014. *KyivPost*. https://www.kyivpost.com/article/content/ukraine-politics/petro-poroshenko-unveils-peace-plan-during-visit-to-east-352786.html (September 26, 2020).

Posner, Eric A, and Jack L Goldsmith. 2003. 'International Agreements: A Rational Choice Approach'. *Virginia Journal of International Law*.

'Poverty line in Ukraine and Europe'. 2010. *Z-Ukraina*. https://zet.in.ua/news/mezha-bidnosti-v-ukra%d1%97ni-ta-yevropi/ (May 29, 2020).

Powell, Robert. 1991. 'Absolute and Relative Gains in International Relations Theory'. *The American Political Science Review* 85(4): 1303–20.

———. 2002. 'Bargaining Theory and International Conflict'. *Annual Review of Political Science* 5(1): 1–30.

President of Russia. 2014a. 'About the beginning of contacts of the public movement "Ukrainian Choice" of Viktor Medvedchuk in Donetsk and Lugansk'. *Kremlin.ru*. http://kremlin.ru/events/president/news/45959 (June 29, 2021).

———. 2014b. Agreement between the Russian Federation and the Republic of Crimea on the admission to the Russian Federation of the Republic of Crimea and the formation of new subjects within the Russian Federation. *Kremlin.ru*. http://kremlin.ru/events/president/news/20605 (January 4, 2019).

———. 2021. "Article by Vladimir Putin "On the Historical Unity of Russians and Ukrainians"." *Kremlin.ru*. http://en.kremlin.ru/events/president/news/66181 (October 9, 2022).

———. 2014c. 'Direct line with Vladimir Putin'. *Kremlin.ru*. http://kremlin.ru/events/president/news/20796 (June 22, 2021).

———. 2014d. 'Meeting with Federal Chancellor of Germany Angela Merkel'. *Kremlin.ru*. http://kremlin.ru/events/president/news/46817 (February 19, 2021).

———. 2014e. 'Telephone conversation with Petro Poroshenko'. *Kremlin.ru*. http://kremlin.ru/events/president/news/45902 (November 13, 2020).

President of Ukraine. 2005. 952/2005 *On the decision of the National Security and Defense Council of Ukraine of May 20, 2005 'On the formation of the Single Economic Space'*. https://zakon.rada.gov.ua/go/952/2005 (February 12, 2021).

———. 2004. *Decree of the President of Ukraine on the Military Doctrine of Ukraine*. https://zakon.rada.gov.ua/go/648/2004 (October 5, 2022).

———. 2005b. *The question of the Military Doctrine of Ukraine dated April 21, 2005*. https://zakon.rada.gov.ua/go/702/2005 (October 5, 2022).

———. 2012. *On the decision of the National Security and Defense Council of Ukraine dated June 8, 2012*. https://www.president.gov.ua/documents/3902012-14403 (October 5, 2022).

———. 2014. *On the decision of the National Security and Defense Council of Ukraine of April 13, 2014 'On urgent measures to overcome the terrorist threat and preserve the territorial integrity of Ukraine'*. https://zakon.rada.gov.ua/go/405/2014 (June 27, 2019).

'Pro-Russian Group in Donetsk Declare Independence from Ukraine'. 2014. *Biharprabha News*. https://news.biharprabha.com/2014/04/pro-russian-group-in-donetsk-declare-independence-from-ukraine/ (September 26, 2020).

Prosch, Bernhard. 2007. 'Vom Kosovo Bis Zum Irak—Internationale Konflikte in Spieltheoretischen Experimenten'. *Historical Social Research / Historische Sozialforschung* 32(4 (122)): 151–65.

'Protocol on the Results of Consultations of the Trilateral Contact Group on Joint Steps Aimed at Implementing Ukrainian President Petro Poroshenko's Peace Plan and Russian President Vladimir Putin's Initiatives'. 2014. *OSCE*. https://www.osce.org/ru/home/123258?download=true.

Pryidun, Stepan. 2018. 'The problem of distribution of the Black Sea Fleet of the USSR in the foreign policy of Ukraine (1991-1997)'. *Novi Zapysky: Seriia 'Istoriia'*: 113–20.

'Putin and Poroshenko: truce in Donbass and gas supplies'. 2014. *BBC News*. https://www.bbc.com/russian/international/2014/10/141017_putin_poroshenko_milan (February 19, 2021).

"Putin Orders Troops into Eastern Ukraine on 'Peacekeeping Duties.'" 2022. *The Guardian*. https://web.archive.org/web/20220223175613/https://www.theguardian.com/world/2022/feb/21/ukraine-putin-decide-recognition-breakaway-states-today (October 9, 2022).

Putin, Vladimir. 2010. 'Highlights - Putin's answers to questions of Russian citizens'. *Reuters*. https://ru.reuters.com/article/topNews/idRURXE6BF0QM20101216 (June 1, 2020).

Putnam, Robert D. 1988. 'Diplomacy and Domestic Politics: The Logic of Two-Level Games'. *International Organization* (3): 427–60.

Raine, Andrew; Lendon, Brad; Picheta, Rob and Khalil, Hafsa "Latest Round of EU Sanctions Includes a Ban on 90% of Russian Oil Imports by End of 2022." 2022. CNN. https://web.archive.org/web/20220531070714/https://edition.cnn.com/europe/live-news/russia-ukraine-war-news-05-30-22/h_49754b3f0bb258b83dbf3612677ac6e7 (October 9, 2022).

Rankin, Jennifer, and Julian Borger. 2023. "Polish Leopard Tanks Arrive in Ukraine as West Piles New Sanctions on Russia." *The Guardian*. https://www.theguardian.com/world/2023/feb/24/ukraine-polish-tanks-arrive-new-sanctions-russia (February 26, 2023).

Rasmussen, Mikkel Vedby. 2014. *The Ukraine Crisis and the End of the Post-Cold War European Order: Options for NATO and the EU*. Centre for Military Studies, University of Copenhagen.

Reynolds, Philip A. 1994. *An Introduction to International Relations*. 3rd ed. London; New York: Longman.

Robinson, Paul. 2016. 'Russia's Role in the War in Donbass, and the Threat to European Security'. *European Politics and Society* 17(4): 506–21.

Ronzheimer, Paul. 2014. 'Petro Poroschenko über die Bedrohung durch Russland'. *Bild*. https://www.bild.de/politik/ausland/petro-poros chenko/petro-poroschenko-im-interview-38593920.bild.html (February 20, 2021).

Roth, Andrew. 2021. "Russia Issues List of Demands It Says Must Be Met to Lower Tensions in Europe." *The Guardian*. https://www.theguardian.com/world/2021/dec/17/russia-issues-list-demands-tensions-europe-ukraine-nato (October 10, 2022).

'Russia is ready to break the friendship treaty with Ukraine over NATO'. 2008. *Kommersant*. https://www.kommersant.ru/doc/899836 (May 30, 2020).

'Russian Consulate General is opened in Simferopol'. 1999. *Kommersant*. https://www.kommersant.ru/doc/227271 (December 1, 2019).

"Russia Planning Massive Military Offensive against Ukraine Involving 175,000 Troops, U.S. Intelligence Warns." 2021. *Washington Post*. https://www.washingtonpost.com/national-security/russia-ukraine-invasion/2021/12/03/98a3760e-546b-11ec-8769-2f4ecdf7a2ad_story.html (October 9, 2022).

'Russian saboteurs shoot at "their" under the guise of the Ukrainian military - The National Security and Defense Council'. 2014. *Ukrainska Pravda*. http://www.pravda.com.ua/news/2014/09/8/7037064/ (February 12, 2021).

'Russian troops captured all Ukrainian military units in the Crimea'. 2014. *BBC News Україна*. https://www.bbc.com/ukrainian/politics/2014/03/140326_russian_control_crimea_dk (April 26, 2020).

Rutland, Peter. 2015. 'An Unnecessary War: The Geopolitical Roots Of The Ukraine Crisis'. In *Ukraine and Russia: People, Politics, Propaganda and Perspectives*, eds. Agnieszka Pikulicka-Wilczewska and Richard Sakwa. E-International Relations, 129–40. /paper/An-Unnecessary-War%3A-The-Geopolitical-Roots-Of-The-Rutland/b426cb719e391294d539f7a1d99a7a0616e425b6 (September 29, 2020).

Sakwa, Richard. 2015a. *Frontline Ukraine: Crisis in the Borderlands*. London: IBTauris.

———. 2015b. 'The Death of Europe? Continental Fates after Ukraine'. *International Affairs* 91(3): 553–79.

Samokhvalov, Vsevolod. 2015. 'Ukraine between Russia and the European Union: Triangle Revisited'. *Europe-Asia Studies* 67(9): 1371–93.

Sasse, Gwendolyn. 1996. 'The Crimean Issue'. *Journal of Communist Studies and Transition Politics* 12(1): 83–100.

———. 2001. 'The "New" Ukraine: A State of Regions'. *Regional & Federal Studies* 11(3): 69–100.

Schelling, Thomas C. 2005. 'Reciprocal Measures for Arms Stabilization'. *Daedalus* 134(4): 101–17.

Security Service of Ukraine. 2014. *Ten Russian Citizens Detained Illegally in Donetsk Region Who Illegally Crossed the Ukrainian Border as Part of a Sabotage Group (Video)*. https://web.archive.org/web/20140828070826/http://www.sbu.gov.ua/sbu/control/uk/publish/article?art_id=130629&cat_id=39574 (September 27, 2020).

Seipel, Hubert. 2014. *Vladimir's Putin interview to the German TV channel ARD*. Vladivostok. http://kremlin.ru/events/president/news/47029 (February 20, 2021).

Sen, Amartya K. 1977. 'Rational Fools: A Critique of the Behavioral Foundations of Economic Theory'. *Philosophy & Public Affairs* (4): 317–44.

Sengupta, Somini, and Andrew E. Kramer. 2016. 'Dutch Inquiry Links Russia to 298 Deaths in Explosion of Jetliner Over Ukraine (Published 2016)'. *The New York Times*. https://www.nytimes.com/2016/09/29/world/asia/malaysia-air-flight-mh17-russia-ukraine-missile.html (November 14, 2020).

'Separatism in Donbass was originally funded by A. Yanukovych - Ponomarev'. 2018. *Interfax*. https://interfax.com.ua/news/general/484995.html (September 27, 2020).

'Severodonetsk Congress: The Truth of an Eyewitness'. 2005. *URA-Inform*. http://ura.dn.ua/28.11.2005/4871.html (August 9, 2020).

Shaffer, Brenda, and Taleh Ziyadov. 2012. *Beyond the Resource Curse*. Philadelphia: University of Pennsylvania Press.

Sherr, James. 2017. 'A Dubious Success: The West's Policy towards Ukraine after Crimea'. In *A Successful Failure. Russia after Crime(a)*, Warsaw: The Centre for Polish-Russian Dialogue and Understanding.

Shevel, Oxana. 2015. 'The Parliamentary Elections in Ukraine, October 2014.' *Electoral Studies (in press)*.

Shmelova, Maria. 2008. 'Ukraine's Multi-Vector Foreign Policy: Attempt at Summary'. *The Polish Quarterly of International Affairs* 17(2): 22–42.

Shulman, Stephen. 2005. 'Ukrainian Nation-Building Under Kuchma'. *Problems of Post-Communism* 52(5): 32–47.

Shyriaev, Valeryi. 2015. 'Crimea. A year after. What do we know now.' *Novayagazeta.ru*. https://novayagazeta.ru/articles/2015/02/20/63128-krym-god-spustya-chto-my-znaem-teper (January 19, 2021).

Shyrokykh, Karina. 2018. 'The Evolution of the Foreign Policy of Ukraine: External Actors and Domestic Factors'. *Europe-Asia studies* 70(5): 832–50.

Simon, Herbert A. 1997. *Administrative Behavior, 4th Edition*. 4th Revised ed. edition. New York: Free Press.

Simon, Michael. 2004. 'Asymmetric Proliferation and Nuclear War: The Limited Usefulness of an Experimental Test'. *International Interactions* 30(1): 69–85.

Skorkin, Konstantin. 2022. "Traitors in the Ranks: Zelensky Purges Ukraine's Security Services." *Carnegie Endowment for International Peace*. https://carnegieendowment.org/politika/87585 (October 25, 2022).

Smith, Adam. 1776. *An Inquiry into the Nature and Causes of the Wealth of Nations*. London: W. Strahan and T. Cadell.

Smith, B. 2016. 'Russian Foreign and Security Policy. Briefing Paper'. *House of Commons Library* (Number CBP 7646).

Smith, Nicholas Ross. 2015. 'The EU and Russia's Conflicting Regime Preferences in Ukraine: Assessing Regime Promotion Strategies in the Scope of the Ukraine Crisis'. *European Security* 24(4): 525–40.

Smith, Steve, Amelia Hadfield, and Tim Dunne, eds. 2016. *Foreign Policy: Theories, Actors, Cases*. 3rd edition. Oxford: OUP Oxford.

Snidal, Duncan. 1985. 'The Game Theory of International Politics'. *World Politics* 38(1): 25–57.

Snyder, Glenn H. 1971. '"Prisoner's Dilemma" and "Chicken" Models in International Politics'. *International Studies Quarterly* 15(1): 66–103.

Snyder, Glenn H., and Paul Diesing. 1977a. *Conflict Among Nations: Bargaining, Decision Making, and System Structure in International Crises*, Princeton University Press.

Snyder, Glenn H., and Paul Diesing. 1977b. 'Formal Models of Bargaining'. In *Conflict Among Nations: Bargaining, Decision Making, and System Structure in International Crises*, Princeton University Press, 33–182.

– – –. 1977b. 'Summary and Synthesis'. In *Conflict Among Nations: Bargaining, Decision Making, and System Structure in International Crises*, Princeton University Press, 471–530.

Snyder, Timothy. 2012. *Bloodlands: Europe Between Hitler and Stalin*. Illustrated edition. New York: Basic Books.

Sobczyk, Kamil. 2015. 'Konflikt na Ukrainie – porażka czy szansa dla Wspólnej Polityki Bezpieczeństwa i Obrony UE?' *Bezpieczeństwo Narodowe* (2015/1): 37–60.

Soltanov, Elnur. 2012. '12. Natural Resources, Domestic Instability, and International Conflicts'. In *Beyond the Resource Curse*, eds. Brenda Shaffer and Taleh Ziyadov. Philadelphia: University of Pennsylvania Press.

Spartz, Victoria. 2022. "Spartz: President Zelensky Must Address the Yermak Issue." *Representative Victoria Spartz*. http://spartz.house.gov/media/press-releases/spartz-president-zelensky-must-address-yermak-issue (February 26, 2023).

'State Statistics Service of Ukraine'. 2020. http://www.ukrstat.gov.ua/ (June 1, 2020).

Stoner, Kathryn, and Michael Mcfaul. 2015. 'Who Lost Russia (This Time)? Vladimir Putin'. *The Washington Quarterly* 38(2): 167–87.

Strelkov, Igor. 2014. 'Alexander Prokhanov, Igor Strelkov: "Who are you," Shooter "?"' *Zavtra*. https://zavtra.ru/blogs/kto-tyi-strelok (December 19, 2020).

"Surkov leaks." 2016. InformNapalm. https://informnapalm.org/29027-vzlom-surkova/ (August 18, 2022).

Szeptycki, Andrzej. 2008. 'Oligarchic Groups and Ukrainian Foreign Policy'. *The Polish Quarterly of International Affairs* 17(2): 43–68.

Taylor, Adam. 2014. 'Why Ukraine Is So Important'. *Business Insider*. https://www.businessinsider.com/why-ukraine-is-so-important-2014-1 (January 4, 2020).

Tenerowicz, Rafał. 2012. 'Wektor euroatlantycki w polityce zagranicznej Ukrainy 1991-2011'. *Kwartalnik Naukowy OAP UW 'e-Politikon'* (1): 153–76.

'Tenyukh: Russia pulled 220 thousand soldiers to the borders of Ukraine'. 2014. *LB.ua*. https://lb.ua/news/2014/03/11/258880_tenyuh_rossiya_podtyanula_granitsam.html (August 9, 2020).

'Terrorists Violated the Minsk Agreements Almost Three and a Half Thousand Times'. 2014. *Novoye Vremya*. https://nv.ua/ukraine/shtab-ato-podschital-skolko-raz-terroristy-narushali-minskie-dogovorennosti-21916.html (February 21, 2021).

'Texts Adopted - Thursday, 6 February 2014 - Situation in Ukraine - P7_TA(2014)0098'. 2014. http://www.europarl.europa.eu/sides/getDoc.do?type=TA&language=EN&reference=P7-TA-2014-0098 (January 9, 2019).

Bibliography

'The agreement on the Settlement of the crisis in Ukraine'. 2014. http://www.pravda.com.ua/articles/2014/02/21/7015533/ (July 10, 2019).

'The CEC processed 100% of the protocols'. 2014. *Ukrainska Pravda*. http://www.pravda.com.ua/news/2014/11/7/7043599/ (February 6, 2021).

The European Council. 2020. 'EU Restrictive Measures in Response to the Crisis in Ukraine'. *European Council*. https://www.consilium.europa.eu/en/policies/sanctions/ukraine-crisis/history-ukraine-crisis/# (January 2, 2019).

The European Union and Ukraine. 2014. *Association Agreement between the European Union and Its Member States, of the One Part, and Ukraine, of the Other Part*. https://eur-lex.europa.eu/legal-content/EN/ALL/?uri=CELEX%3A22014A0529%2801%29 (November 22, 2021).

'The European Union's Eastern Partnership'. 2019. *Council on Foreign Relations*. https://www.cfr.org/backgrounder/european-unions-eastern-partnership (December 8, 2018).

'The Federation Council agreed to use the Russian Armed Forces on the territory of Ukraine'. 2014. http://council.gov.ru/events/news/39851/?hl=%D0%9E%D0%B1%20%D0%B8%D1%81%D0%BF%D0%BE%D0%BB%D1%8C%D0%B7%D0%BE%D0%B2%D0%B0%D0%BD%D0%B8%D0%B8%20%D0%92%D0%BE%D0%BE%D1%80%D1%83%D0%B6%D0%B5%D0%BD%D0%BD%D1%8B%D1%85%20%D0%A1%D0%B8%D0%BB%20%D0%A0%D0%BE%D1%81%D1%81%D0%B8%D0%B9%D1%81%D0%BA%D0%BE%D0%B9%20%D0%A4%D0%B5%D0%B4%D0%B5%D1%80%D0%B0%D1%86%D0%B8%D0%B8%20%D0%BD%D0%B0%20%D1%82%D0%B5%D1%80%D1%80%D0%B8%D1%82%D0%BE%D1%80%D0%B8%D0%B8%20%D0%A3%D0%BA%D1%80%D0%B0%D0%B8%D0%BD%D1%8B (October 23, 2020).

"The Federation Council Allowed Putin to Use the Russian Army Abroad." 2022. *BBC News*. https://web.archive.org/web/20220224082352/https://www.bbc.com/ukrainian/news-60482687 (October 9, 2022).

'The Full Text of the New Minsk Document Has Been Published'. 2015. *LB.ua*. https://lb.ua/news/2015/02/12/295325_opublikovan_polniy_tekst_novogo.html (February 11, 2021).

'The Meeting between Poroshenko and Putin Ended in Minsk'. 2014. *LB.ua*. https://lb.ua/news/2014/08/26/277318_minske_zavershilas_vstrecha.html (February 12, 2021).

'The vast majority of Ukrainian citizens believe that Russia is an aggressor state, a party to the conflict in eastern Ukraine (71.8%), and the DPR and LPR - terrorist organizations that have no right to represent the population of the respective territories (66.1%) - Razumkov Center'. 2015. *Ilko Kucheriv Democratic Initiatives Foundation*. https://dif.org.ua/article/perevazhna-bilshist-gromadyan-ukraini-vvazhayut-shcho-rosiya-e-derzhavoyu-agresorom-storonoyu-konfliktu-na-skhodi-ukraini-718-a-dnr-ta-lnr-teroristichni-organizatsii-yaki-ne-mayut-prava-predstavlyati-naselennya-vidpovidnikh-teritoriy-661-tsentr-razumkova (February 12, 2021).

Thompson, Alexander. 2002. 'Applying Rational Choice Theory to International Law: The Promise and Pitfalls'. *The Journal of Legal Studies* 31: 285–306.

Thompson, Leigh. 1995. '"They Saw a Negotiation": Partisanship and Involvement'. *Journal of Personality and Social Psychology* 68(5): 839–53.

Thoughts and Views of Residents of the South-Eastern Regions of Ukraine: April 2014. 2014b. Kyiv International Institute of Sociology. http://www.kiis.com.ua/?lang=rus&cat=reports&id=302&page=3 (February 24, 2021).

Tikhonova, Polina. 2015. 'Ukraine Ex-Army Chief: Russian Occupation of Crimea Was Spontaneous'. *ValueWalk*. http://www.valuewalk.com/2015/02/ukraine-ex-army-russia-crimea/ (February 14, 2020).

Tingley, Dustin H., and Barbara F. Walter. 2011. 'The Effect of Repeated Play on Reputation Building: An Experimental Approach'. *International Organization* 65(2): 343–65.

'Trading Insults'. 2013. *The Economist*. https://www.economist.com/europe/2013/08/24/trading-insults (June 1, 2020).

Treaty on European Union. 1992.

Trudolyubov, Maxim. 2015. 'Russia's Grand Choice to Be Feared as a Superpower or Prosperous as a Nation?' In *Roots of Russia's War in Ukeaine*, Washington, D.C: New York: Woodrow Wilson Center Press / Columbia University Press.

Tsebelis, George. 1990. *Nested Games: Rational Choice in Comparative Politics*. University of California Press.

Tsitsuashvili, Nodari. 2009. 'Ethnopolitical role of the Black Sea Fleet of the Russian Federation in Ukraine'. *State and Law* (46): 673–79.

Tsygankov, Andrei. 2015. 'Vladimir Putin's Last Stand: The Sources of Russia's Ukraine Policy'. *Post-Soviet Affairs* 31(4): 279–303.

'Turchynov is ready to free the separatists without crime if they lay down their arms'. 2014. *Novosti.dn.ua*. http://novosti.dn.ua/news/205252-turchynov-gotov-osvobodyt-separatystov-bez-krymynala-esly-ony-slozhat-oruzhye (September 26, 2020).

'Turchynov fired 42 advisers to the President'. 2014. *Ukrainska Pravda*. https://www.ukrinform.ua/rubric-polytics/1623335-turchinov_zvilniv_42_radniki_prezidenta_1911827.html (December 12, 2020).

'Tymoshenko criticized the Armistice Protocol'. 2014. *UaPress*. https://uapress.info/uk/news/show/38075 (February 9, 2021).

'Ukraine and the Customs Union: Victory of the Diplomacy Style of Viktor Yanukovych'. 2013. *LB.ua*. https://lb.ua/news/2013/05/30/202741_ukraina_tamozhenniy_soyuz_pobeda.html (June 1, 2020).

"Ukraine Broke off Diplomatic Relations with Russia - Zelensky." 2022. *Suspilne*. https://web.archive.org/web/20220224101927/https://suspilne.media/210264-ukraina-rozirvala-dipvidnosini-z-rosieu-zelenskij/ (October 9, 2022).

'Ukraine Crisis: Kiev Talks Open without Rebels'. 2014. *BBC News*. https://www.bbc.com/news/world-europe-27403109 (September 26, 2020).

'Ukraine: EU Support up Again'. 2013. *Deutsche Welle*. https://www.dw.com/en/ukraine-eu-support-up-again/a-16924061 (July 29, 2021).

Ukraine, Russian Federation. 1994. *Agreement between the Russian Federation and Ukraine on a Phased Settlement of the Black Sea Fleet Problem, the International Agreement of April 15, 1994*. http://docs.cntd.ru/document/901778482 (November 10, 2019).

———. 1997. *Agreement between Ukraine and the Russian Federation on the status and conditions of the stationing of the Black Sea Fleet of the Russian Federation on the territory of Ukraine*. https://zakon.rada.gov.ua/go/643_076 (May 15, 2020).

———. 1998. *Treaty on Friendship, Cooperation and Partnership between Ukraine and the Russian Federation*. https://zakon.rada.gov.ua/go/643_006 (July 28, 2019).

Ukraine, Russian Federation, the United Kingdom of Great Britain and Northern Ireland, the United States of America. 1994. *Memorandum on Security Assurances in connection with Ukraine's accession to the Treaty on the Non-Proliferation of Nuclear Weapons*. https://zakon.rada.gov.ua/go/998_158 (July 25, 2019).

'Ukrainian Insurgent Army'. 1993. *Internet Encyclopedia of Ukraine*. http://www.encyclopediaofukraine.com/display.asp?linkpath=pages%5CU%5CK%5CUkrainianInsurgentArmy.htm (September 20, 2020).

'Ukrainian Society 1994–2004: Sociological Monitoring'. 2004. *Ilko Kucheriv Democratic Initiatives Foundation.* https://dif.org.ua/article/ukrainske-suspilstvo-19942004-sotsiologichniy-monitoring (May 28, 2020).

'Ukrainians renewed the Rada by 56%'. 2014. *Ukrainska Pravda.* http://www.pravda.com.ua/news/2014/10/31/7042837/ (February 6, 2021).

United Nations. 2014. 'UN General Assembly Resolution 68/262 on Territorial Integrity of Ukraine'. http://digitallibrary.un.org/record/767565 (November 14, 2020).

"US Intel Predicted Russia's Invasion Plans. Did It Matter?" 2022. *AP NEWS.* https://apnews.com/article/russia-ukraine-vladimir-putin-business-europe-8acc2106b95554429e93dfee5e253743 (October 9, 2022).

'Varangian Route'. 1993. *Internet Encyclopedia of Ukraine.* http://www.encyclopediaofukraine.com/display.asp?linkpath=pages%5CV%5CA%5CVarangianroute.htm (December 19, 2019).

Veebel, Viljar, and Raul Markus. 2016. 'Will Sanctions Against Russia Be Successful: Will Russia Fall Before Ukraine?' *Journal of Security and Sustainability Issues* 5(4): 465–80.

Verkhovna Rada of the ARC. 2014. *On the Organization and Conduct of a Republican (Local) Referendum on Improving the Status and Powers of the Autonomous Republic of Crimea.* https://web.archive.org/web/20140329214951/http://www.rada.crimea.ua/act/11610 (April 26, 2020).

Verkhovna Rada of Ukraine. 1991. *On declaration of independence of Ukraine.* https://zakon.rada.gov.ua/go/1427-12 (July 24, 2019).

— — —. 2019. *Law of Ukraine dated February 7, 2019 No. 2680-VIII On making changes to the Constitution of Ukraine (regarding the state's strategic course towards full membership of Ukraine in the European Union and the North Atlantic Treaty Organization).* https://zakon.rada.gov.ua/go/2680-19 (October 5, 2022).

— — —. 1993. *On the Military Doctrine of Ukraine.* https://zakon.rada.gov.ua/go/3529-12 (December 8, 2019).

— — —. 1995. 96/95-ВР *On the Autonomous Republic of Crimea.* https://zakon.rada.gov.ua/go/95/95-%D0%B2%D1%80 (December 1, 2019).

— — —. 1996. 254к/96-ВР *Constitution of Ukraine.* https://zakon.rada.gov.ua/go/254%D0%BA/96-%D0%B2%D1%80 (January 3, 2020).

— — —. 1997. *On the Concept (Principles of State Policy) of National Security of Ukraine.* https://zakon.rada.gov.ua/go/3/97-%D0%B2%D1%80 (May 27, 2020).

— — —. 1998. *On approval of the Strategy of integration of Ukraine into the European Union.* http://zakon.rada.gov.ua/go/615/98 (December 4, 2018).

———. 2010. *On the Foundations of Internal and Foreign Policy*. https://zakon.rada.gov.ua/go/2411-17 (December 2, 2019).

———. 2014. 'Ceremonial Session of the Verkhovna Rada of Ukraine Dedicated to the Oath of Newly Elected President of Ukraine Petro Poroshenko'. https://www.rada.gov.ua/news/Top-novyna/94013.html (November 11, 2020).

Vynogradova, Ilona, and Vitalii Chervonenko. 2017. '25 years of Ukraine-Russia relations: how the friendship disappeared'. *BBC News Ukraine*. https://www.bbc.com/ukrainian/features-38965793 (January 6, 2020).

Wagner, R. Harrison. 2000. 'Bargaining and War'. *American Journal of Political Science* 44(3): 469–84.

Walker, Edward E. 2015. 'Between East & West: NATO Enlargement & the Geopolitics of the Ukraine Crisis'. In *Ukraine and Russia: People, Politics, Propaganda and Perspectives*, eds. Agnieszka Pikulicka-Wilczewska and Richard Sakwa. E-International Relations. https://www.e-ir.info/2015/04/13/between-east-west-nato-enlargement-the-geopolitics-of-the-ukraine-crisis/ (September 30, 2020).

Werner, Suzanne. 2000. 'Deterring Intervention: The Stakes of War and Third-Party Involvement'. *American Journal of Political Science* 44(4): 720–32.

'What Hollande said about the Minsk agreements and Putin's plans for Ukraine'. 2018. *BBC News Ukraine*. https://www.bbc.com/ukrainian/features-45374522 (February 11, 2021).

Wheeler, Nicholas J. 2018. *Trusting Enemies: Interpersonal Relationships in International Conflict*. Oxford University Press.

Wiegand, Gunnar, and Evelina Schulz. 2015. 'The EU and Its Eastern Partnership: Political Association and Economic Integration in a Rough Neighbourhood'. In book: *Trade Policy between Law, Diplomacy and Scholarship*, 321–58.

Wiegrefe, Klaus. 2022. "NATO's Eastward Expansion: Is Vladimir Putin Right?" *Der Spiegel*. https://www.spiegel.de/international/world/nato-s-eastward-expansion-is-vladimir-putin-right-a-bf318d2c-7aeb-4b59-8d5f-1d8c94e1964d (October 6, 2022).

Wilson, Andrew. 2015. 'Ukrainian Politics since Independence'. In *Ukraine and Russia: People, Politics, Propaganda and Perspectives*, E-International Relations Publishing Bristol, 101–8.

———. 2016. 'The Donbas in 2014: Explaining Civil Conflict Perhaps, but Not Civil War'. *Europe-Asia Studies* 68(4): 631–52.

Wood, Elizabeth. 2015a. 'A Small, Victorious War? The Symbolic Politics of Vladimir Putin'. In *Roots of Russia's War in Ukraine*, Washington, D.C: New York: Woodrow Wilson Center Press / Columbia University Press.

———. 2015b. 'Introduction'. In *Roots of Russia's War in Ukraine*, Washington, D.C: New York: Woodrow Wilson Center Press / Columbia University Press.

Wood, Elizabeth, William Pomeranz, E. Wayne Merry, and Maxim Trudolyubov. 2015. *Roots of Russia's War in Ukraine*. Washington, D.C: New York: Woodrow Wilson Center Press / Columbia University Press.

Yaffa, Joshua. 2022. "Inside the U.S. Effort to Arm Ukraine." *The New Yorker*. https://www.newyorker.com/magazine/2022/10/24/inside-the-us-effort-to-arm-ukraine (October 23, 2022).

Yanitsky, Andriy. 2011. 'Russian-Ukrainian trade war'. *LB.ua*. https://lb.ua/economics/2011/07/26/107729_rossiyskoukrainskaya_torgovaya_vo.html (June 1, 2020).

Yatseniuk, Arseniy. 2014. *Appeal to Citizens of Ukraine, in Particular Residents of the South and East of the Country*. https://www.youtube.com/watch?time_continue=18&v=GedblzwJXLs&feature=emb_logo (August 9, 2020).

Yelisieiev, Kostiantyn. 2013. 'Seven Myths on EU-Ukraine Association Agreement'. *Ministry of Foreign Affairs of Ukraine*. https://ukraine-eu.mfa.gov.ua/en/press-center/news/9473-7-mifiv-shhodo-ugodi-pro-asociaciju-mizh-ukrajinoju-ta-jes (December 7, 2018).

Zagorski, Andrei. 2011. 'Eastern Partnership from the Russian Perspective'. *Friedrich Ebert Stiftung*: 25.

Zaluzhnyi, Valerii, and Mykhailo Zabrodskyi. 2022. "Prospects for securing the military campaign of 2023: the Ukrainian view." *Ukrinform News*. https://www.ukrinform.ua/rubric-ato/3566162-ak-zabezpeciti-voennu-kampaniu-u-2023-roci-ukrainskij-poglad.html (October 9, 2022).

"Zelensky's Full Speech at Munich Security Conference." 2022. *The Kyiv Independent*. https://kyivindependent.com/national/zelenskys-full-speech-at-munich-security-conference (October 10, 2022).

"Zelensky Signs Decree Formally Ruling out Negotiations with Putin." 2022. *CommonSpace.EU*. https://www.commonspace.eu/news/zelensky-signs-decree-formally-ruling-out-negotiations-putin (October 25, 2022).

Zon, Hans van. 2005. 'Political Culture and Neo-Patrimonialism Under Leonid Kuchma'. *Problems of Post-Communism* 52(5): 12–22.

UKRAINIAN VOICES

Collected by Andreas Umland

1   *Mychailo Wynnyckyj*
    Ukraine's Maidan, Russia's War
    A Chronicle and Analysis of the Revolution of Dignity
    With a foreword by Serhii Plokhy
    ISBN 978-3-8382-1327-9

2   *Olexander Hryb*
    Understanding Contemporary Ukrainian and Russian Nationalism
    The Post-Soviet Cossack Revival and Ukraine's National Security
    With a foreword by Vitali Vitaliev
    ISBN 978-3-8382-1377-4

3   *Marko Bojcun*
    Towards a Political Economy of Ukraine
    Selected Essays 1990–2015
    With a foreword by John-Paul Himka
    ISBN 978-3-8382-1368-2

4   *Volodymyr Yermolenko (ed.)*
    Ukraine in Histories and Stories
    Essays by Ukrainian Intellectuals
    With a preface by Peter Pomerantsev
    ISBN 978-3-8382-1456-6

5   *Mykola Riabchuk*
    At the Fence of Metternich's Garden
    Essays on Europe, Ukraine, and Europeanization
    ISBN 978-3-8382-1484-9

6   *Marta Dyczok*
    Ukraine Calling
    A Kaleidoscope from Hromadske Radio 2016–2019
    With a foreword by Andriy Kulykov
    ISBN 978-3-8382-1472-6

7   *Olexander Scherba*
    Ukraine vs. Darkness
    Undiplomatic Thoughts
    With a foreword by Adrian Karatnycky
    ISBN 978-3-8382-1501-3

8   *Olesya Yaremchuk*
    Our Others
    Stories of Ukrainian Diversity
    With a foreword by Ostap Slyvynsky
    Translated from the Ukrainian by Zenia Tompkins and Hanna Leliv
    ISBN 978-3-8382-1475-7

9   *Nataliya Gumenyuk*
    Die verlorene Insel
    Geschichten von der besetzten Krim
    Mit einem Vorwort von Alice Bota
    Aus dem Ukrainischen übersetzt von Johann Zajaczkowski
    ISBN 978-3-8382-1499-3

10 *Olena Stiazhkina*
    Zero Point Ukraine
    Four Essays on World War II
    Translated from the Ukrainian by Svitlana Kulinska
    ISBN 978-3-8382-1550-1

11 *Oleksii Sinchenko, Dmytro Stus, Leonid Finberg (compilers)*
    Ukrainian Dissidents
    An Anthology of Texts
    ISBN 978-3-8382-1551-8

12 *John-Paul Himka*
    Ukrainian Nationalists and the Holocaust
    OUN and UPA's Participation in the Destruction of Ukrainian Jewry, 1941–1944
    ISBN 978-3-8382-1548-8

13 *Andrey Demartino*
    False Mirrors
    The Weaponization of Social Media in Russia's Operation to Annex Crimea
    With a foreword by Oleksiy Danilov
    ISBN 978-3-8382-1533-4

14 *Svitlana Biedarieva (ed.)*
    Contemporary Ukrainian and Baltic Art
    Political and Social Perspectives, 1991–2021
    ISBN 978-3-8382-1526-6

15 *Olesya Khromeychuk*
    A Loss
    The Story of a Dead Soldier Told by His Sister
    With a foreword by Andrey Kurkov
    ISBN 978-3-8382-1570-9

16 *Marieluise Beck (Hg.)*
    Ukraine verstehen
    Auf den Spuren von Terror und Gewalt
    Mit einem Vorwort von Dmytro Kuleba
    ISBN 978-3-8382-1653-9

17 *Stanislav Aseyev*
    Heller Weg
    Geschichte eines Konzentrationslagers im Donbass 2017–2019
    Aus dem Russischen übersetzt von
    Martina Steis und Charis Haska
    ISBN 978-3-8382-1620-1

18 *Mykola Davydiuk*
    Wie funktioniert Putins Propaganda?
    Anmerkungen zum Informationskrieg des Kremls
    Aus dem Ukrainischen übersetzt von Christian Weise
    ISBN 978-3-8382-1628-7

19 *Olesya Yaremchuk*
    Unsere Anderen
    Geschichten ukrainischer Vielfalt
    Aus dem Ukrainischen übersetzt von Christian Weise
    ISBN 978-3-8382-1635-5

20 *Oleksandr Mykhed*
    „Dein Blut wird die Kohle tränken"
    Über die Ostukraine
    Aus dem Ukrainischen übersetzt von Simon Muschick
    und Dario Planert
    ISBN 978-3-8382-1648-5

21   *Vakhtang Kipiani (Hg.)*
     Der Zweite Weltkrieg in der Ukraine
     Geschichte und Lebensgeschichten
     Aus dem Ukrainischen übersetzt von Margarita Grinko
     ISBN 978-3-8382-1622-5

22   *Vakhtang Kipiani (ed.)*
     World War II, Uncontrived and Unredacted
     Testimonies from Ukraine
     Translated from the Ukrainian by Zenia Tompkins and Daisy Gibbons
     ISBN 978-3-8382-1621-8

23   *Dmytro Stus*
     Vasyl Stus
     Life in Creativity
     Translated from the Ukrainian by Ludmila Bachurina
     ISBN 978-3-8382-1631-7

24   *Vitalii Ogiienko (ed.)*
     The Holodomor and the Origins of the Soviet Man
     Reading the Testimony of Anastasia Lysyvets
     With forewords by Natalka Bilotserkivets and Serhy Yekelchyk
     Translated from the Ukrainian by Alla Parkhomenko and Alexander J. Motyl
     ISBN 978-3-8382-1616-4

25   *Vladislav Davidzon*
     Jewish-Ukrainian Relations and the Birth of a Political Nation
     Selected Writings 2013-2021
     With a foreword by Bernard-Henri Lévy
     ISBN 978-3-8382-1509-9

26   *Serhy Yekelchyk*
     Writing the Nation
     The Ukrainian Historical Profession in Independent Ukraine and the Diaspora
     ISBN 978-3-8382-1695-9

27   *Ildi Eperjesi, Oleksandr Kachura*
     Shreds of War
     Fates from the Donbas Frontline 2014-2019
     With a foreword by Olexiy Haran
     ISBN 978-3-8382-1680-5

28 *Oleksandr Melnyk*
    World War II as an Identity Project
    Historicism, Legitimacy Contests, and the (Re-)Construction of
    Political Communities in Ukraine, 1939–1946
    With a foreword by David R. Marples
    ISBN 978-3-8382-1704-8

29 *Olesya Khromeychuk*
    Ein Verlust
    Die Geschichte eines gefallenen ukrainischen Soldaten,
    erzählt von seiner Schwester
    Mit einem Vorwort von Andrej Kurkow
    Aus dem Englischen übersetzt von Lily Sophie
    ISBN 978-3-8382-1770-3

30 *Tamara Martsenyuk, Tetiana Kostiuchenko (eds.)*
    Russia's War in Ukraine 2022
    Personal Experiences of Ukrainian Scholars
    ISBN 978-3-8382-1757-4

31 *Ildikó Eperjesi, Oleksandr Kachura*
    Shreds of War. Vol. 2
    Fates from Crimea 2015–2022
    With a foreword by Anton Shekhovtsov and an interview of
    Oleh Sentsov
    ISBN 978-3-8382-1780-2

32 *Yuriy Lukanov, Tetiana Pechonchik (eds.)*
    The Press: How Russia destroyed Media Freedom in
    Crimea
    With a foreword by Taras Kuzio
    ISBN 978-3-8382-1784-0

33 *Megan Buskey*
    Ukraine Is Not Dead Yet
    A Family Story of Exile and Return
    ISBN 978-3-8382-1691-1

34 *Vira Ageyeva*
    Behind the Scenes of the Empire
    Essays on Cultural Relationships between Ukraine and Russia
    With a foreword by Oksana Zabuzhko
    ISBN 978-3-8382-1748-2

35 *Marieluise Beck (ed.)*
Understanding Ukraine
Tracing the Roots of Terror and Violence
With a foreword by Dmytro Kuleba
ISBN 978-3-8382-1773-4

36 *Olesya Khromeychuk*
A Loss
The Story of a Dead Soldier Told by His Sister, 2nd edn.
With a foreword by Philippe Sands
With a preface by Andrii Kurkov
ISBN 978-3-8382-1870-0

37 *Taras Kuzio, Stefan Jajecznyk-Kelman*
Fascism and Genocide
Russia's War Against Ukrainians
ISBN 978-3-8382-1791-8

38 *Alina Nychyk*
Ukraine Vis-à-Vis Russia and the EU
Misperceptions of Foreign Challenges in Times of War, 2014–2015
With a foreword by Paul D'Anieri
ISBN 978-3-8382-1767-3

39 *Sasha Dovzhyk (ed.)*
Ukraine Lab
Global Security, Environment, Disinformation Through the Prism of Ukraine
With a foreword by Rory Finnin
ISBN 978-3-8382-1805-2

40 *Serhiy Kvit*
Media, History, and Education
Three Ways to Ukrainian Independence
With a preface by Diane Francis
ISBN 978-3-8382-1807-6

41 *Anna Romandash*
Women of Ukraine
Reportages from the War and Beyond
ISBN 978-3-8382-1819-9

42 *Dominika Rank*
Matzewe in meinem Garten
Abenteuer eines jüdischen Heritage-Touristen in der Ukraine
ISBN 978-3-8382-1810-6

43 *Myroslaw Marynowytsch*
    Das Universum hinter dem Stacheldraht
    Memoiren eines sowjet-ukrainischen Dissidenten
    Mit einem Vorwort von Timothy Snyder und einem Nachwort
    von Max Hartmann
    ISBN 978-3-8382-1806-9

44 *Konstantin Sigow*
    Für Deine und meine Freiheit
    Europäische Revolutions- und Kriegserfahrungen im heutigen
    Kyjiw
    Mit einem Vorwort von Karl Schlögel
    Herausgegeben von Regula M. Zwahlen
    ISBN 978-3-8382-1755-0

45 *Kateryna Pylypchuk*
    The War that Changed Us
    Ukrainian Novellas, Poems, and Essays from 2022
    With a foreword by Victor Yushchenko
    ISBN 978-3-8382-1859-5

46 *Kyrylo Tkachenko*
    Rechte Tür Links
    Radikale Linke in Deutschland, die Revolution und der Krieg in
    der Ukraine, 2013-2018
    ISBN 978-3-8382-1711-6

47 *Alexander Strashny*
    The Ukrainian Mentality
    An Ethno-Psychological, Historical and Comparative Exploration
    With a foreword by Antonina Lovochkina
    ISBN 978-3-8382-1886-1

Book series "Ukrainian Voices"

Collector
Andreas Umland, National University of Kyiv-Mohyla Academy

Editorial Board
Lesia Bidochko, National University of Kyiv-Mohyla Academy
Svitlana Biedarieva, George Washington University, DC, USA
Ivan Gomza, Kyiv School of Economics, Ukraine
Natalie Jaresko, Aspen Institute, Kyiv/Washington
Olena Lennon, University of New Haven, West Haven, USA
Kateryna Yushchenko, First Lady of Ukraine 2005-2010, Kyiv
Oleksandr Zabirko, University of Regensburg, Germany

Advisory Board
Iuliia Bentia, National Academy of Arts of Ukraine, Kyiv
Natalya Belitser, Pylyp Orlyk Institute for Democracy, Kyiv
Oleksandra Bienert, Humboldt University of Berlin, Germany
Sergiy Bilenky, Canadian Institute of Ukrainian Studies, Toronto
Tymofii Brik, Kyiv School of Economics, Ukraine
Olga Brusylovska, Mechnikov National University, Odesa
Mariana Budjeryn, Harvard University, Cambridge, USA
Volodymyr Bugrov, Shevchenko National University, Kyiv
Olga Burlyuk, University of Amsterdam, The Netherlands
Yevhen Bystrytsky, NAS Institute of Philosophy, Kyiv
Andrii Danylenko, Pace University, New York, USA
Vladislav Davidzon, Atlantic Council, Washington/Paris
Mykola Davydiuk, Think Tank "Polityka," Kyiv
Andrii Demartino, National Security and Defense Council, Kyiv
Vadym Denisenko, Ukrainian Institute for the Future, Kyiv
Oleksandr Donii, Center for Political Values Studies, Kyiv
Volodymyr Dubovyk, Mechnikov National University, Odesa
Volodymyr Dubrovskiy, CASE Ukraine, Kyiv
Diana Dutsyk, National University of Kyiv-Mohyla Academy
Marta Dyczok, Western University, Ontario, Canada
Yevhen Fedchenko, National University of Kyiv-Mohyla Academy
Sofiya Filonenko, State Pedagogical University of Berdyansk
Oleksandr Fisun, Karazin National University, Kharkiv
Oksana Forostyna, Webjournal "Ukraina Moderna," Kyiv
Roman Goncharenko, Broadcaster "Deutsche Welle," Bonn
George Grabowicz, Harvard University, Cambridge, USA
Gelinada Grinchenko, Karazin National University, Kharkiv
Kateryna Härtel, Federal Union of European Nationalities, Brussels
Nataliia Hendel, University of Geneva, Switzerland
Anton Herashchenko, Kyiv School of Public Administration
John-Paul Himka, University of Alberta, Edmonton
Ola Hnatiuk, National University of Kyiv-Mohyla Academy
Oleksandr Holubov, Broadcaster "Deutsche Welle," Bonn
Yaroslav Hrytsak, Ukrainian Catholic University, Lviv
Oleksandra Humenna, National University of Kyiv-Mohyla Academy
Tamara Hundorova, NAS Institute of Literature, Kyiv
Oksana Huss, University of Bologna, Italy
Oleksandra Iwaniuk, University of Warsaw, Poland
Mykola Kapitonenko, Shevchenko National University, Kyiv
Georgiy Kasianov, Marie Curie-Skłodowska University, Lublin
Vakhtang Kebuladze, Shevchenko National University, Kyiv
Natalia Khanenko-Friesen, University of Alberta, Edmonton
Victoria Khiterer, Millersville University of Pennsylvania, USA
Oksana Kis, NAS Institute of Ethnology, Lviv
Pavlo Klimkin, Center for National Resilience and Development, Kyiv
Oleksandra Kolomiiets, Center for Economic Strategy, Kyiv

Sergiy Korsunsky, Kobe Gakuin University, Japan
Nadiia Koval, Kyiv School of Economics, Ukraine
Volodymyr Kravchenko, University of Alberta, Edmonton
Oleksiy Kresin, NAS Koretskiy Institute of State and Law, Kyiv
Anatoliy Kruglashov, Fedkovych National University, Chernivtsi
Andrey Kurkov, PEN Ukraine, Kyiv
Ostap Kushnir, Lazarski University, Warsaw
Taras Kuzio, National University of Kyiv-Mohyla Academy
Serhii Kvit, National University of Kyiv-Mohyla Academy
Yuliya Ladygina, The Pennsylvania State University, USA
Yevhen Mahda, Institute of World Policy, Kyiv
Victoria Malko, California State University, Fresno, USA
Yulia Marushevska, Security and Defense Center (SAND), Kyiv
Myroslav Marynovych, Ukrainian Catholic University, Lviv
Oleksandra Matviichuk, Center for Civil Liberties, Kyiv
Mykhailo Minakov, Kennan Institute, Washington, USA
Anton Moiseienko, The Australian National University, Canberra
Alexander Motyl, Rutgers University-Newark, USA
Vlad Mykhnenko, University of Oxford, United Kingdom
Vitalii Ogiienko, Ukrainian Institute of National Remembrance, Kyiv
Olga Onuch, University of Manchester, United Kingdom
Olesya Ostrovska, Museum "Mystetskyi Arsenal," Kyiv
Anna Osypchuk, National University of Kyiv-Mohyla Academy
Oleksandr Pankieiev, University of Alberta, Edmonton
Oleksiy Panych, Publishing House "Dukh i Litera," Kyiv
Valerii Pekar, Kyiv-Mohyla Business School, Ukraine
Yohanan Petrovsky-Shtern, Northwestern University, Chicago
Serhii Plokhy, Harvard University, Cambridge, USA
Andrii Portnov, Viadrina University, Frankfurt-Oder, Germany
Maryna Rabinovych, Kyiv School of Economics, Ukraine
Valentyna Romanova, Institute of Developing Economies, Tokyo
Natalya Ryabinska, Collegium Civitas, Warsaw, Poland
Darya Tsymbalyk, University of Oxford, United Kingdom
Vsevolod Samokhvalov, University of Liege, Belgium
Orest Semotiuk, Franko National University, Lviv
Viktoriya Sereda, NAS Institute of Ethnology, Lviv
Anton Shekhovtsov, University of Vienna, Austria
Andriy Shevchenko, Media Center Ukraine, Kyiv
Oxana Shevel, Tufts University, Medford, USA
Pavlo Shopin, National Pedagogical Dragomanov University, Kyiv
Karina Shyrokykh, Stockholm University, Sweden
Nadja Simon, freelance interpreter, Cologne, Germany
Olena Snigova, NAS Institute for Economics and Forecasting, Kyiv
Ilona Solohub, Analytical Platform "VoxUkraine," Kyiv
Iryna Solonenko, LibMod - Center for Liberal Modernity, Berlin
Galyna Solovei, National University of Kyiv-Mohyla Academy
Sergiy Stelmakh, NAS Institute of World History, Kyiv
Olena Stiazhkina, NAS Institute of the History of Ukraine, Kyiv
Dmitri Stratievski, Osteuropa Zentrum (OEZB), Berlin
Dmytro Stus, National Taras Shevchenko Museum, Kyiv
Frank Sysyn, University of Toronto, Canada
Olha Tokariuk, Center for European Policy Analysis, Washington
Olena Tregub, Independent Anti-Corruption Commission, Kyiv
Hlib Vyshlinsky, Centre for Economic Strategy, Kyiv
Mychailo Wynnyckyj, National University of Kyiv-Mohyla Academy
Yelyzaveta Yasko, NGO "Yellow Blue Strategy," Kyiv
Serhy Yekelchyk, University of Victoria, Canada
Victor Yushchenko, President of Ukraine 2005-2010, Kyiv
Oleksandr Zaitsev, Ukrainian Catholic University, Lviv
Kateryna Zarembo, National University of Kyiv-Mohyla Academy
Yaroslav Zhalilo, National Institute for Strategic Studies, Kyiv
Sergei Zhuk, Ball State University at Muncie, USA
Alina Zubkovych, Nordic Ukraine Forum, Stockholm
Liudmyla Zubrytska, National University of Kyiv-Mohyla Academy

Friends of the Series

Ana Maria Abulescu, University of Bucharest, Romania
Łukasz Adamski, Centrum Mieroszewskiego, Warsaw
Marieluise Beck, LibMod—Center for Liberal Modernity, Berlin
Marc Berensen, King's College London, United Kingdom
Johannes Bohnen, BOHNEN Public Affairs, Berlin
Karsten Brüggemann, University of Tallinn, Estonia
Ulf Brunnbauer, Leibniz Institute (IOS), Regensburg
Martin Dietze, German-Ukrainian Culture Society, Hamburg
Gergana Dimova, Florida State University, Tallahassee/London
Caroline von Gall, Goethe University, Frankfurt-Main
Zaur Gasimov, Rhenish Friedrich Wilhelm University, Bonn
Armand Gosu, University of Bucharest, Romania
Thomas Grant, University of Cambridge, United Kingdom
Gustav Gressel, European Council on Foreign Relations, Berlin
Rebecca Harms, European Centre for Press & Media Freedom, Leipzig
André Härtel, Stiftung Wissenschaft und Politik, Berlin/Brussels
Marcel Van Herpen, The Cicero Foundation, Maastricht
Richard Herzinger, freelance analyst, Berlin
Mieste Hotopp-Riecke, ICATAT, Magdeburg
Nico Lange, Munich Security Conference, Berlin
Martin Malek, freelance analyst, Vienna
Ingo Mannteufel, Broadcaster "Deutsche Welle," Bonn
Carlo Masala, Bundeswehr University, Munich
Wolfgang Mueller, University of Vienna, Austria
Dietmar Neutatz, Albert Ludwigs University, Freiburg
Torsten Oppelland, Friedrich Schiller University, Jena
Niccolò Pianciola, University of Padua, Italy
Gerald Praschl, German-Ukrainian Forum (DUF), Berlin
Felix Riefer, Think Tank Ideenagentur-Ost, Düsseldorf
Stefan Rohdewald, University of Leipzig, Germany
Sebastian Schäffer, Institute for the Danube Region (IDM), Vienna
Felix Schimansky-Geier, Friedrich Schiller University, Jena
Ulrich Schneckener, University of Osnabrück, Germany
Winfried Schneider-Deters, freelance analyst, Heidelberg/Kyiv
Gerhard Simon, University of Cologne, Germany
Kai Struve, Martin Luther University, Halle/Wittenberg
David Stulik, European Values Center for Security Policy, Prague
Andrzej Szeptycki, University of Warsaw, Poland
Philipp Ther, University of Vienna, Austria
Stefan Troebst, University of Leipzig, Germany

[Please send address requests for changes, corrections, and additions to this list to andreas.umland@stanforalumni.org.]

***ibidem**.eu*